FLAGSTAFF

HIKES

Revised Fifth Edition, 2001

by
Richard & Sherry Mangum

PRESS

Non Liability Statement

While we have worked hard to guarantee accuracy and have personally taken every one of these hikes, errors in field notes, transcription and typesetting can occur. Changes also occur on the land and some descriptions that were accurate when written may become inaccurate. One storm, for example, can change a trail or road. In addition to the problem of accuracy, there is the problem of injury. It is always possible that hikers may sustain harm while on a hike. The authors, publishers and all those associated with this book, directly or indirectly, disclaim any liability for accidents, injuries, damages or losses that may occur to anyone using this book. The responsibility for good health and safety while hiking is that of the user.

Look for Our Companion Book

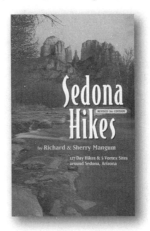

Cover photo, *San Francisco Peaks from Hart Prairie*
by Sherry G. Mangum
Cover design by Joan Carstensen
Produced by Northland Graphics, Flagstaff

Revised Fifth Edition 2001
First Edition, April 1992
Revised Second Edition, June 1992
Revised Third Edition, April 1995
Revised Fourth Edition November 1997
ISBN 1-891517-50-3

Table of Contents

Foreword

In April, 1992 we published the first edition of *Flagstaff Hikes*, followed in June 1992 by the revised second edition, the third revised edition in 1995 and the fourth revised edition in 1997. Now we present the fifth revised edition for 2001.

We constantly monitor the trails, looking for changes and scouting for something new, different and better. With every edition we have refined our data and presented more hikes, expanding the coverage of the area and appealing to more tastes and abilities. We have seven new hikes in this edition. These are the changes we have made for the fifth edition:

New (7): Arizona Trail—Allan Lake, Deer Hill Trail, Old Caves Crater, Soldiers Trail, Vista Loop Trail, Wildlife Trail, and Wood Trail.

Deleted (7): Bald Hill (required bushwhacking, also fire damaged), Blue Canyon (closed by Hopi Tribe), East Pocket (required bushwhacking), Hog Hill (hard to follow), Kelly Canyon (bushwhack), Old Munds Highway (nonsystem trail), Ott Lake (difficult to find).

Revised: Wendell Duffield, expert volcanologist and author of *Volcanoes of Northern Arizona*, kindly offered to contribute to this book, taking several of the hikes and adding information about them. These hikes are: A-1 Mountain, Anderson Mesa, Doney Trail, Grand Falls, Slate Mountain, and Strawberry Crater. We have revised the Griffiths Spring hike to incorporate the new trail made there by the Forest Service. The Strawberry Crater Trail has also been revised, since the trail was changed.

Upcoming: The Forest Service is still working on the Arizona Trail, with more segments being added to the system each year. The goal of having final completion by the year 2000 was not reached, with estimates of completion now being 2002. Planners are examining the entire area around Flagstaff and many proposed trails are now on the drawing board, some of which look very exciting. We will continue to work hard to keep up to date on these and pass the information on to you with future revisions of this book. The forests around Flagstaff are changing and the Forest Service is changing with them. In years past the forests were seen as the source of logs for the lumber industry and the Forest Service placed its main emphasis on timber management. Now the emphasis has shifted to recreational uses and we believe that this trend will strengthen. This is good news for hikers as the Forest Service devotes more and more resources to recreation, with hiking trails being one of the principal beneficiaries.

About the Authors

Richard K. (Dick) Mangum

Dick was born in Flagstaff. From his childhood he has enjoyed getting out into the woods, canyons, hills and mountains surrounding his birthplace.

After graduating from Flagstaff High School, he attended the University of Arizona, where he obtained his BS and law degrees. He returned to Flagstaff and engaged in the general practice of law for fifteen years, then became a Superior Court Judge in Flagstaff in 1976.

He retired in November 1993 in order to devote full time to his two favorite hobbies, hiking and writing. He wrote the articles, drew the maps and typeset the book.

Sherry G. Mangum

Although Sherry was not born in Flagstaff, she has lived there since she was seven years old. Like Dick, she enjoyed getting into the outdoors from the time she was a toddler.

Inheriting her love for photography from her parents, both professionals, she has refined her skills to produce the photographs used in this book.

Adept at all aspects of photography, she prefers landscapes. Her work has been published in books and periodicals since 1978. Sherry's camera of choice is a Nikon F5.

The couple was given the Copper Quill Award by the Friends of the Public Library in 2000 for their significant contribution to literature of the Flagstaff area.

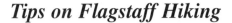

Tips on Flagstaff Hiking

Water

Don't count on finding water anywhere. Take your water with you.

High Elevation

Hikes in Flagstaff start at 7,000 feet and go all the way up to 12,643 feet, the highest point in Arizona. High elevations mean: l. You won't have the energy you are used to, 2. Hiking will be a lot harder on your heart, 3. You will be drier than usual, 4. You will sunburn more easily, 5. It will be much colder than normal, especially at night, 6. Alcohol is more intoxicating.

The Terrain

Flagstaff country is generally benign. You can get lost in the woods, but you won't if you stay on the hikes described in this book.

Rock Climbing

We do not provide any rock climbing information. If you want to go rock climbing, you are on your own.

Varmints

Because Flagstaff is cool and has long winters, you won't find many mosquitoes. Pests like chiggers are absent. Ticks are rare in the high country. There are a few black widow spiders around, but no scorpions. Rattlesnakes are not entirely out of their life zone but they are not plentiful. Even so, don't do anything stupid like reaching blindly under a rock or brush pile.

Weather

Flagstaff's normal snow season is anytime between Halloween and Easter. Don't count on hiking in the high country then. Summers are perfection, though rain is common between the Fourth of July and Labor Day. We indicate the best times for hiking with a graphic on each map, as you see here, to the right.

🖋 SPRING ☀️ SUMMER	
OK from April 15	BEST Nice & Cool
🍂 FALL ❄️ WINTER	
GOOD until Nov. 15	POOR Snowy

Access

Some of these hikes are totally unavailable in winter. Hikes in the high mountains are impossible then because of snow. The average snowfall in Flagstaff is 110 inches, and the mountains get even more. In addition to the obvious road problems caused by snow, some of the back roads are barred by locked gates during the winter. Call the Forest Service for road data.

Handy Charts & Data

Hours of Daylight

☼☽	JAN	FEB	MAR	APR	MAY	JUN	JUL	AUG	SEPT	OCT	NOV	DEC
SUNRISE	7:35	7:26	6:57	6:14	5:36	5:14	5:16	5:35	5:59	6:21	6:48	7:16
SUNSET	5:26	5:55	6:22	6:48	7:12	7:35	7:45	7:30	6:54	6:11	5:33	5:15

Normal Precipitation—inches

JAN	FEB	MAR	APR	MAY	JUN	JUL	AUG	SEP	OCT	NOV	DEC
2.04	2.09	2.55	1.48	0.72	0.40	2.78	2.75	2.03	1.61	1.95	2.40

Normal Temperatures—High and Low

JAN	FEB	MAR	APR	MAY	JUN	JUL	AUG	SEP	OCT	NOV	DEC
42.2	45.3	49.2	57.8	67.4	78.2	50.5	79.3	73.2	63.4	61.0	51.1
15.2	17.7	21.3	26.7	33.3	41.4	50.5	48.9	41.2	31.0	22.4	15.8

Converting Feet to Meters

Meters	910	1212	1515	1818	2121	2424	2727	3030	3333	3636
Feet	3000	4000	5000	6000	7000	8000	9000	10000	11000	12000

Average Walking Rates

Time	1 Hour	30 Min.	15 Min.	7.5 Min.
Miles	2.0	1.0	0.5	0.25
KM	3.2	1.6	0.8	0.4

CLIMATE

Flagstaff, elevation 7,000 feet, is situated on a volcanic plateau at the base of the highest mountains in Arizona. The climate may be classified as vigorous with cold winters, mild, pleasantly cool summers, moderate humidity, and considerable diurnal temperature change. The stormy months are January, February, March, July, and August.

Based on the 1951-1980 period, the average first occurrence of 32 degrees Fahrenheit in the fall is September 21 and the average last occurrence in the spring is June 13.

Temperatures in Flagstaff are characteristic of high elevation climates. The average daily range of temperature is relatively high, especially in the winter months, October to March, as a result of extensive snow cover and clear skies. Winter minimum temperatures frequently reach zero or below and temperatures of -25 degrees or less have occurred. Summer maximum temperatures are often above 80 degrees and occasionally, temperatures have exceeded 95 degrees.

The Flagstaff area is semi-arid. Several months have recorded little or no precipitation. Over 90 consecutive days without measurable precipitation have occurred. Annual precipitation ranges from less than 10 inches to more than 35 inches. Winter snowfalls can be heavy, exceeding 100 inches during one month and over 200 inches during the winter season. However, accumulations are quite variable from year to year. Some winter months may experience little or no snow and the winter season has produced total snow accumulations of less than 12 inches.

How To Use This Book

Alphabetical arrangement. The 146 hikes in this book are arranged from A-Z.

Index. The index starts at page 286. It groups the hikes by geographical area and by special features.

Layout. The text describing a hike and the map of the hike are on facing pages so that you can take in everything at once.

Maps. The maps are not to scale but their proportions are generally correct. The main purpose of the maps is to get you to the trailhead. The maps show mileage point-to-point. The text gives cumulative mileage.

Larger scale maps. For the big picture, we recommend using a Forest Service recreation map.

Bold type. When you see a trail name in **bold** type it means that the hike is described in this book.

Ratings. We show hikes rated as *easy, moderate* and *hard.* We are middle-aged hikers in normal condition—not highly conditioned athletes who never tire. Hikers should adjust our ratings for their own fitness level. The hike-in-a-box on each map may best show how hard a hike is.

Mileage. Driving distance was measured from Flagstaff City Hall located at the junction of Route 66

and Humphreys Street. All hikes start from this point. Milepost locations are also shown on the maps (as MP) on highways that have them. Hike mileage was measured by a pedometer and map scaling.

Access roads. To reach many of these hikes, you will have to travel unpaved roads, some of them rough. Our vehicle has 4-wheel drive but not much clearance. Our access ratings were based on how well our car handled the roads. Some drives require a high clearance vehicle.

Safety. We avoid taking risks on hikes. None of these hikes requires technical climbing.

Wilderness Areas. The Flagstaff area is blessed by having many of its hiking places included within federally designated Wilderness Areas. This is great for the hiker. Please read the Leave No Trace Outdoor Ethics on page 9.

Cairns. These are stacks of rocks used as trail markers. Some are officially placed, while others are made by hikers. Do not disturb them.

Mileposts. Major Arizona highways are marked every mile by a sign about three feet high on the right side of the road.

Leave No Trace Outdoor Ethics

Plan Ahead And Prepare
• Know the regulations and special concerns for the area you'll visit.
• Prepare for extreme weather, hazards, and emergencies.
• Schedule your trip to avoid times of high use.
• Visit in small groups. Split larger parties into groups of 4-6.
• Repackage food to minimize waste.
• Use a map and compass; eliminate the use of rock cairns, flagging, marking paint.

Travel And Camp On Durable Surfaces
• Durable surfaces: established trails & campsites, rock, gravel, dry grasses, snow.
• Protect riparian areas by camping at least 200 feet from lakes, streams.
• Good campsites are found, not made. Altering a site is not necessary.

In popular areas:
• Concentrate use on existing trails and campsites.
• Walk single file in the middle of the trail, even when wet or muddy.
• Keep campsites small. Focus activity in areas where vegetation is absent.

In pristine areas:
• Disperse use to prevent the creation of campsites and trails.
• Avoid places where impacts are just beginning.

Dispose Of Waste Properly
• Pack it in, pack it out. Inspect your campsite and rest areas for trash or spilled foods. Pack out all trash, leftover food, and litter.
• Deposit solid human waste in catholes dug 6 to 8 inches deep at least 200 feet from water, camp, and trails. Cover and disguise the cathole when finished.
• Pack out toilet paper and hygiene products.
• To wash yourself or your dishes, carry water 200 feet away from streams or lakes and use small amounts of biodegradable soap. Scatter strained dishwater.

Leave What You Find
• Preserve the past: examine, but do not touch, cultural or historic structures and artifacts.
• Leave rocks, plants and other natural objects as you find them.
• Avoid introducing or transporting non-native species.
• Do not build structures, furniture, or dig trenches.

Minimize Campfire Impacts
• Campfires can cause lasting impacts to the backcountry. Use a lightweight stove for cooking and enjoy a candle lantern for light.
• Where fires are permitted, use established fire rings, fire pans, or mound fires.
• Keep fires small. Only use sticks from the ground that can be broken by hand.
• Burn all wood and coals to ash, put out campfires fully, then scatter cool ashes.

Respect Wildlife
• Observe wildlife from a distance. Do not follow or approach them.
• Never feed animals. Feeding wildlife damages their health, alters natural behaviors, and exposes them to predators and other dangers.
• Protect wildlife and your food by storing rations and trash securely.
• Control pets at all times, or leave them at home.
• Avoid wildlife during sensitive times: mating, nesting, raising young, or winter

Be Considerate Of Other Visitors
• Respect other visitors and protect the quality of their experience.
• Be courteous. Yield to other users on the trail.
• Step to the downhill side of the trail when encountering pack stock.
• Take breaks and camp away from trails and other visitors.
• Let nature's sounds prevail. Avoid loud voices and noises.

Access Map

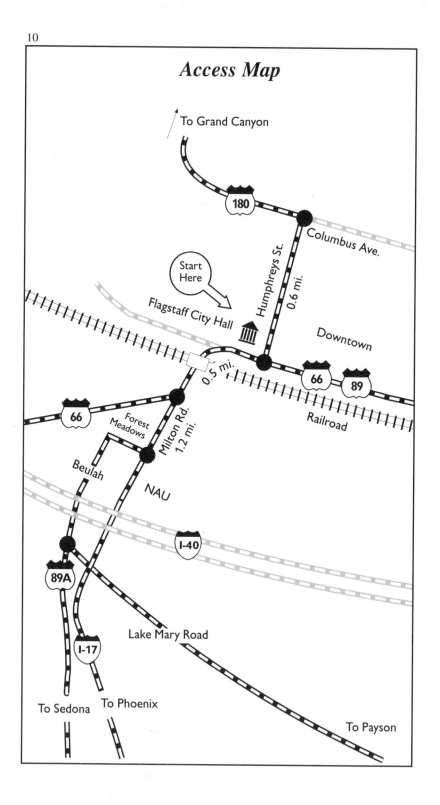

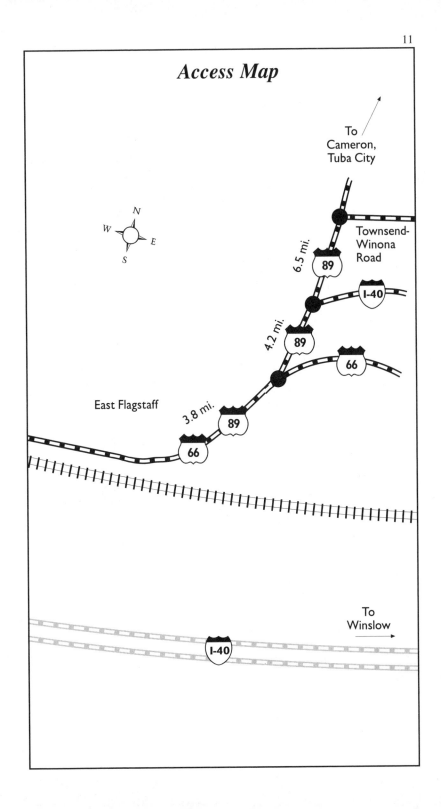

Access Map

Hike Locator

B2
Bright Angel Trail
Grandview Trail
Hermit Trail
South Kaibab Trail
C2
Coconino Rim
Red Butte
C4
Coal Mine Canyon
D2
Red Mountain
D3
SP Crater
Strawberry Crater
D4
Doney Trail
Wupatki Ruin
E1
Three Sisters
E2
A-1 Mountain
Antelope Hills
Beale Road—Govt. Pr.
Beale Road—Laws
Bull Basin Trail
Chalender X-Country (3)
Connector
Crater Lake
Eagle Rock
Government Knoll
Kendrick Mountain
Keyhole Sink
Lava River Cave
Pumpkin Trail
Route 66
RS Hill
Slate Mountain
Wild Bill Hill
Wildlife Trail
Wing Mt.
E3
Abineau Canyon
Abineau Pipeline
Bear Jaw Canyon
Bismarck Lake
Brookbank Trail
Buffalo Park (3)
Christmas Tree Trail
Deer Hill Trail
Elden Lookout
Elden Pueblo
Elden Skyline
Elden Springs Loop
Fat Man's Loop

Flagstaff Spring
Heart Trail
Humphreys Peak
Inner Basin
Kachina Trail
Little Bear Trail
Little Elden—Heart
LittleElden-Schultz Tank
Little Spring
Lookout Trail
Old Caves Crater
Oldham Trail #1
Rocky Ridge Trail
Saddle Mountain
Sandy Seep Trail
Schultz Creek Trail
Snow Bowl Hikes
Sunset Trail
Tunnel Road
Upper Oldham Trail
Veit Springs
Walker Lake
Weatherford Canyon
Weatherford Trail
White Horse Hills
Wilson Meadow
E4
Grand Falls
Lava Flow Trail
O'Leary Peak
F1
Bear Canyon
Benham Trail
Bill Williams Mt.
Bixler Saddle
Buckskinner Trail
Clover Spring
Davenport Hill (3)
Dogtown Lake
JohnsonCrater-Canyon
Overland Road
Ponderosa Nature Trail
Secret Pocket
Summit Mountain
F2
Babe's Hole
Casner Mt. North
Dorsey Spring
Geronimo Spring
Kelsey Spring
Kelsey-Winter Cabin
Lonesome Pocket
Secret Mountain
Sycamore Rim Trail
Taylor Cabin Trail

West Fork Head
Winter Cabin
F3
Anderson Mesa
Flagstaff-North Trail
Griffiths Spring
Island Trail
James Canyon
Ledge Trail
Marshall Lake
McMillan Mesa Trail
Museum Nature Trail
Oak Creek Vista
Old Lowell Observatory
Pipeline Trail
Ranger Trail
Rim Trail
Rio de Flag Trail
Sandys Canyon
Sinclair Wash (2)
Soldiers Trail
Turkey Hill
Vista Loop Trail
Walnut Canyon Link
Walnut Canyon Trails (4)
Wildcat Hill
Wood Trail
G2
Sycamore Basin Trail
G3
Arizona Trail—Allan Lake
Crystal Point Trail
Hutch Mountain
Lakeview Trail
Ledges Trail
Mormon Mountain
G4
Calloway Trail
Fossil Springs
General Springs Trail
Horse Crossing
Houston Brothers
Kinder Crossing
Mack's Crossing
Maxwell Trail
Pivot Rock
Point Trail
Railroad Tunnel Trail
Tramway Trail
Wildcat Spring
Willow Crossing

13

LOCATION MAP

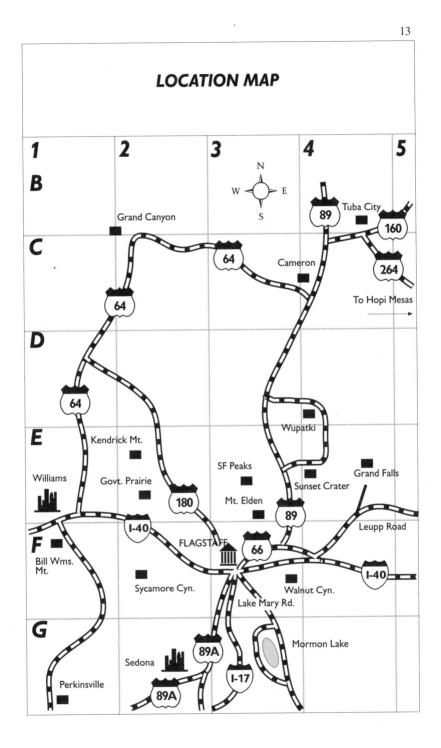

14

Hikes Grouped by Difficulty

Easy
Anderson Mesa
Arizona Trail—Allan Lk.
Beale Rd—Govt. Prairie
Beale Rd.—Laws Spring
Buffalo Park
Coconino Rim Trail
Crystal Point Trail
Dogtown Lake Trail
Elden Pueblo
Flagstaff-North Trail
Griffith Springs Cyn.
Houston Bros. Trail
Johnson Crater/Canyon
Keyhole Sink
Lava Flow Trail
McMillan Mesa Trail
Museum Nature Trail
Oak Creek Vista
Pivot Rock
Ponderosa Nature Trail
Rio de Flag Trail
Route 66
Sandy Seep
Sinclair Wash Trail
Veit Springs
Walker Lake
Walnut Canyon (Rim)
Wildcat Spring
Wildlife Trail
Wilson Meadow
Wood Trail
Wupatki Ruin Trail

Moderate
Abineau Pipeline
Antelope Hills
Babe's Hole
Bear Cyn.—Overland Tr.
Bismarck Lake
Buckskinner Trail
Buffalo Park
Casner Mt. North
Chalender X-Country
Christmas Tree Trail
Clover Spring Trail
Coal Mine Canyon
Connector Trail
Crater Lake

Davenport Hill Trail
Deer Hill Trail
Doney Trail
Elden Skyline Trail
Elden Spring Loop
Fat Man's Loop
General Springs Trail
Government Knoll
Grand Falls
Hutch Mountain
James Canyon
Kelsey Spring Trail
Kinder Crossing Trail
Lakeview Trail
Lava River Cave
Ledges Trail
Little Elden—Heart
Little Elden-Schultz Tnk
Little Springs
Lookout Trail
Mack's Crossing
Marshall Lake
Mormon Mountain
Old Caves Crater
Old Lowell Obsv. Road
Oldham Trail #1
Overland Road
Pipeline Trail
Railroad Tunnel Trail
Red Butte
Red Mountain
Rocky Ridge Trail
SP Crater
Saddle Mountain
Sandys Canyon Trail
Schultz Creek Trail
Secret Mountain Trail
Secret Pocket Trail
Slate Mountain
Soldiers Trail
Summit Mountain
Sycamore Basin Trail
Three Sisters
Turkey Hill
Vista Loop Trail
Walnut Canyon Link
Walnut Canyon (Island)
Walnut Canyon (Ledge)
Walnut Canyon (Ranger)
Weatherford Canyon

West Fork Head
White Horse Hills
Wild Bill Hill
Wildcat Hill
Willow Crossing Trail
Winter Cabin Trail

Hard
A-1 Mountain
Abineau Canyon Trail
Bear Jaw Canyon Trail
Benham Trail
Bill Williams Mtn. Trail
Bixler Saddle Trail
Bright Angel Trail
Brookbank Trail
Bull Basin Trail
Calloway Trail
Dorsey Spring Trail
Elden Lookout Trail
Flagstaff Spring
Fossil Spring Trail
Geronimo Spring Trail
Grandview Trail
Heart Trail
Hermit Trail
Horse Crossing Trail
Humphreys Peak Trail
Inner Basin Trail
Kachina Trail
Kelsey-Winter Trail
Kendrick Mtn. Trail
Little Bear Trail
Lonesome Pocket Trail
Maxwell Trail
O'Leary Peak
Point Trail
Pumpkin Trail
South Kaibab Trail
Strawberry Crater
Sunset Trail
Sycamore Rim Trail
Taylor Cabin Trail
Tramway Trail
Tunnel Road
Upper Oldham Trail
Weatherford Trail
Wing Mountain

Hikes Grouped by Driving Distance

(One Way) Less Than 10 Mi.

A-1 Mountain
Brookbank Trail
Buffalo Park (3)
Christmas Tree
Elden Lookout Trail
Elden Pueblo
Elden Skyline
Elden Springs Loop
Fat Man's Loop
Flagstaff-North Trail
Griffiths Spring
Heart Trail
McMillan Mesa
Museum Nature Trail
Old Caves Crater
Old Lowell Road
Oldham Trail
Pipeline Trail
Rio de Flag Trail
Rocky Ridge
Sandy Seep
Sandys Canyon
Schultz Creek
Sinclair Wash (2)
Soldiers Trail
Sunset Trail
Tunnel Trail
Turkey Hill
Upper Oldham Trail
Vista Loop Trail
Weatherford Cyn.
Wildcat Hill

11—20 Mi.

Anderson Mesa
Antelope Hills
Bismarck Lake
Deer Hill Trail
Humphreys Trail
James Canyon
Lava River Cave
Little Bear
Little Elden—Heart
Little Elden—Schultz
Lookout Trail
Marshall Lake
Oak Creek Vista
Route 66
Veit Spring
Walnut Canyon (4)

Walnut Canyon Link
Weatherford Trail
Wildlife Trail
Wilson Meadow
Wing Mountain
Wood Trail

21—30 Mi.

Abineau Canyon
Abineau Pipeline
Babe's Hole
Beale-Government
Bear Jaw
Casner Mtn.
Chalender X-Country (3)
Crater Lake
Crystal Point
Dorsey Spring
Flagstaff Spring
Geronimo Spring
Government Knoll
Inner Basin
Kachina Trail
Kelsey Spring
Kelsey-Winter Cabin
Kendrick Mtn.
Keyhole Sink
Lakeview Trail
Lava Flow Trail
Ledges Trail
Little Spring
Mormon Mtn.
O'Leary Peak
Pumpkin Trail
Saddle Mtn
Secret Mountain
Slate Mountain
Strawberry Crater
Sycamore Rim
Taylor Cabin
Walker Lake
West Fork Head
White Horse Hills
Wild Bill Hill
Winter Cabin

31—40 Mi.

Arizona Trail—Allan Lk.
Beale—Laws
Benham Trail
Bill Williams
Buckskinner Trail
Bull Basin

Clover Spring
Connector
Grand Falls
Hutch Mountain
Red Mountain
SP Crater
Three Sisters
Wupatki Trail

41—50 Mi.

Bear Cyn.—Overland
Bixler Saddle
Davenport Hill (3)
Doney Trail
Johnson Crater
Overland Road
Summit Mountain

51—60 Mi.

Lonesome Pocket
Maxwell Trail
Secret Pocket
Tramway Trail
Willow Crossing

61—70 Mi.

Pivot Rock
Red Butte
Wildcat Spring

71—80 Mi.

Calloway
General Springs
Horse Crossing
Houston Brothers
Kinder Crossing
Mack's Crossing
Point Trail
Railroad Tunnel
Sycamore Basin

81—90 Mi.

Bright Angel
Coconino Rim
Fossil Springs
Grandview
Hermit
South Kaibab

91 Plus Mi.

Coal Mine Cyn.

16

A-1 Mountain

General Information
Location Map E2
Bellemont and Flagstaff West USGS Maps
Coconino Forest Service Map

Driving Distance One Way: 9.9 miles *15.84 km* (Time 30 minutes)
Access Road: All cars, Last 4.4 miles *7.04 km* good gravel road
Hiking Distance One Way: 1.0 miles *1.6 km* (Time 40 minutes)
How Strenuous: Hard
Features: Landmark hill north of Flagstaff

NUTSHELL: This hike takes you to the top of a prominent landmark on the Flagstaff horizon.

DIRECTIONS:
From Flagstaff City Hall Go:
West a block on Route 66, then south, beneath the railroad overpass, see Access Map, page 10. At 0.5 miles *0.8 km* you will reach a Y intersection. The right fork is Route 66. Take it. You will soon leave town, driving on a stretch of fabled Highway 66. At the 5.0 mile *8.0 km* point you will merge onto Interstate-40 West. Look for Exit 190 at the 5.3 mile *8.5 km* point, and take it. Turn right at the stop sign and take gravel road FR 506. Follow it to the 7.5 mile *12 km* point, where you will be on top of Observatory Mesa. Here you will meet FR 515 forking to the right. Go left here, staying on FR 506, the main road. It will curl around toward A-1 Mountain. At 8.2 miles *13.12 km* there is a fork. Go left, again on the main road, which is now FR 518B. At 9.7 miles *15.5 km* you will come to a radio tower. Go past it on the left side on a rocky road. Take the first turn to the left and continue to the 9.9 mile *15.84 km* point, where you will see a rough road going up the east side of the mountain. Park nearby. To your right you will see a large metal object inside a barbed wire fence.

TRAILHEAD: Walk the road going uphill.

DESCRIPTION: Before you walk up the mountain, take a minute to look at the object inside the fence, which you will find to be a stock tank. You will see what looks like a large corrugated metal shed roof resting on the ground sloping downward. A gutter catches all the rain water that runs off the roofing and channels it into a pipe that flows into a large round metal tank from where it feeds out into a trough. This is an upscale version of the old rain barrel and is called a trick tank. We have encountered many of these scattered throughout the woods around Flagstaff.

Flagstaff Hikes

A-1 Mountain is a basaltic volcano with a nicely shaped crater but with a breach where part of its east side is missing. Some of the missing material may have been blown out during explosive eruption. Also, some may have simply floated out on the A-1 lava flow. A small rounded-top hill just northeast of the breach is probably such a floater. The lava flow advanced about 4 miles to the east where its abrupt edge forms the 200-foot-tall hill behind the Museum of Northern Arizona and all along the west side of Flagstaff. Lowell observatory sits atop the lava near this edge.

In spring, the crater basin may be a small lake, and can be a charming place then. In the crater you will see a gravel road going up the north rim. This makes an easy hike but the views are not good from the top there. Work your way around the rim (no trail) counterclockwise and you will find that from the west and south faces there are fine views. Explore the top and then return on the road you first followed.

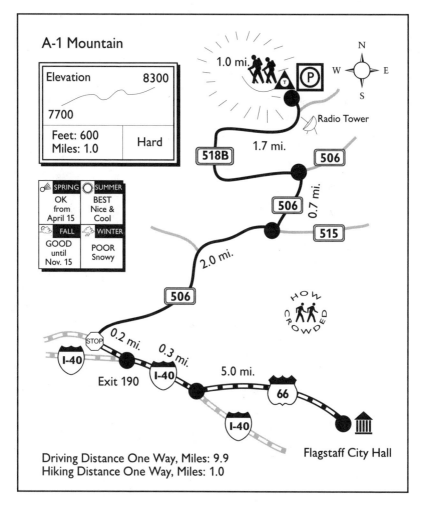

A-1 Mountain

Elevation	8300
7700	
Feet: 600 Miles: 1.0	Hard

☘ SPRING	☀ SUMMER
OK from April 15	BEST Nice & Cool
☁ FALL	❄ WINTER
GOOD until Nov. 15	POOR Snowy

N
W — E
S

1.0 mi.

Radio Tower

518B   1.7 mi.   506

506   0.7 mi.   515

2.0 mi.

506

HOW CROWDED

STOP
0.2 mi.   0.3 mi.
I-40   I-40   5.0 mi.
Exit 190   66

I-40

Flagstaff City Hall

Driving Distance One Way, Miles: 9.9
Hiking Distance One Way, Miles: 1.0

Mangum

Abineau Canyon #127

General Information
Location Map E3
Humphreys Peak and White Horse Hills USGS Maps
Coconino Forest Service Map

Driving Distance One Way: 24.7 miles *39.52 km* (Time 50 minutes)
Access Road: All cars, Last 5.3 miles *8.5 km* gravel, in medium condition
Hiking Distance One Way: 2.3 miles *3.68 km* (Time 2 hours)
How Strenuous: Hard, Steep trail, High elevations
Features: Alpine scenery, Vast views

NUTSHELL: This is a strenuous hike up the north face of the San
Francisco Peaks about 25 miles *40 km* north of Flagstaff.

DIRECTIONS:
From Flagstaff City Hall Go:
North on Humphreys Street, 0.60 miles *1.0 km* to the stoplight. See
Access Map, page 10. Turn left on Columbus Avenue and follow it north
around a curve, where it changes name to Ft. Valley Road, and then to
Highway 180. At 19.4 miles *31.04 km* (MP 235.2) turn right on the upper
Hart Prairie Road, FR 151. At 21.0 miles *33.6 km*, turn left on FR 418 and
continue on it to the 24.1 miles *38.56 km* point, where you will see a sign for
the Bear Jaw and Abineau Trails. The road to the trailhead is marked FR
9123-J. Turn right onto it and follow it to the 24.6 miles *39.36 km* point,
where you fork left, then to the 24.7 miles *39.52 km* point, where you will
reach the parking area. Park at the parking lot.

TRAILHEAD: The cinder road on which you drove in is blocked by a big
boulder at the parking lot. Walk past the boulder and go down near the end
of the road. The trail takes off to your right, uphill, and is marked.

DESCRIPTION: From the parking area you hike a connecting trail that
goes about 0.3 miles *0.48 km* from the parking lot to a junction of the
Abineau and Bear Jaw Trails. Here you turn right and go uphill.
   From the junction the trail starts rather mildly, moving through a nice
forest, then the pitch changes to a steeper grade. Soon it will become obvi-
ous to you that you are in a canyon. Just above the 9,000 foot level, the for-
est is entirely spruce and the trail is very rocky and steep.
   Near the top, you break out into a small park, which is treeless in spots.
The view is quite breathtaking. Ahead of you (S), is the towering top of Mt.
Humphreys, highest point in Arizona at 12,643 feet. Behind you (N), you

can see forever. From this spot it's a hard climb up to FR 146, the end of the trail, at 2.3 miles *3.68 km* from the parking area.

If you want to do a loop, walk along east on FR 146, downhill, for a distance of 2.0 miles *3.2 km* to the Bear Jaw Trail and go down it. Look carefully, as it may not be signed. Cairns may be the only marker. If you overrun it, you will be in trouble. Taking the Bear Jaw trail will add 2.0 miles *3.2 km* to this hike, for a loop total of 6.85 miles *10.96 km*, compared to a total of 4.6 miles *7.36 km* going up and down the Abineau Trail only. (There is no access to Humphreys Peak from Abineau).

The canyon, the trail and a peak in the area were named for Julius Aubineau, who was the Flagstaff mayor in 1898, and is regarded as the father of the Flagstaff municipal water system which brought water to town from the Peaks. They got his name right on the Humphreys Peak USGS Quad map, but some careless cartographer spelled it "Abineau" on the White Horse Hills map and the Forest Service unfortunately copied the error.

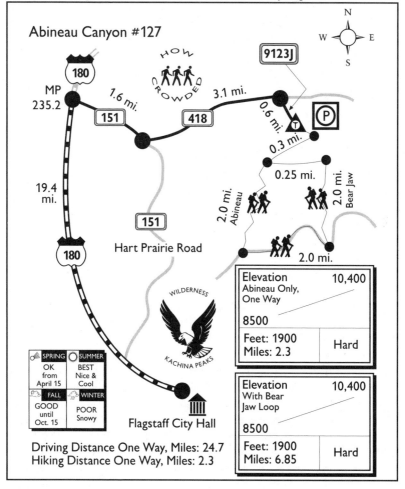

Mangum

Abineau Pipeline Trail

General Information
Location Map E3
Humphreys Peak, Sunset Crater West, and White Horse Hills USGS Maps
Coconino Forest Service Map

Driving Distance One Way: 21.6 miles *34.6 km* (Time 45 minutes)
Access Road: All cars, Last 4.5 miles *7.2 km* medium dirt road
Hiking Distance One Way: 6.7 miles *10.7 km* (Time 4 hours)
How Strenuous: Moderate, except for high elevations
Features: Beautiful forests, marvelous views

NUTSHELL: Start this hike on Locket Meadow, high on the east side of the San Francisco Peaks 21.6 miles *34.6 km* north of town. From the meadow you follow the Inner Basin Trail (old service road) to Jack Smith Spring then branch off onto another closed road that takes you around the north side of the peaks through a beautiful forest to a clearing where you have vast views. A great trail in October when aspen leaves are turning.

DIRECTIONS:
From Flagstaff City Hall Go:
East on Route 66. This will take you through the city, heading first easterly and then north out of town. See Access Map, pages 10-11. Route 66 veers off to the right in about 3.8 miles *6.08 km*. Go straight here, on Highway 89. At 17.1 miles *27.4 km* (MP 431.2)—just past the entrance to Sunset Crater—turn left onto FR 552 and take it to the 18.3 mile *29.3 km* point, where you will see a sign for Lockett Meadow. Go right. From here the road is a winding narrow gravel route which zigzags up the face of the mountain, giving great views of the Painted Desert as you go. At 21.3 miles *34 km* you reach Lockett Meadow. Go to your right into the campground. Park in the day use area at the 21.6 mile *34.6 km* point.

TRAILHEAD: Use the Inner Basin trailhead, which you will find by driving all the way back into the trees among the campsites. The trailhead is posted with a big sign to the left of a toilet.

DESCRIPTION: The first part of this hike follows the **Inner Basin Trail** for 1.5 miles *2.4 km* to Jack Smith Spring. This is a beautiful part of the trail, a lush alpine habitat with plenty of aspens, firs, ferns and other vegetation. You are walking along a maintenance road used by the City of Flagstaff. Its purpose is to allow city vehicles to get to the springs in the Inner Basin, which are part of Flagstaff's water supply. The road is closed to all other vehicular traffic, so it makes an excellent hiking trail. It is heavily used by mountain bikers, so stay alert.

At Jack Smith Spring you will find a couple of old green cabins and a supply dump with water pipe and other materials lying about. A road comes in from the left here. It is FR 146, which goes down to the Schultz Pass Road. FR 146 road is used as a hiking trail, see **Tunnel Road.** What you want to do at this point is take FR 146 to the right, which goes uphill. You will soon see that this extension of FR 146 is not maintained.

This old road goes around to the north side of the Peaks and makes a fine hiking trail. It takes you on a gradual climb, curving around to the north. The **Bear Jaw** and **Abineau Canyon** hiking trails intersect this road near its end.

You will pass through heavy aspen forests, so it is a great place to come in the fall to see the changing leaves. Mid-October is the right time for this. The trail ends at a bare spot on the side of the mountain, where there are sweeping views to the north.

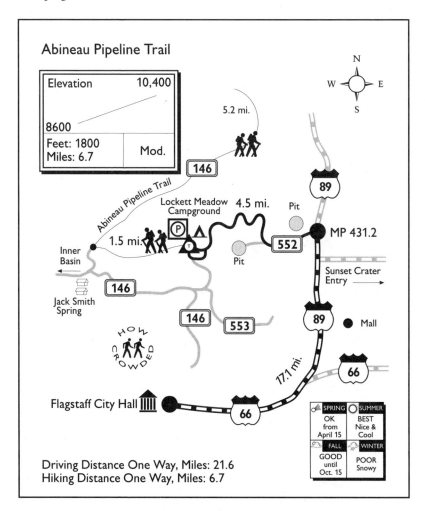

Mangum

Anderson Mesa

General Information
Location Map F3
Ashurst Lake, Lower Lake Mary USGS Maps
Coconino Forest Service Map

Driving Distance One Way: 13.55 miles *21.68 km* (Time 25 minutes)
Access Road: All cars, All paved
Hiking Distance One Way: 1.0 miles *1.6 km* (Time 30 minutes)
How Strenuous: Easy
Features: Easy to reach, Charming lake, Views

NUTSHELL: This hike takes you along a leg of The Arizona Trail. It starts on Anderson Mesa near the Lowell Observatory facility and then winds south and east toward Ashurst Lake. We have selected a portion of this long trail that makes a good day hike, with a lake and interesting views.

DIRECTIONS:
From Flagstaff City Hall Go:
West, then south on Route 66 under the railroad overpass. See Access Map, page 10. At 0.50 miles *0.8 km*, a stoplight at a Y intersection, leave Route 66 here and go straight on Milton Road. At 1.70 miles *2.72 km* turn right at the stoplight at Forest Meadows. At the next corner turn left on Beulah and follow it out of town. Beulah will connect onto Highway 89A. At the 2.4 miles *3.84 km* point (MP 401.6) you will see the turnoff to the Lake Mary Road to your left at the last stoplight in town. Turn left and follow the Lake Mary Road to the 12.0 miles *19.2 km* point (MP 334.3) where you will see the paved Marshall Lake road to your left going uphill. Turn left and take it to the 13.55 mile *21.68 km* point, the top of the mesa, taking the curve to the right toward the Lowell Observatory facility. The paving curves right at a place where there is a wide loop parking lot (cindered) to your left. Pull in here and park.

TRAILHEAD: At the parking place. You will see an Arizona Trail sign immediately at the parking loop, with a segment of trail headed north. Do not take this. Instead, walk across the dirt road, where you will see another Arizona Trail marker going through a fence made of criss-crossed logs. This is the part of the trail to take.

DESCRIPTION: The trail skirts the Lowell Observatory installation and almost immediately brings you near Prime Lake (named after pioneer George Prime). This lake is a scenic little gem, and is one of several lakes atop Anderson Mesa. It is a great place for water birds.

Soon after you leave the lake you veer away from a dirt road and head toward the edge of the mesa. Here you will see the typical Anderson Mesa landscape, with many shrubs and lots of open spaces. It is extremely rocky, with broken basalt lava rock all over the place. The rocks have been mostly cleared from the trail, so the walking is easy.

At a distance of 1.0 miles *1.6 km* is a great viewpoint where the trail runs to the edge of a bare rock outcrop. You look down onto the area between Upper and Lower Lake Mary, just west of the Upper Lake Mary dam. The abrupt step down to Lake Mary is the result of a fault, or break, in the Earth's crust across which the rocks on the southwest side have dropped down about 200 feet. The original continuation of the basalt lava under your feet can be found in rocky outcrops just beyond Lake Mary. We stop the hike here for a short but interesting day hike. You may want to wander back and forth along the rim in this area to find different viewpoints.

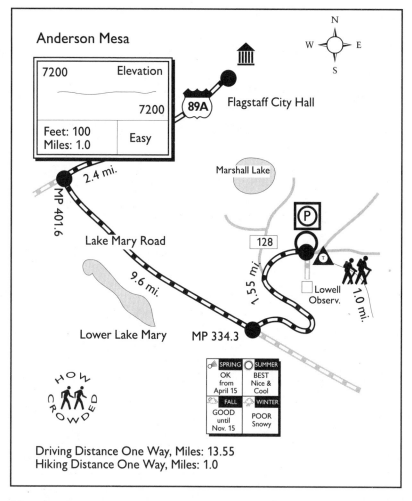

Mangum

Antelope Hills

General Information
Location Map E2
Wing Mountain USGS Map
Coconino Forest Service Map

Driving Distance One Way: 18.3 miles *29.28 km* (Time 40 minutes)
Access Road: All cars, Last 3.9 miles *6.24 km* good gravel road
Hiking Distance One Way: 0.8 miles *1.3 km* (Time 45 minutes)
How Strenuous: Moderate
Features: Views

NUTSHELL: This mountain 18.3 miles *29.28 km* north of Flagstaff is located at the northeast end of Government Prairie and gives tremendous views of the prairie to the south.

DIRECTIONS:
From Flagstaff City Hall Go:
North on Humphreys Street for 0.60 miles *1.0 km*. See Access Map, page 10. Turn left at the stoplight onto Columbus Avenue and follow it around a big curve to the north. You will see the street signs call this road Columbus at first, then Ft. Valley Road and then Highway 180. Stay on Highway 180 to the 14.4 miles *23.04 km* point (MP 230.1), where a road takes off to the left. Turn left onto this road, FR 245, and follow it to the 17.4 mile *27.84 km* point where it intersects FR 171. Turn left onto FR 171 and follow it to the 18.05 mile *28.9 km* point, where FR 812 goes off to the right. Turn right on FR 812 and take it to the 18.3 mile *29.28 km* point. Park there.

TRAILHEAD: You will see the Antelope Hills to your right (north). You will also see a primitive road going to it and then going straight up the side of the mountain. Hike near this road.

DESCRIPTION: There are several hills surrounding Government Prairie. While they all have features in common, each has its own distinct characteristics and personality. The Antelope Hills are the farthest north of the group, situated at the north end of the prairie, close to Kendrick Peak.
     The trail was not made for hiking. Kamikaze four-wheelers created it by charging straight up the mountain in a *falter-and-die* test of their machines. Government Prairie is now closed to off-road travel, so the scar is healing. Help it heal by hiking alongside it, but not on it.
     The Antelope Hills have two knobs. The southern knob that you climb first is bare. As a result it provides some great views. You can see particularly well to the south, where the whole sweep of the Government Prairie is

in view, although your ability to see beyond the midpoint is restricted to the opening between Klostermeyer Hill and Rain Tank Hill. The views east are also fine, as you look onto the western side of the San Francisco Peaks. We were here in October and saw a great display of yellow and red aspen leaves on the slopes of the peaks.

Once you reach the top you will find that there is only a small drop in elevation to the saddle between the knobs and that it is easy to walk down to the saddle and then up to the top of the north knob. Sad to say, the views to the north are not good because of heavy timber on the north knob.

On your way up or down, check out the ruins of an old cabin and out-buildings at the foot of the hill to the east of the trail about thirty yards. You will also see a couple of platforms about eight feet high. These are part of an NAU research project into the life of the prairie dog. There is a large prairie dog colony surrounding the platforms.

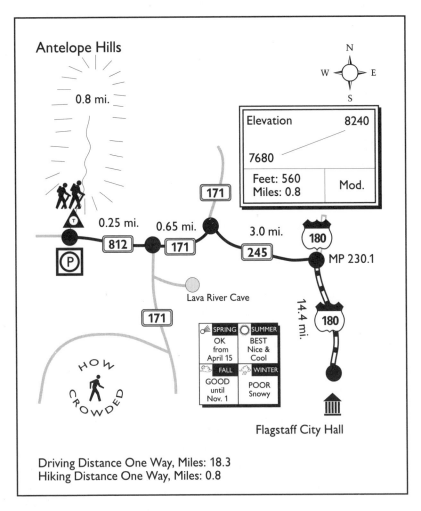

Antelope Hills

0.8 mi.

Elevation	8240
7680	

| Feet: 560 Miles: 0.8 | Mod. |

0.25 mi. 0.65 mi. 3.0 mi.

812   171   245   180   MP 230.1

14.4 mi.

Lava River Cave

171   180

☘ SPRING	☀ SUMMER
OK from April 15	BEST Nice & Cool
☁ FALL	❄ WINTER
GOOD until Nov. 1	POOR Snowy

HOW CROWDED

Flagstaff City Hall

Driving Distance One Way, Miles: 18.3
Hiking Distance One Way, Miles: 0.8

Mangum

Arizona Trail—Allan Lake

General Information
Location Map G3
Hutch Mountain USGS Map
Coconino Forest Service Map

Driving Distance One Way: 32.1 miles *51.36 km* (Time 1 hour)
Access Road: All cars, Last 0.5 miles *0.8 km* good gravel road
Hiking Distance One Way: 0.8 miles *1.3 km* (Time 45 minutes)
How Strenuous: Easy
Features: Old logging railroad bed, Two springs, Beautiful pine forest

NUTSHELL: This part of the Arizona Trail works its way through the tall timber country southeast of Flagstaff, on top of a logging railroad bed.

DIRECTIONS:
From Flagstaff City Hall Go:
 West, then south on Route 66 under the railroad overpass. See Access Map, pages 10-11. At 0.5 miles *0.8 km*, leave Route 66 and go straight on Milton Road. At 1.7 miles *2.72 km* you will reach a stoplight at Forest Meadows Street. Turn right onto Forest Meadows and go one block to Beulah. Turn left on Beulah and follow it south. Beulah merges onto Highway 89A. At 2.4 miles *3.84 km* (MP 401.6), turn left onto the Lake Mary-Mormon Lake Road. Follow this road past both of the entrance roads to Mormon Lake and at the 31.6 mile *50.56 km* point MP 313.3 turn right on FR 91. Drive this good gravel road to the 32.1 mile *51.36 km* point, where you turn right into a little campground, the place where you will park.

TRAILHEAD: There are lath-type signs for the Arizona Trail on both sides of FR 91 where you turned into the parking area. For this hike we recommend that you take the trail on the south side of the road. The trail on the north side runs for many miles for more good hiking.

DESCRIPTION: This area is similar to Flagstaff but it is somewhat higher and gets more moisture and as a result the pine forest is especially thick and healthy. The abundance of prime trees attracted the attention of the operators of Flagstaff's lumber mills, who logged the area for years.
 The trail winds through the forest, being a bit hard to see at first because of the heavy pine needle drop, but at 0.25 miles *0.4 km* you come to a high embankment and climb to the top of it, turning left. You are now on the old logging railroad grade and will have absolutely no trouble following the trail from this point. We love finding and hiking old logging railroad grades and really enjoy this one, which is one of the most interesting. It was built in

1948 as a joint venture of the Southwest and Saginaw-Manistee Lumber companies of Flagstaff, and was used until March 30, 1966, when engine #25 brought the last load of logs into the mill at Flagstaff.

Just across the grade the green area with a couple of ponds that you see is Van Deren Spring. As you walk along the grade you will see many old ties but no steel. At 0.66 miles *1.0 km* you reach the most interesting place. It is also green and is the site of another spring, but more importantly, it is the site of a wye for the railroad. You will see a curved extension of the railroad bed going to your right into the forest. This goes to a point, from which there is another curved extension which you reach after a few minutes more hiking. This wye made it possible to turn a train around.

At 0.8 miles *1.3 km* you come to a fence where you leave the woods and emerge into an open field, across which the trail goes about 0.4 miles *0.64 km* to a point on the Mormon Lake Road. We end the hike at the fence.

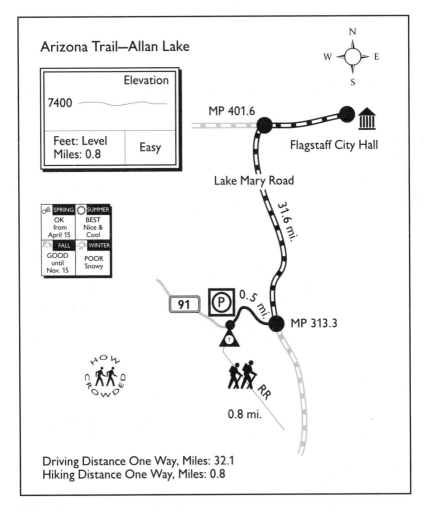

Mangum

Babe's Hole

General Information
Location Map F2
Sycamore Point USGS Map
Coconino Forest Service Map

Driving Distance One Way: 24.1 miles *38.6 km* (Time 1 hour)
Access Road: High clearance needed for last 1.8 miles *2.9 km*
Hiking Distance One Way: 1.2 miles *1.9 km* (Time 1 hour)
How Strenuous: Moderate
Features: Remote hidden spring, Virgin forests in a Wilderness

NUTSHELL: Located 24.1 miles *38.6 km* southwest of Flagstaff, this trail takes you to a remote and beautiful spring hidden away on the east side of Sycamore Canyon.

DIRECTIONS:
From Flagstaff City Hall Go:
    West one block on Route 66, then left (south) beneath the railroad overpass. See Access Map, page 10. At 0.5 miles *0.8 km* you will reach a Y intersection. The right fork is named Route 66. Take it. You will soon leave town. At 2.6 miles *4.2 km* you will reach a road going to the left. This is the Woody Mountain Road, FR 231. Take it. It is paved about a mile and then turns into a cinder road. At 16.6 miles *26.6 km* you will intersect FR 538. Turn right onto FR 538 and follow it to the 22.3 mile *35.7 km* point, where it intersects FR 538E. Turn right on 538E. The road is rough beyond here. At 22.7 miles *36.3 km* you hit another intersection, where FR 538E forks to the left, going to Dorsey Spring Road. Keep straight, now on FR 538G, and follow it to its end at 23.7 miles *37.9 km*, where it meets FR 527A. Turn left onto the Kelsey Trail road, going to the 24.1 mile *38.6 km* point, the parking area. This last 0.4 mile *0.64 km* stretch is terrible, a real tire-eater. You might want to walk this bit.

TRAILHEAD: You will see a big sign at the parking area.

DESCRIPTION: This trail shares the same right of way with the **Kelsey Spring Trail**, and you have to pass through Kelsey Spring to reach Babe's Hole. The comments about the Kelsey Spring hike apply here.
    The parking lot is located right on the edge of the rim, so the trail immediately plunges down into the canyon. It is steep but not slippery. It passes through a beautiful forest, which gets more beautiful and interesting as you go.
    Kelsey Spring is easily reached in 0.5 miles *0.8 km*, on a shelf of level

land. Enjoy it and then continue down the canyon. As you leave Kelsey Spring, you enter an unusual life zone where the prevailing pines disappear, to be replaced with oaks and other deciduous trees. The area seems to get a lot of moisture, so the vegetation is heavy.

At Babe's Hole several hill folds come together to make a small protected pocket of land. You can see why it got the name "hole" as it really is a small and enclosed area. Babe's Hole is a beautiful place. It looks otherwordly, with many bent trees overarching and protecting the spring, which is lined with a small circle of rocks and roofed over with poles. It is very quiet. A fantastic place.

From Babe's Hole you can continue downhill another 0.15 miles *0.24 km*, where there is a trail junction. The **Kelsey-Winter Trail** takes off to the left, to **Dorsey Spring** and then **Winter Cabin Spring**, while the trail to **Geronimo Spring** goes down to the bottom of the canyon.

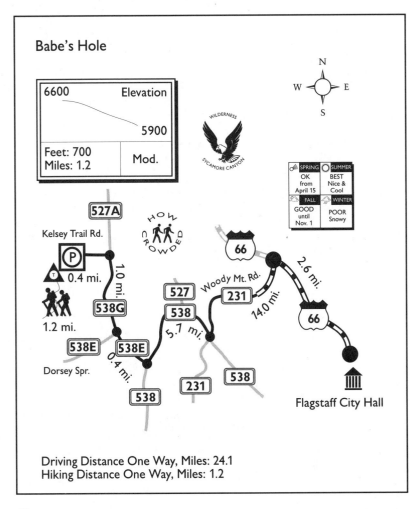

Babe's Hole

6600   Elevation   5900

Feet: 700
Miles: 1.2   Mod.

	SPRING	SUMMER
	OK from April 15	BEST Nice & Cool
	FALL	WINTER
	GOOD until Nov. 1	POOR Snowy

527A

Kelsey Trail Rd.

P   0.4 mi.

HOW CROWDED

66

527   231

Woody Mt. Rd.

1.0 mi.

14.0 mi.

2.6 mi.

1.2 mi.

538G   538

5.7 mi.

66

538E   538E

Dorsey Spr.

0.4 mi.

538   231   538

Flagstaff City Hall

Driving Distance One Way, Miles: 24.1
Hiking Distance One Way, Miles: 1.2

Mangum

Beale Road On Government Prairie

General Information
Location Map E2
Parks and Wing Mt. USGS Maps
Kaibab (Williams) Forest Service Map

Driving Distance One Way: 24.3 miles *38.9 km* (Time 40 minutes)
Access Road: All cars, Last 11.0 miles *17.6 km* good gravel road
Hiking Distance One Way: 2.3 miles *3.7 km* (Time 1.5 hours))
How Strenuous: Easy
Features: Historic road, Views

NUTSHELL: This stretch of the Beale Road crosses Government Prairie. The old wagon tracks are visible and have been marked. A hike across the prairie would be worthwhile in its own right, but with the added bonus of the wagon road, it becomes a fascinating experience.

DIRECTIONS:
From Flagstaff City Hall Go:
   West a block on Route 66, then south, beneath the railroad overpass. See Access Map, page 10. At 0.5 miles *0.8 km* you will reach a Y intersection. The right fork is Route 66. Take it. You will soon leave town. At the 5.0 mile *8.0 km* point you will merge onto Interstate-40 West. Look for Exit 185, "Transwestern Rd., Bellemont" and take it. It is at the 10.8 mile *17.3 km* point. From the exit turn right and go to the frontage road, where you turn left onto FR 146. You are now following another stretch of U.S. 66. Stay on this to the 18 mile *28.8 km* point, where you will see FR 107 fork right. Take FR 107 and follow it to the 24.3 mile *38.9 km* point, where FR 107 and FR 100 join. Park off FR 107 on the right (east) just below the intersection.

TRAILHEAD: At the gate.

DESCRIPTION: The Beale Road was scouted in 1857 by a government party led by Lt. Edward Beale. It was this *government* sponsorship leading to the establishment of a *government* road that gave the name Government Prairie. Beale returned with work crews in 1858 and 1859 to develop the road and it was used as a major east-west road until the coming of the railroad in 1882. On the first expedition Beale used twenty camels, an experiment to see how well they could handle American deserts. This explains why a camel is used as a symbol for the road. You will see the camel burned onto the posts that mark the trail. Beale loved the camels but the cowboys (camelboys?) hated them and they never caught on.
   At the junction of FR 107 and FR 100 you will see a fence to your right

with a gate. Go through the gate to begin walking the Beale Road. You will pick up markers there. The right of way is marked with posts, rock cairns, blazes and brass caps. In 0.15 miles *0.24 km* you will come upon an old homestead to your left. There isn't much left, but you can make out the outlines of stones that were used as footings.

At 0.3 miles *0.48 km* you will leave the road you are walking and go across country. This takes you from open land, through woods. At 1.3 miles *2.1 km*, you break out onto the main part of the prairie where you will see the wagon tracks clearly and follow them. You cross FR 793 at the 1.4 mile *2.3 km* point. When you reach the 2.3 mile point, the road leaves the prairie and enters a wooded area in front of **Wild Bill Hill**. We end the hike here (the road continues) as crossing the prairie makes a good day hike.

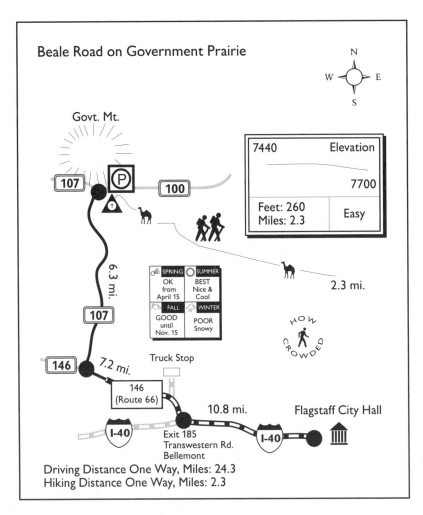

Beale Road—Laws Spring

General Information
Location Map E2
Sitgreaves Mountain and Squaw Mountain USGS Maps
Kaibab (Williams) Forest Service Map

Driving Distance One Way: 37.6 miles *60 km* (Time 1 hour)
Access Road: All cars, Last 10.3 miles *16.5 km* good gravel roads
Hiking Distance One Way: 0.25 miles *0.4 km* (Time 30 minutes)
How Strenuous: Easy
Features: Spring with petroglyphs, Historical 1850s wagon route

NUTSHELL: This hike takes you to Laws Spring, an attractive historical site with an interpretive sign, rock art (both ancient and modern), and then onto the Beale Road.

DIRECTIONS:
From Flagstaff City Hall Go:
West a block on Route 66, then south, beneath the railroad overpass. See Access Map, page 10. At 0.5 miles *0.8 km* you will reach a Y intersection. The right fork is Route 66. Take it. You will soon leave town. At the 5.0 mile *8.0 km* point you will merge onto Interstate-40 West. Drive I-40 West to the 24.5 mile *39.2 km* point (MP 172), where you will take Exit 171 for Pittman Valley. Turn left at the stop sign and take paved road FR 74, toward the Compressor Station. The paving will end at 27.3 miles *43.7 km*. At 32.2 miles *51.5 km* you will intersect FR 141 and go right on it. At 32.7 miles *52.3 km* you will see a sign for Boulin Tank and intersect FR 730. Turn left on FR 730 and follow it to the 34.95 mile *55.9 km* point where you join FR 115. Turn left onto FR 115 and follow it to the 36.85 mile *58.9 km* point. There you turn to your left on FR 2030. You will see a Laws Spring sign. Take this road to the parking lot, where you park at 37.6 miles *60 km*.

TRAILHEAD: Posted at the parking lot.

DESCRIPTION: The Beale Road was a heroic undertaking. The United States acquired Arizona north of the Gila River in 1848 after the Mexican War, and Congress sent Beale to explore it and find a travel route across northern Arizona to California in 1857. Beale's party included camels to deal with deserts. Beale located a good route roughly following the thirty-fifth parallel. In 1858 and 1859 he returned under a Congressional grant and developed the road for travel. About seventy-five percent of the old road has been located, thanks largely to the efforts of Flagstaff's Jack Beale Smith. The Forest Service joined with Smith in the project of marking the road, and their efforts made this hike possible.

The trail takes you gently down the bank of a small stream, where you will find a rock basin at the bottom. Look for Indian rock art along the way, and you will see a few symbols. Laws Spring fills the rock basin, and seems to be perennial. It was an important water source for travelers on the Beale Road. The words, "Laws Spring" were chiseled into a rock in 1859 by a member of Beale's crew. Look carefully and you will see other rock art, both ancient Indian and modern. The Forest Service has placed a nice explanatory plaque on the face of a boulder at the spring.

After you have enjoyed the spring, take the rest of the trail, up the other bank, again a gentle climb. At the 0.25 mile *0.4 km* point, you will find the Beale Road marker in a field. This is officially the end of the hike, but you might want to walk part of the old road. Turn right at the marker and follow the cairns and posts as far as you wish.

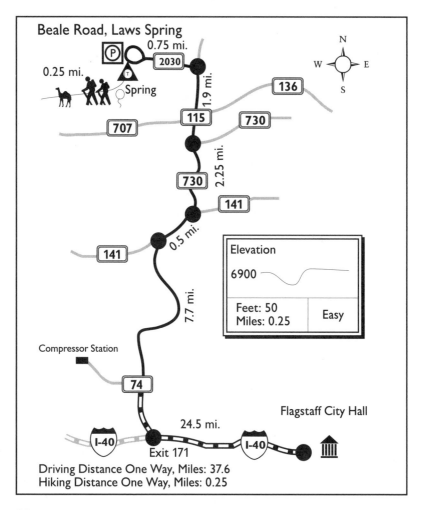

Mangum

Bear Canyon, Overland Road

General Information
Location Map F1
Williams South, May Tank Pocket USGS Maps
Kaibab Forest Service Map

Driving Distance One Way: 46.55 miles *74.5 km* (Time 1.25 hours)
Access Road: High clearance needed for last 0.9 miles *1.44 km*
Hiking Distance One Way: 2.5 miles *4.0 km* (Time 1.5 hours)
How Strenuous: Moderate
Features: Historic Overland Road (1863), Beautiful wild canyons

NUTSHELL: The Overland Road was built in 1863 to give access from the Beale Road (at a point where Flagstaff was founded 17 years later) to the gold fields near Prescott. It was used until rail transportation made it obsolete in 1882. In 1988 the portion of the old road through the Kaibab Forest was located and marked. On this hike you will enjoy hiking part of the Overland Road, as it crosses the head of Bear Canyon and then goes across country to join the paved Perkinsville Road south of Williams.

DIRECTIONS:
From Flagstaff City Hall Go:
South on Route 66 under the railroad overpass. Be sure to follow Route 66 when it turns right at the second stoplight. See Access Map, page 10. In about five miles *8.0 km* you will merge onto I-40 West and stay on it to the 30.3 miles *48.5 km* point, the Williams Exit, #165. Take that exit and at the stop sign go left to Williams. Go into town on Railroad Avenue to the 32.9 mile point *52.6 km* where you will find Fourth Street. Turn left on Fourth Street. As it leaves town its name changes to the Perkinsville Road (73). Stay on this road to the 45.65 mile *73.0 km* point, where you will turn left on FR 175 (fka FR 57). At the 45.85 mile *73.4 km* point, you reach the junction with FR 176. Turn right (south) on 176 and follow it to the 46.55 mile *74.5 km* point, where you will find a cattle guard. Park off the road there.

TRAILHEAD: Start hiking at the cattle guard.

DESCRIPTION: The Overland Road is marked with 4x4 posts, large cairns (rock piles), brass pins and blazes. You will see some of these along FR 176, which was part of the Overland Road. Walk down FR 176 to a point 0.5 miles *0.8 km* from the cattle guard, where you will see a burro marker on a 4x4 post. Walk 25 paces beyond it and you will see markers where you leave the roadway and take off cross country to your right (west). Follow these markers from now on. You can seldom see the path, so be sure to follow the markers. They are well located. Never guess where the hike is going. Keep a marker in sight at all times.

The Overland Road's builders had many challenges. One of the major ones was the problem of avoiding the canyons that seem to cut this area everywhere. You will see how they met this challenge, as you go across Bear Canyon at its head, where it is a tiny ravine. You will skirt three other canyons as you go.

Once the road builders had dodged the canyons, they got onto a finger ridge that took them from the top of the Mogollon Rim down to the Verde Valley, the route still used by the present Perkinsville Road, which you will meet at the end of this hike. Since the 3d edition of our book, the Forest Service has created the Bandit trailhead at the terminus of this hike, a nice paved parking area with an interpretive sign. We think our 2.5 mile *4.0 km* hike is a better day hike than the 6.0 mile *9.6 km* hike they show on the sign.

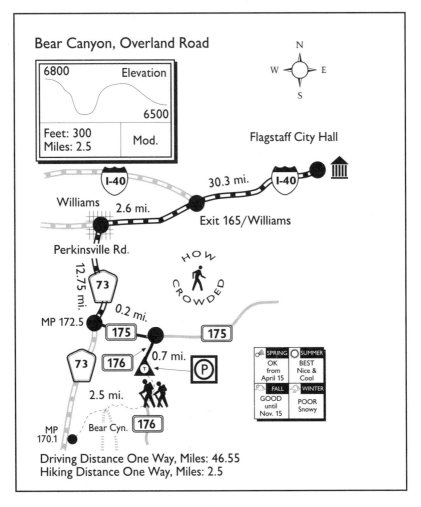

Mangum

Bear Jaw Canyon #26

General Information
Location Map E3
Humphreys Peak and White Horse Hills USGS Maps
Coconino Forest Service Map

Driving Distance One Way: 24.7 miles *39.5 km* (Time 50 minutes)
Access Road: All cars, Last 5.3 miles *8.5 km* gravel, in medium condition
Hiking Distance One Way: 2.55 miles *4.1 km* (Time 2 hours)
How Strenuous: Hard, Steep trail, High elevations
Features: Alpine scenery, Vast views

NUTSHELL: This is a strenuous hike up the north face of the San Francisco Peaks about 25 miles *40 km* north of Flagstaff.

DIRECTIONS:
From Flagstaff City Hall Go:
North on Humphreys Street, 0.6 miles *1.0 km* to the stoplight. See Access Map, page 10. Turn left on Columbus Avenue and follow it north around a curve, where it changes name to Ft. Valley Road, and then to Highway 180. At 19.4 miles *31.04 km* (MP 235.2) turn right on the upper Hart Prairie Road, FR 151. At 21.0 miles *33.6 km*, turn left on FR 418 and continue on it to the 24.1 miles *38.6 km* point, where you will see a sign for the Bear Jaw and Abineau Trails. The road to the trailhead is marked FR 9123-J. Turn right onto it and follow it to the 24.6 miles *39.36 km* point, where you fork left, then to the 24.7 miles *39.5 km* point, where you will reach the parking area. Park at the parking lot.

TRAILHEAD: The cinder road on which you drove in is blocked by a row of boulders at the parking lot. Walk past the boulders and go on down to the end of the road. The trail takes off to your right, uphill, and is marked.

DESCRIPTION: From the parking area you will hike up a connector trail which meets a junction of the Bear Jaw and Abineau Trails in 0.3 miles *0.48 km*. From here go left. You will hike 0.25 miles *0.4 km* down and around to another signed trail junction, where the signs are confusing: disregard any information about Reese Tank and FR 418. Turn uphill.

From here the trail moves on old roads through beautiful woods, featuring heavy stands of aspens. You will pass through some old sheep camps, complete with herders' names carved on the aspens. The trail is steep and goes up and up without respite.

You will climb through these woods for about 2.0 miles *3.2 km*, to the end of the trail at the 9,800 foot point, where it ends at Forest Road FR 146.

You will see a sign there showing the Abineau Trail 2.0 miles *3.2 km* to your right (W). You can return the way you came for a 5.1 mile *8.2 km* total hike or you can make the hike a 6.85 mile *10.96 km* loop using FR 146 as a connector to the Abineau Trail.

To use the Abineau loop, walk west (to your right) on FR 146 a distance of 2.0 miles *3.2 km*, a beautiful climb through a magnificent forest. The Abineau Trail intersects FR 146 in a treeless park, a great view platform. FR 146 continues beyond the Abineau connection and ends against the side of Mt. Humphreys where some digging has taken place, where the City of Flagstaff tapped a spring.

The Abineau Trail is 2.3 miles *3.68 km* long, the upper portion being very steep and rocky.

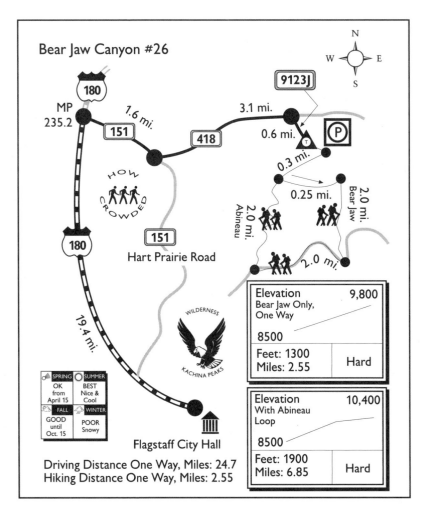

Mangum

Benham Trail #38

General Information
Location Map F1
Williams South USGS Map
Kaibab (Williams District) Forest Service Map

Driving Distance One Way: 36.85 miles *59.0 km* (Time 60 minutes)
Access Road: All cars, All paved except last 0.25 miles *0.40 km*
Hiking Distance One Way: 4.5 miles *7.2 km* (Time 2.75 hours)
How Strenuous: Hard
Features: Beautiful forest, High mountain, Views

NUTSHELL: This hike takes you to the top of Bill Williams Mountain outside the Town of Williams, about 30 miles *48 km* west of Flagstaff.

DIRECTIONS:
From Flagstaff City Hall Go:
South on Route 66 under the railroad overpass. Be sure to follow Route 66 when it turns right at the second stoplight. See Access Map, page 10. In 5.0 miles *8.0 km* you will merge onto I-40 West and stay on it to the 30.3 miles *48.5 km* point, the Williams Exit, #165. Take that exit and at the stop sign go left to Williams. Go into town on Railroad Avenue to the 32.9 mile point *52.6 km* where you will find Fourth Street. Turn left on Fourth Street. As it leaves town its name changes to the Perkinsville Road (73). Stay on this road to the 36.6 miles *58.6 km* point, where you turn right onto the signed trail access road, which is paved. Take this road to the 36.85 miles *59.0 km* point, the trail parking area, which is equipped with a restroom and also has horse facilities: corrals and trailer parking.

TRAILHEAD: You will see a sign marking the trailhead at the parking area.

DESCRIPTION: The sign at the trailhead indicates that this trail was built in 1920. It was abandoned in 1951 when the nearby FR 111 (the present road to the top) was built. It was reopened as a recreational trail in 1976. The trail was named after H. L. Benham, who was the Ranger for the Williams District from 1910 to 1911.

It is hard to tell whether this trail was built as a road or as a pack trail. There are places where it is wide enough for a road, but the upper half looks only wide enough to have been a pack or foot trail. In any event, the trail was well engineered so that it climbs 1950 feet gradually. This means a lot of zigging and zagging.

The trail goes up the east and south faces of the mountain. It does not get as much moisture as the **Bill Williams Mountain Trail** on the north side. Consequently, the forest is mostly pine with a lot of oak, until you reach aspen groves in the last mile *1.6 km*. There are some open areas for views, but generally the forest is heavy.

At about the 1.5 mile *2.4 km* point you will enter into a gorgeous grove of oaks, really special. Mile posts have been inserted along the trail to mark your way. According to Dick's pedometer, they are accurate. You will cross the road, FR 111, five times as you go up the mountain. The fifth time is at the 4.0 mile *6.4 km* point, where the trail ends. You then walk the road the final half mile *0.8 km* to get to the lookout tower. Until you reach the 3.5 mile *5.6 km* point, views are scarce because the forest is so heavy. At the top, however, the views are open and glorious.

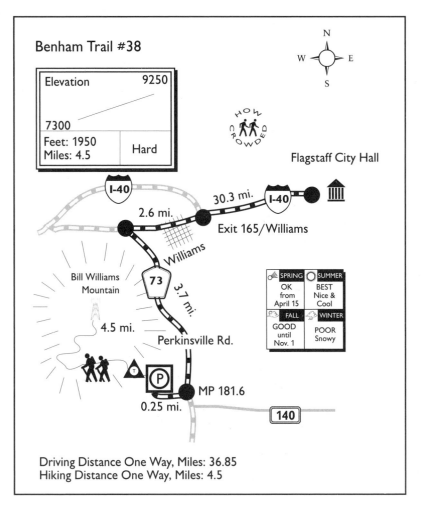

Mangum

Bill Williams Mountain Trail #21

General Information
Location Map F1
Williams South USGS Map
Kaibab (Williams District) Forest Service Map

Driving Distance One Way: 35.0 miles *56.0 km* (Time 50 minutes)
Access Road: All cars, All paved
Hiking Distance One Way: 4.4 miles *7.04 km* (Time 3 hours)
How Strenuous: Hard
Features: Beautiful forest, High mountain, Views

NUTSHELL: This hike takes you to the top of Bill Williams Mountain outside the Town of Williams.

DIRECTIONS:
From Flagstaff City Hall Go:
South on Route 66 under the railroad overpass. Take Route 66 when it turns right at the second stoplight. See Access Map, page 10. In 5.0 miles *8.0 km* you will merge onto I-40 West. Stay on I-40 to the Williams Exit, #165. Take that exit. It is 30.3 miles *48.5 km* to the stop sign. Go left to Williams, and drive through town, where the main street is divided into Railroad Avenue (westbound) and Route 66 (eastbound). Stay on Railroad Avenue. The two streets merge and become old Highway 66. At the 34.1 miles *54.56 km* point, turn left, for the Forest Service's Williams District Ranger Office. Watch carefully for the sign, as it comes up suddenly. Go uphill around a curve and keep going east. At 34.7 miles *55.5 km*, turn left on the road going to the Forest Service facility. Immediately after you turn, you will see a sign for the Bill Williams Mtn. Trail. The road to the trailhead goes toward the camp and then turns left. At the 35.0 mile *56.0 km* point, you will see the trailhead parking area to your right.

TRAILHEAD: A sign marks the trailhead at the parking area.

DESCRIPTION: This trail was built in 1902 as a toll trail for horse riders, and was operated for several years. Then it fell into disuse and was taken over by the Forest Service as a means of reaching the fire lookout on the top of Bill Williams Mountain. Later a vehicle road was built, and the old trail was turned into a hiking trail. It is a very good one.

At the trailhead you will see a large wooden sign containing a map of trails on the mountain. It shows the **Benham** and **Bixler** trails as well as the Bill Williams Mountain trail. Not shown are the **Clover Spring Trail** and the two trails radiating from it, the City of Williams Link Trail #124 and the

Buckskinner Trail. The sign says that the Bill Williams Trail is 3.0 miles *4.8 km* long. We have found it to be longer than that. Whatever the true mileage, the trail is long, hard and steep.

At the 0.15 mile *0.24 km* point you will come to the trail junction where the Clover Spring Trail takes off to the left. At 0.9 miles *1.44 km* you will meet this trail again. As you hike, you wind your way up through a nice pine forest. The trail climbs sharply and the forest changes character as you climb higher, becoming almost a rain forest, with lots of fir and spruce and incredible stands of tall aspens.

At 4.0 miles *6.4 km* the trail intersects FR 111, the road to the lookout tower. Because of the heavy forest you won't have any views until you reach this road, but from here upward, the views are marvelous. You could quit here, but we urge you hike 0.4 miles *0.64 km* up to the tower. If there is someone on duty, ask if you can come up, for the spectacular views.

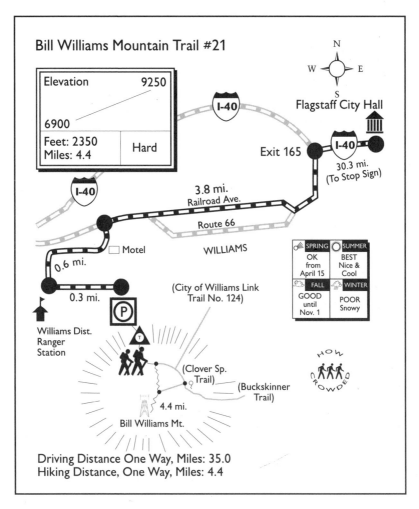

Bismarck Lake Elk Preserve

General Information
Location Map E3
Humphreys Peak and Wing Mountain USGS Maps
Coconino Forest Service Map

Driving Distance One Way: 17.2 mile *27.5 km* (Time 35 minutes)
Access Road: All cars, Last 7.0 miles *11.2 km* gravel, in good condition
Hiking Distance One Way: 1.0 mile *1.6 km* (Time 30 minutes)
How Strenuous: Moderate
Features: Aspen groves, Meadow views

NUTSHELL: Located on the San Francisco Peaks, about 15 miles *24 km* north of Flagstaff, this hike displays the alpine beauty of the area.

DIRECTIONS:
From Flagstaff City Hall Go:
North on Humphreys Street for 0.6 miles, *1.0 km* to the stoplight. See Access Map, page 10. Then take a left onto a street marked Columbus Avenue, which changes to Ft. Valley Road as it makes a curve to the north. Outside the city limits, the road becomes Highway 180, a major route to the Grand Canyon. At 10.2 miles *16.3 km* (MP 225.1), turn right onto FR 151, the lower Hart Prairie Road, and follow it to the l6.6 mile *26.6 km* point, where it intersects FR 627. Take FR 627 to the right and drive to the 17.2 mile *27.5 km* point, where you will find a fenced parking place. Park there.

TRAILHEAD: You will see a sign at a gate in the parking area fence.

DESCRIPTION: The Hart Prairie Road is a loop road that intersects Highway 180 at two points. One point is 10.2 miles *16.3 km* north of Flagstaff and the other is 19.4 miles *31.0 km* north. If you hear someone talking about taking the Hart Prairie Road, be sure to find out whether they are talking about the upper or lower end of the loop.

To make this hike, you walk through the fence and follow a road which has been closed, as no vehicle traffic is allowed inside the Bismarck Lake Elk Preserve. At 0.3 miles *0.5 km* you will come to Ki Tank. Don't take the fork to the right that appears there. At 0.7 miles, *1.1 km* the trail forks again. Take the left fork, which goes uphill to a grassy ledge.

When you top out on the ledge you find yourself on a sizable meadow ringed with aspen, pine and fir. The lake is hardly deserving of the name most of the time, usually appearing as a cattle tank about 20 feet in diameter except during the spring thaw, when it is at its fullest. In dry Arizona any body of water more than ten feet across is likely to be called a lake.

The forest is beautiful here. The area gets a lot of moisture, so in addition to the trees, there are many ferns, mosses, mushrooms and flowers.

The hike is an easy one for the Peaks area, as the climb is gentle, the trail is short, and the elevation is not terribly high.

This is a perfect place for elk, as they have everything they need here: grass, water and shelter. Best time to see them is just at dusk. We have been here five times and have heard but not seen elk each time. If you are in elk country in the autumn, you may hear the bull elks bugling. We have heard this twice at Bismarck Lake Elk Preserve, both times in mid-October. Once it erupted from a thick grove of trees nearby and made us jump. The elk bugle is a weird sound and if you are unprepared for it, you would have no idea what you are hearing. It sounds like the hokey trumpeting of elephants that you hear in a Tarzan movie. The bulls, normally passive, are quite aggressive when they are bugling, so don't bugle back.

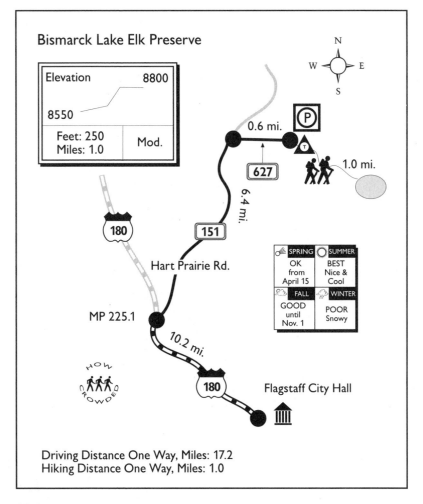

Bixler Saddle Trail #72

General Information
Location Map F1
McLellan Reservoir, Williams South USGS Maps
Kaibab (Chalender) Forest Service Map

Driving Distance One Way: 44.15 miles *70.64 km* (Time 1 hour)
Access Road: High clearance recommended for last 2.5 miles *4.0 km*
Hiking Distance One Way: 2.5 miles *4.0 km* (Time 1 hour)
How Strenuous: Hard
Features: Beautiful forest, Views

NUTSHELL: Bill Williams Mountain dominates the skyline of the Town of Williams, located about 30 miles *48 km,* west of Flagstaff, in the same way that the San Francisco Peaks dominate Flagstaff. The **Benham Trail** takes you up the east and south faces of Bill Williams Mountain, and the **Bill Williams Mountain Trail** takes you up the north face. This little known but excellent new trail takes you around the west face of the mountain.

DIRECTIONS:
From Flagstaff City Hall Go:
South on Route 66 under the railroad. See Access Map, page 10. Turn right at the stoplight at 0.5 miles *0.8 km.* You will merge onto I-40 headed west in about 5.0 miles *8.0 km.* Go past Williams, to the 39.1 mile *62.6 km* point, the Devil Dog Exit 157, and turn off onto a loop which will bring you to a stop sign. Take the fork to the right here and go south under I-40. You will come to another intersection at 39.6 miles *63.3 km.* Take the left fork (S). The paving ends soon at a cattle guard. You're now driving FR 108. At 40.0 miles *64.0 km* you will come to a junction where FR 744 goes to your right. Stay on FR 108 and turn left (E). At 40.4 miles *64.6 km* you reach a corner where the road ahead is blocked by a barrier. Turn right here, still on FR 108. At 40.55 miles *65.0 km* you will meet FR 45 to your left (E), look sharp, as the entrance is not very obvious. At 41.65 miles *66.6 km* FR 45 makes a 90° turn to the right. Turn right on FR 45, which begins to climb to the 44.15 mile *70.64 km* point, its end. The road has recently been improved, but there are exposed rocks in some places. You can drive it in a passenger car, but will feel more comfortable with a high clearance vehicle. You will top out at Bixler Saddle, a bare shelf surrounded by forest.

TRAILHEAD: At the saddle.

DESCRIPTION: The trail heads northerly toward a gap between two immense, spectacular lave reefs. It winds through a pretty forest of aspen, oak and fir. In places it seems almost as if you are walking through a tunnel of green.

One of the nice things about this trail is the variety of vegetation. The trail moves through different exposures and the forest changes depending on the situation. There are also many viewpoints, some of which are quite breathtaking. From the 1.5 mile *2.4 km* point there are wonderful views to the south. The trail is also quiet and not heavily used.

After a long climb, the trail levels off and heads toward its end. Although the Forest Service rates this trail as 2.0 miles *3.2 km* long, we found it to be closer to 2.5 miles *4.0 km*. It ends in a heavy grove of fir and aspen where it intersects the **Bill Williams Mountain Trail**. The distance to the end of the Bill Williams Mountain Trail is not stated on the sign at the trail junction, but we estimate it to be about 0.5 miles *0.8 km* from the point where it intersects the road to the lookout.

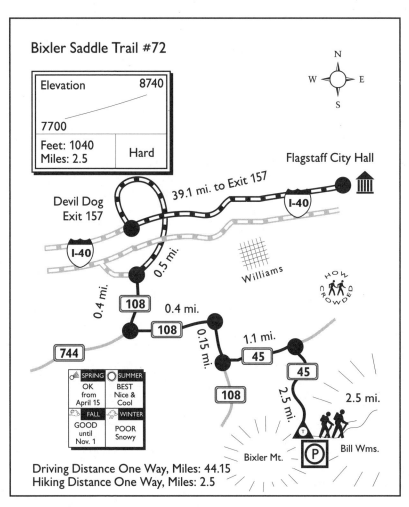

Bixler Saddle Trail #72

Elevation	8740
7700	
Feet: 1040 Miles: 2.5	Hard

Flagstaff City Hall

Devil Dog Exit 157

39.1 mi. to Exit 157

I-40

I-40

0.5 mi.

Williams

HOW CROWDED

0.4 mi.

108

0.4 mi.

108

744

0.15 mi.

1.1 mi.

45

45

2.5 mi.

2.5 mi.

108

SPRING	SUMMER
OK from April 15	BEST Nice & Cool
FALL	WINTER
GOOD until Nov. 1	POOR Snowy

Bixler Mt.

Bill Wms.

Driving Distance One Way, Miles: 44.15
Hiking Distance One Way, Miles: 2.5

Mangum

Bright Angel Trail

General Information
Location Map B2
Grand Canyon USGS Map
Kaibab (Tusayan) Forest Service Map

Driving Distance One Way: 82.8 miles *132.5 km* (Time 2 hours)
Access Road: All cars, All paved
Hiking Distance One Way: 1.5 miles *2.4 km* (Time 1.5 hours)
How Strenuous: Hard
Features: The main Grand Canyon trail

NUTSHELL: You will sample the most famous hiking trail in the world, by taking a day hike down the first 1.5 miles *2.4 km*. You will enjoy the color, history and romance of the Grand Canyon.

DIRECTIONS:
From Flagstaff City Hall Go:
North on Humphreys Street 0.6 miles *1.0 km* to a stoplight. See Access Map, page 10. Go left on Columbus Avenue and follow the curve north. Street signs will show the street first as Ft. Valley Road, then Highway 180. This is a major road to the Grand Canyon. At 50.4 miles *80.7 km* (MP 265.8), you will intersect Highway 64, coming out of Williams, at Valle. Go right at this junction and follow the highway to the south entrance to the Grand Canyon National Park, where you will have to pay an entrance fee. Once inside the park, go to the 79.8 mile *128 km* point, where you intersect the East Rim Drive. Turn left, toward Grand Canyon Village. You will reach the village area, then stay on the main road just past the Bright Angel Lodge, which is uphill, to your right, at 82.8 miles *132.5 km*. Look for a trail sign at the end of the Bright Angel parking lot and turn right, going past the cottages to the trail parking lot at the rim. Parking is scarce in high season and you may have to hunt for a place in the area.

TRAILHEAD: Follow the signs at the parking area.

DESCRIPTION: The Bright Angel Trail began as an ancient Indian path. In 1890 it was developed as a privately-owned mining trail, later converted into a tourist toll-trail. The Hermit Trail, built by the Santa Fe Railroad; and the South Kaibab Trail, built by the Park Service, were created to avoid these tolls. The Park Service acquired Bright Angel in 1928.

This is the trail used by the famous mule rides to go down to Phantom Ranch. It is crowded, not a wilderness experience.

Serious hikers backpack on this trail, using it as access for a multi-day experience. Overnight hikes require permits (which are scarce) and a great deal of preparation and training. For a day hike, you do not need a permit, but please be prepared. Take water (one quart per person), wear suitable shoes, and allow enough time for a comfortable experience.

As you descend, the temperature increases. Take this into account in deciding how much water to carry and how to dress.

You will pass through two tunnels, and end your hike at the First Rest House. This is a hike of 1.5 miles *2.4 km*, which seems mild, but it requires a steep climb of 1131 feet on the way back up. You will enjoy gorgeous views of the canyon all the way.

We recommend that every able-bodied visitor go down into the Grand Canyon, even if it is for a very short distance, for it is the only way to get a feel for the canyon's immensity. A good shorter hike is to go to the Second Tunnel, a hike of 0.87 miles *1.4 km*, a drop of 597 feet.

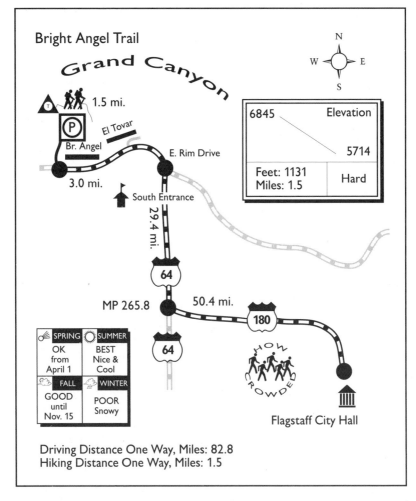

Driving Distance One Way, Miles: 82.8
Hiking Distance One Way, Miles: 1.5

Mangum

Brookbank Trail #2

General Information
Location Map E3
Flagstaff West, Humphreys Peak & Sunset Crater West USGS Maps
Coconino Forest Service Map

Driving Distance One Way: 6.5 miles *10.4 km* (Time 30 minutes)
Access Road: All cars, Last 1.9 miles *3.0 km* medium gravel road
Hiking Distance One Way: 5.0 miles *8.0 km* (Time 3 hours)
How Strenuous: Hard
Features: Views, Forests

NUTSHELL: This is a marked and maintained trail that starts at a point on the Elden Lookout Road and climbs to Sunset Park near the top of Mt. Elden north of Flagstaff.

DIRECTIONS:
From Flagstaff City Hall Go:
North on Humphreys Street for 0.6 miles *1.0 km.* See Access Map, page 10. Turn left at the stoplight onto Columbus Avenue and follow it around a big curve to the north. You will see the street signs call this road Columbus Avenue at first, then Ft. Valley Road and then Highway 180. Stay on Highway 180 to the 3.1 miles *5.0 km* point (MP 218.6), where the Schultz Pass Road, FR 420, goes to the right. Follow FR 420. At the 3.6 mile *5.8 km* point it curves left where you will see the paved Elden Lookout Road (FR 557) going straight. Take the right fork and follow FR 557 to the 6.5 mile *10.4 km* point, where you will park.

TRAILHEAD: There is a closed road to your left. The sign is located about twenty yards up this road.

DESCRIPTION: This trail is part of the Dry Lake Hills-Mt. Elden trail system, so it is marked and maintained. The trail goes up a closed ranch road for about a mile *1.6 km*, beyond which it turns into a footpath. At the 1.1 mile *1.8 km* point you will reach a trail junction. The unmarked trail to your left goes uphill into private property in the Dry Lake Hills.

Take the right fork here. It goes around a long loop that hugs the shoulder of one of the hills. At the toe of the loop you will have good views of the San Francisco Peaks. Then you curve south, toward Mt. Elden, walking through high north-facing forests of spruce and fir.

At the 3.4 mile *5.5 km* point you will reach a trail junction. Here you want to turn right onto the Sunset Trail. The signs here are confusing, so please follow our directions.

The trail will take you down a fold between the Dry Lake Hills and Mt. Elden and will then climb up a slope of Mt. Elden through a very nice alpine forest. You will reach a ridge crest on Elden in about a mile *1.6 km*. From here the trail goes over the crest a short distance and then follows along on the shoulder of the crest to Sunset Park.

This last half mile *0.8 km* burned in a huge forest fire caused by human carelessness in 1978. Only now is the forest starting to heal. The fire made the mountain bare here so you have clear views to the east. They are spectacular.

We end the hike at Sunset Park, where there is a trail junction, just above the Elden Lookout Road. You can go on a mile *1.6 km* to the lookout tower. We like this as a two-car hike, parking one car at the 6.5 mile *10.4 km* point and the other at the 9.4 mile *15.0 km* point on the Elden Lookout Road, then hiking downhill.

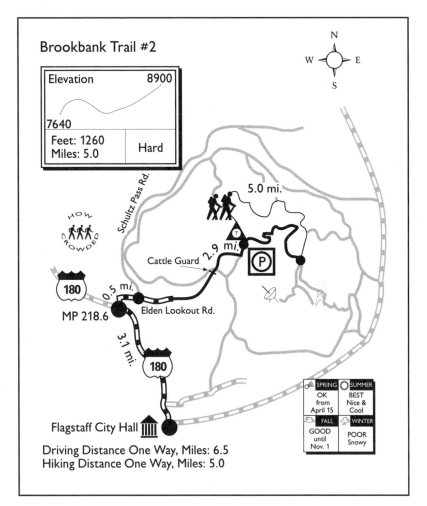

Brookbank Trail #2

Elevation	8900
7640	
Feet: 1260 Miles: 5.0	Hard

5.0 mi.

Cattle Guard 2.9 mi.

0.5 mi.

180

MP 218.6

Elden Lookout Rd.

3.1 mi.

180

Flagstaff City Hall

Driving Distance One Way, Miles: 6.5
Hiking Distance One Way, Miles: 5.0

HOW CROWDED

SPRING	SUMMER
OK from April 15	BEST Nice & Cool
FALL	WINTER
GOOD until Nov. 1	POOR Snowy

Mangum

Buckskinner Trail #130

General Information
Location Map F1
Williams South USGS Map
Kaibab (Williams District) Forest Service Map

Driving Distance One Way: 36.05 miles 57.68 *km* (Time 60 minutes)
Access Road: All cars, Last 0.5 miles *0.8 km* good gravel roads
Hiking Distance One Way: 1.0 miles *1.6 km* (Time 35 minutes)
How Strenuous: Moderate
Features: Beautiful forest, Spring, Easy-to-reach

NUTSHELL: This trail starts at Buckskinner Park and climbs through a nice mixed forest of pine and oak to Clover Spring. From Clover Spring, the hiker has several choices.

DIRECTIONS:
From Flagstaff City Hall Go:
   South on Route 66 under the railroad overpass. Be sure to follow Route 66 when it turns right at the second stoplight. See Access Map, page 10. In 5.0 miles *8.0 km* you will merge onto I-40 West and stay on it to the 30.3 miles *48.5 km* point, the Williams Exit, #165. Take that exit and at the stop sign go left to Williams. Go into town on Railroad Avenue to the 34.9 mile point *55.84 km* where you will find Seventh Street. Turn left and drive one block to Route 66. Turn left and drive one block to Sixth Street. Turn right on Sixth Street. You cannot turn directly from Railroad Avenue onto Sixth Street, because there is a drainage ditch where Sixth Street would be—you must loop around to get onto Sixth. From the junction of Sixth Street and Route 66 it is 1.1 miles *1.76 km* to Buckskinner Park. Just stay on Sixth Street and follow the signs.

TRAILHEAD: You will see a trailhead sign at the parking area.

DESCRIPTION: This trail was opened in August, 1997 and provides the sort of opportunity that many hikers seek, a moderate, short hike that is interesting enough to hold their attention.
   Buckskinner Park is a developed and maintained facility with picnic tables, toilet and other amenities. This allows the possibility of planning a picnic followed by a nice hike. You will see the turnoff and the picnic facilities clearly as you approach. (If you stay on the gravel road instead of turning in to Buckskinner Park, you will reach the Saginaw Reservoir in another 0.1 mile *0.16 km*. This is a scenic little lake set down in a bowl, with a nice grove of aspens at the far end. We recommend including a visit to it).

From the picnic tables, the trail heads generally SW, up a gentle grade. Soon after the hike begins you will see through the trees what looks like a long wall. This was a water diversion weir constructed for city water storage purposes, and no longer in use. After a climb of 0.6 miles *0.96 km* you will be on top of a knob and will see a canyon before you.

You will hike part way down the canyon and then climb up again, moving laterally to get to Clover Spring. We have been here several times and water was always running, but not much. Apparently this spring and many others in northern Arizona contained much more water in the old days than they do now. The spring has been captured in a concrete box. The water flows across the trail. There is a big metal plate which acts as a bridge across the water channel, which is very shallow.

Look at the map for the **Clover Spring Trail #46** and you will see your choices for finishing the hike.

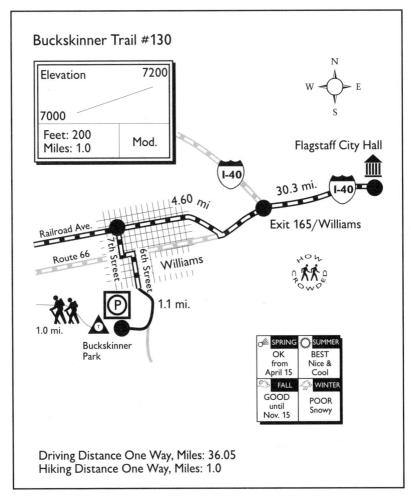

Buffalo Park

General Information
Location Map E3
Flagstaff West USGS Map
Coconino Forest Service Map

Driving Distance One Way: 2.3 miles *3.7 km* (Time 10 minutes)
Access Road: All cars, All paved
Hiking Distances: 3 Trails. **Trail #1** is 0.5 mi. *0.8 km*, **Trail #2** is a 2.0 mi. *3.2 km* loop, **Trail #3** runs 0.5 miles *0.8 km* downhill.
How Strenuous: Easy/Easy/Moderate
Features: Urban Trails, Easy to reach, Easy to walk

NUTSHELL: Buffalo Park is owned by the City of Flagstaff. Located on top of a flat mesa, it features three well maintained trails. *One* is a straight half-mile road. *Two* loops around a Vita Course. *Three* follows the old road alignment downhill.

DIRECTIONS:
From Flagstaff City Hall Go:
North on Humphreys Street to the stoplight at 0.60 miles *1.0 km.* See Access Map, page 10. Turn right here onto Columbus Avenue and go one block east to the next stop sign, which is at Beaver Street. Turn left onto Beaver Street and go up the hill. At the 1.0 mile *1.6 km* point you will reach Forest Avenue. Turn right on Forest and follow it to the top of the hill. Here, at 1.9 miles *3.04 km*, you will find Gemini Drive. Turn left onto it and at 2.3 miles *3.7 km*, you will come to Buffalo Park. Park in the parking lot.

TRAILHEADS: At the entrance arch.

DESCRIPTION: Buffalo Park is an open plain extending back about a half mile from the archway at its entrance. In the 1960s it was run as a zoo but failed due to lack of funds. You can see some vestiges of this operation near the entrance, where a welcoming arch and buffalo statue survive.
Trail No. 1: As you stand under the arch and look ahead, you will see the main trail running in a straight line due north. This trail runs almost exactly 0.5 miles *0.8 km* to the fence marking the rear boundary of the park. There is nothing fancy about this trail. It runs across the open park like an arrow. You will find a couple of metal buildings behind a chain link fence near the trail's end, where it veers to the northeast and you come to a gate where the **Oldham Trail No. 1** begins. If you are doing a timed or measured mile, you simply turn around and go back the way you came.
Trail No. 2: This trail is a Vita Course. You will encounter 20 stations

with placards describing some kind of exercise to be done on each spot. In some places there are devices such as chinning bars. There are mileage markers every quarter mile. The course runs in a loop. If you do the entire loop you will do two miles *3.2 km*. Walk north from the archway about 100 yards, where you will see a cindered path forking to your right (NE). Turn right onto the path. From here it is easy to follow your way because you can see the exercise stations ahead. The first leg of the trail loops around to the east of Trail No. 1, then turns west and crosses it. The second leg loops around west of Trail No. 1 and is more scenic. Near the end of this trail take the right fork that goes down into dense woods.

Trail No. 3: This trail does not go into the park. Follow the old alignment of Cedar Road from outside the gate. You will go downhill to the corner of McPherson Park, then curve south to join the new road at its intersection with Turquoise Drive, a distance of 0.5 miles *0.8 km*.

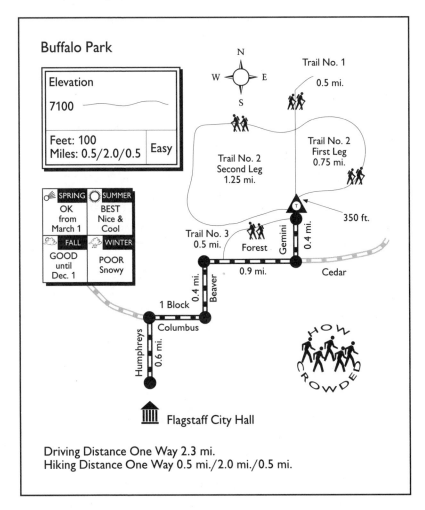

Bull Basin Trail #40

General Information
Location Map E2
Kendrick Peak, Moritz Ridge and Wing Mt. USGS Maps
Kaibab Forest Service Map

Driving Distance One Way: 34.35 miles *54.96 km* (Time 1.25 hours)
Access Road: All cars, Last 20 miles *32 km* good gravel road
Hiking Distance One Way: 4.5 miles *7.2 km* (Time 3.0 hours)
How Strenuous: Hard
Features: Fine forests, Ten thousand foot peak, Views

NUTSHELL: This trail takes you up the north side of Kendrick Peak, the second highest mountain in the region. Terrible fire damage in 2000 has altered it. Call the Forest Service at 800-863-0546 for trail conditions.

DIRECTIONS:
From Flagstaff City Hall Go:
     North on Humphreys Street for 0.60 miles *1.0 km*. See Access Map, page 10. Turn left at the stoplight onto Columbus Avenue and follow it around a big curve to the north. You will see the street signs call this road Columbus at first, then Ft. Valley Road and then Highway 180. Stay on Highway 180 to the 14.4 miles *23.04 km* point (MP 230.1), where a gravel road takes off to the left. Turn left onto this road, FR 245, and follow it to the 17.4 mile *27.84 km* point where it intersects FR 171. Turn right on FR 171 and follow it to the 24.6 mile *39.36 km* point, where you will see a sign for the Pumpkin Trail. Go just beyond this, to the 24.7 mile *39.52 km* point and turn left on FR 171. Follow it to the 27.5 mile *44.0 km* point, where it meets FR 144 and turn right on FR 144, taking it to the 29.0 miles *46.4 km* point, where it intersects FR 90. Turn right on FR 90 and drive it to the 33.7 mile *53.92 km* point, where you will see FR 90A to the right. Take FR 90A to the 34.25 mile *54.8 km* point, where you will see a sign marking a road to the right to the Bull Basin trailhead. You can see the parking lot from this point. Turn right, downhill, and you will reach the parking area at 34.35 miles *54.96 km*.

TRAILHEAD: Well marked with a sign at the parking area.

DESCRIPTION: There are three trails that take you to the top of Kendrick Peak: The Bull Basin Trail, The **Kendrick Mt. Trail** and The **Pumpkin Trail**. We think Bull Basin is the best, with Pumpkin running a poor third.
     From the parking area you will walk a closed road along the west side of Bull Basin, a large grassy meadow. At 0.9 miles *1.4 km* you will come to a trail junction where you will see the **Connector Trail** to the right.

Up to this point the land has been flat. Beyond it you begin to climb the mountain, with the trail following some old logging roads up to the 1.5 mile *2.4 km* point. The forest on this north side of the mountain has many spruces and firs, and seems to have recovered from logging better than pure pine forests do.

Beyond the 1.5 mile *2.4 km* point the trail becomes a footpath and climbs steeply. The trail is well designed so that the grades are not too steep. Soon you are in a forest of spruce, fir and aspen. NOTE: This area was badly damaged in a 2000 forest fire, after this description was written.

At 3.0 miles *4.8 km* you will emerge onto a small saddle and follow a ridge line to the top. From here the forest is all spruce and there are many huge boulders. You will emerge from this dark forest at 4.0 miles *6.4 km* at the Old Ranger Cabin, built in 1911-1912 and in remarkably good shape. From the cabin it is another half mile *0.8 km* to the lookout tower.

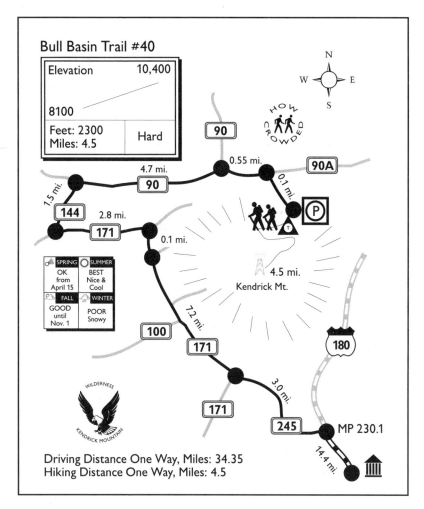

Calloway Trail #33

General Information
Location Map G4
Calloway Butte USGS Map
Coconino Forest Service Map

Driving Distance One Way: 79.75 miles *127.6 km* (Time 1.5 hours)
Access Road: High clearance for last 8.25 miles *13.2 km*
Hiking Distance One Way: 0.70 miles *1.12 km* (Time 30 minutes)
How Strenuous: Hard, due to steepness
Features: Perennial stream in wild deep canyon

NUTSHELL: This trail is short but steep. At the bottom you will enjoy the pure rushing waters of West Clear Creek in an unspoiled canyon.

DIRECTIONS:
From Flagstaff City Hall Go:
West, then south on Route 66, under the railroad overpass. At 0.5 miles *0.8 km*, go straight on Milton Road. See Access Map, page 10. At 1.7 miles *2.72 km* you will reach a stoplight at Forest Meadows Street. Turn right here onto Forest Meadows and go one block to Beulah. Turn left on Beulah and follow it south. Beulah merges onto Highway 89A. At 2.4 miles *3.84 km* (MP 401.6), turn left onto the Lake Mary Road. Follow the Lake Mary Road (also known as FH 3) to its end at the junction with State Route 87, 56.6 miles *90.6 km*. Turn right here on Highway 87, a paved road, and follow it to the 68.4 mile *109.44 km* point (MP 278.3), where you turn right on Highway 260, which is well posted. Follow Highway 260 to the 71.5 mile *114.4 km* point (MP 249) and turn right onto FR 144, a good forest road. Take FR 144 to the 73.3 mile *117.28 km* point, where you turn left onto FR 149, also a good road. Stay on FR 149 to the 74.55 mile *119.28 km* point, where you turn left onto FR 142, a road that is not quite so good. At the 77.35 mile *123.76 km* point, turn right onto FR 142B. You are now 2.4 miles *3.84 km* from the trailhead. The roads up to this point have been good, but FR 142B is terrible, with deep ruts and many exposed sharp rocks. We got in about a mile before we decided to save our tires and park, walking the rest of the way. If you are a kamikaze, you can drive all the way to the trailhead, where there is a turnaround loop and ample parking.

TRAILHEAD: At the end of FR 142B. There is a fence marking the West Clear Creek Wilderness and a big Forest Service sign at the head of the trail with a notebook in which you are invited to register. The path is easy to find, though not marked as a trail.

DESCRIPTION: At the trailhead you can see into the canyon and hear the stream flowing. The canyon shows high desert vegetation, and the walls are of a rust-tinted buff limestone.

The trail is maintained, and you will even find that steps have been created out of sandstone slabs. It is very steep, dropping 640 feet in 0.7 miles *1.12 km*. The footing is a little tricky in places due to the presence of many small loose rocks. Contrary to the desert landscape impression one gets at the top, you will pass through an attractive lush forest of pine and spruce that provides shade all the way to the bottom.

At the end of the trail you emerge onto the creek. There is no sandy beach here, but there are some nice rock ledges. In order to explore, you have to do some boulder hopping. If you seriously want to check out the area, you will want to wear Tevas or similar footgear so that you can walk in the water at times. The streamside area feels really wild and remote.

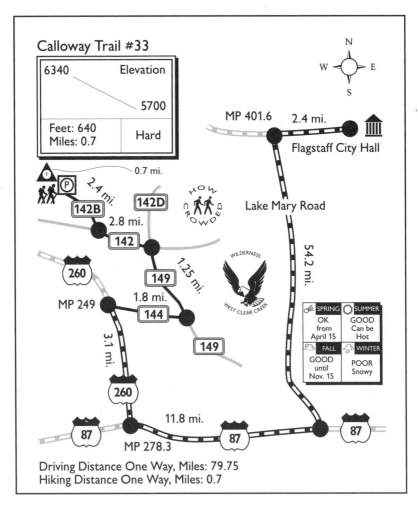

Mangum

58

Casner Mountain Trail North

General Information
Location Map F2
Loy Butte, Sycamore Point USGS Maps
Coconino Forest Service Map

Driving Distance One Way: 29.0 miles *46.4 km* (Time 60 minutes)
Access Road: High clearance only, Last 25.4 miles *40.6 km* unpaved,
 rough spots
Hiking Distance One Way: 4.0 miles *6.4 km* (Time 2.5 hours)
How Strenuous: Moderate
Features: Views

NUTSHELL: Located 29.0 miles *46.4 km* southwest of Flagstaff, this hike
follows the top of a ridge connecting Casner Mountain to the Mogollon Rim.

DIRECTIONS:
From Flagstaff City Hall Go:
 West a block on Route 66, then south, beneath the railroad overpass. See
Access Map, page 10. At 0.5 miles *0.8 km* you will reach a Y intersection.
The right fork is Route 66. Take it. You will soon leave town. At 2.6 miles
4.2 km you will reach a road going to the left. This is the Woody Mountain
Road, FR 231. Take it. It is paved about a mile *1.6 km* and then turns into a
cinder road. At 16.6 miles *26.6 km* you will intersect FR 538. Turn right onto
FR 538 and follow it to the 26.1 mile *41.8 km* point, where FR 538B branches off to the right. Take FR 538B. It follows the path of the huge power line
you can see overhead. The road is pretty good down to the 28.25 mile *45.2
km* point but from there it becomes very rough with lots of exposed tire-eat-
ing rock. It ends at 29.0 miles *46.4 km* at a bare spot on the ridge, where you
park, near the power line.

TRAILHEAD: You walk the power line service road.

DESCRIPTION: This trail began as a sheep driveway. Later engineers followed this same route to bring a major power line down to the Verde Valley
and the sheep trail was converted into a service road for the line.
 A major attraction of this trail is that the ridge you walk is so narrow that
you can see off into the Sycamore side or the Sedona side in many places.
Both are spectacular. There are very few trees growing along the side of this
trail, so it is mostly unshaded and can be hot. Take lots of water.
 At the 0.25 mile *0.4 km* point on the hike you will come to a three-point
wilderness trail intersection where the Casner Mountain, Mooney and
Taylor Cabin trails meet. You can see the Mooney Trail going down diag-

Flagstaff Hikes

onally to your left into the Sedona back country. The Taylor Cabin Trail drops down steeply into Sycamore Canyon on your right.

The Casner Mountain Trail is not level. As it follows the contours of the ridge it dips and rises. At 2.0 miles *3.2 km* it makes a major dip into a saddle where you reach bottom at 2.5 miles *4.0 km*. From there you begin the mile *1.6 km*-long ascent that will take you onto Casner Mountain.

You reach a false top on Casner at 3.5 miles *5.6 km* and then make the final push to hike's end, the real top, at 4.0 miles *6.4 km*.

The trail continues, going down the mountain on its south face. It is about 3.0 miles *4.8 km* to the bottom on the south. Instead of trying to make this a killer day hike, we think it is better described as two hikes. The **Casner Mountain Trail South** and **Mooney Trail** are described in our other book, *Sedona Hikes*.

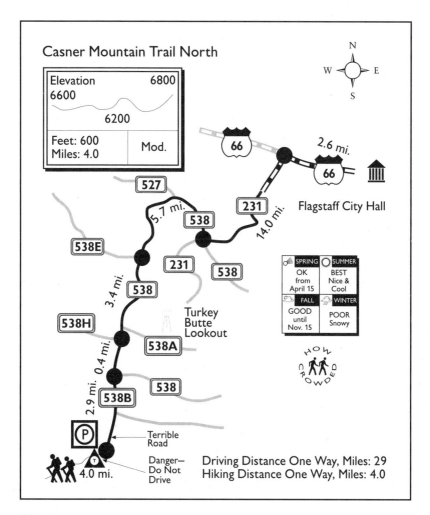

Mangum

Chalender Cross-Country Trails (3)

General Information
Location Map E2
Parks USGS Map
Kaibab (Chalender) Forest Service Map

Driving Distance One Way: 24.7 miles *39.5 km* (Time 40 minutes)
Access Road: All cars, All paved
Hiking Distances: See map
How Strenuous: Moderate
Features: Three trails loop through a fine forest, Beautiful meadows, Views

NUTSHELL: These hikes take you on loop routes in the Spring Valley area west of Flagstaff.

DIRECTIONS:
From Flagstaff City Hall Go:
West a block on Route 66, then south, beneath the railroad overpass. The street name changes to Milton Rd. At 0.5 miles *0.8 km* there's a Y intersection. The right fork is Route 66. Take it. You will soon leave town. At the 5.0 mile *8.0 km* point you merge onto Interstate-40 West. Look for Exit 178 "Parks" at the 18.0 mile *28.8 km* point, and take it. Turn right at the stop sign and go to the 18.4 mile *29.5 km* point, at a second stop sign. Turn left and go to the Parks Store at 19.0 mile *30.4 km* point. Turn right here, on the Spring Valley Road (FR 141). It is paved all the way to the trailhead. At 24.7 miles *39.5 km* you will see a sign for the Cross Country Ski Trail. Turn left here into the parking lot and park.

TRAILHEAD: You will see a large wooden signboard with a trail map. We—and the Forest Service—previously called these trails the Spring Valley X-Country Trails.

DESCRIPTION: Three cross-country ski trails in this area make good hiking trails. The **RS Hill Trail** is the easiest. The **Eagle Rock Trail** is harder and a bit longer. The **Spring Valley Trail** is longest.
For all three trails, you start on a road, then at 0.40 miles *0.64 km* veer off into the woods. You will at times be on roads and at other times off road on this hike. Follow the triangle trail makers in the trees.
At 0.75 miles *1.2 km* you will reach a beautiful meadow beyond an aspen grove in the middle of which is Shoot-Em-Up-Dick Tank. At the other side you will come onto FR 76 and walk it to the 1.25 mile *2.0 km* point, where there is a trail fork. At this point, you have options. The best way to understand your choices is to look at the map. Depending on which route you

choose, you can add up the mileage to get the total for the hike you select.

Eagle Rock: Turn left. The trail soon emerges from the woods to join FR 104, which you hike to Eagle Rock Pass. Eagle Rock is to your left just before the pass. You do not go to Eagle Rock. From the gate at the pass you descend steeply on a footpath to join another road, where you turn to the right. We like Eagle Rock best, and recommend it.

RS Hill: This 1.0 mile *1.6 km* trail goes through a typical pine forest. It has a nice rise and fall, then joins the Eagle Rock trail on the old road.

Spring Valley: This starts where the Eagle Rock and RS Hill trails meet near RS Tank. The trail soon leaves the road and goes uphill on a shoulder of RS Hill, through an area rich in obsidian.

As you round the hill you see Spring Valley to your left. From here you walk a road back to the junction of FR 76 and FR 104, then retrace your steps to the parking lot. You never climb RS Hill.

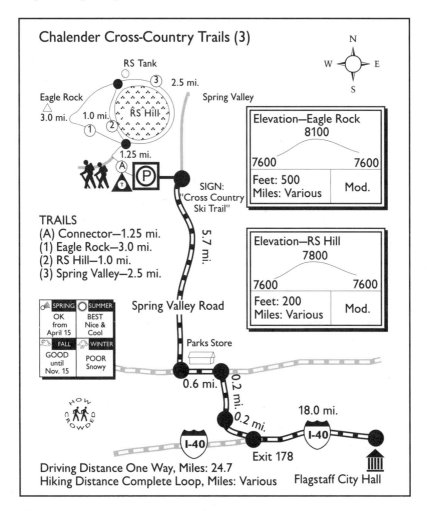

Chalender Cross-Country Trails (3)

RS Tank

(3) 2.5 mi.

Eagle Rock
3.0 mi.   1.0 mi.   RS Hill

Spring Valley

(1) (2)

1.25 mi.

(A)   P

1.25 mi.

SIGN:
"Cross Country Ski Trail"

Elevation—Eagle Rock 8100		
7600		7600
Feet: 500 Miles: Various	Mod.	

5.7 mi.

TRAILS
(A) Connector—1.25 mi.
(1) Eagle Rock—3.0 mi.
(2) RS Hill—1.0 mi.
(3) Spring Valley—2.5 mi.

Elevation—RS Hill 7800		
7600		7600
Feet: 200 Miles: Various	Mod.	

Spring Valley Road

SPRING	SUMMER
OK from April 15	BEST Nice & Cool
FALL	WINTER
GOOD until Nov. 15	POOR Snowy

Parks Store

HOW CROWDED

0.6 mi.   0.2 mi.

0.2 mi.

18.0 mi.

I-40   I-40

Exit 178

Flagstaff City Hall

Driving Distance One Way, Miles: 24.7
Hiking Distance Complete Loop, Miles: Various

Christmas Tree Trail

General Information
Location Map E3
Flagstaff East USGS Map
Coconino Forest Service Map

Driving Distance One Way: 5.2 miles *8.3 km* (Time 15 minutes)
Access Road: All cars, All paved
Hiking Distance One Way: 2.0 miles *3.2 km* (Time 1.0 hour)
How Strenuous: Moderate
Features: Easy to reach, Pleasant forest

NUTSHELL: This trail is a connector between the **Fat Man's Loop** and the **Sandy Seep** and **Heart,** and **Little Elden-Heart** Trails. It is located at the base of Mt. Elden in East Flagstaff.

DIRECTIONS:
From Flagstaff City Hall Go:
East, then north on Highway 89. See Access Map, pages 10-11. At 5.2 miles *8.3 km* (MP 419.5) just past the Flagstaff Mall, you will see a sign for the "Mt. Elden Trailhead" and a paved driveway to your left into a parking lot bounded by a pole fence. Pull in there and park.

TRAILHEAD: There are trail signs at the gate in the parking lot fence.

DESCRIPTION: From the parking lot, start off on the main trail. In 0.2 miles *0.32 km*, you will come to the Fat Man's Loop, which is marked. Follow the sign and take the Fat Man's trail, to your right.

At the 0.5 mile *0.8 km* point, you will come to a trail junction, also marked with a sign, though the sign does not show that you have come to the Christmas Tree Trail, mentioning only Little Elden Spring. Turn right (N) here.

From this point, the Christmas Tree Trail runs along parallel to the base of Mt. Elden, heading generally north. It is easy to walk. There are many side trails, which are unofficial and unmaintained, but you should not have any trouble getting confused by these, as the main trail is easy to follow due to the markers. Without the markers, there would be some places where it would be difficult to determine which trail to take.

At 1.1 miles *1.76 km*, you will see a small concrete block building to your left, and a large earthen tank.

From this point, you have 0.5 miles *0.8 km* to go, intersecting the Sandy Seep Trail at the 2.0 mile *3.2 km* point. There is a sign at this trail junction showing that you have been on the Christmas Tree Trail. The Heart Trail is

0.3 miles *0.48 km* ahead. The Christmas Tree Trail is not as scenic as the Fat Man's Loop, as you have no views, but it makes a welcome bit of variety and is useful as a connector.

Mountain bikers love the trails around Mt. Elden, so keep a lookout for them. The trails are also favored by people living in the area, who often come out to take a nice stroll in the cool of the evening. The Christmas Tree Trail is very well suited for this purpose, as it is easy and pleasant.

The Christmas Tree Trail also serves to provide access to other trails in the Mt. Elden system. It joins the Sandy Seep Trail at the end of the Little Elden-Heart Trail and is only 0.2 miles *0.32 km* from the bottom of the Heart Trail.

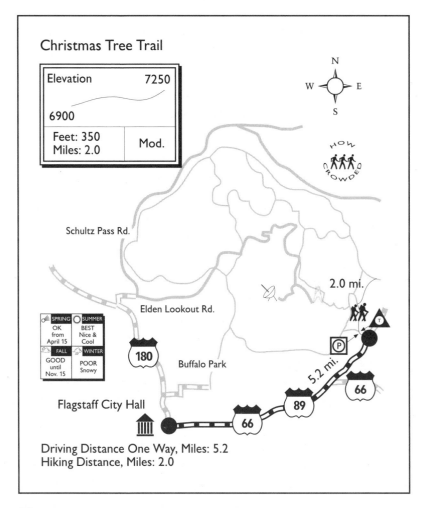

Mangum

Clover Spring Trail #46

General Information
Location Map F1
Williams South USGS Map
Kaibab (Williams District) Forest Service Map

Driving Distance One Way: 35.0 miles *56.0 km* (Time 50 minutes)
Access Road: All cars, All paved
Hiking Distance, Complete Loop: 2.5 miles *4.0 km* (Time 1 hour)
How Strenuous: Moderate
Features: Beautiful forest, Views, Spring

NUTSHELL: This loop hike takes you to a spring on the flank of Bill Williams Mountain outside the Town of Williams. Not only is it a refreshing hike in itself, but it provides connections to other trails (see map).

DIRECTIONS:
From Flagstaff City Hall Go:
South on Route 66 under the railroad overpass. Take Route 66 when it turns right at the second stoplight. See Access Map, page 10. In 5.0 miles *8.0 km* you will merge onto I-40 West. Take the Williams Exit, #165. It is 30.3 miles *48.5 km* to the stop sign. Go left to Williams, and drive through town. At the 34.1 miles *54.56 km* point, turn left, for the Forest Service's Williams District Ranger Office. Watch carefully for the sign, as it comes up suddenly. Go uphill around a curve and keep going east. At 34.7 miles *55.5 km*, turn left on the road going to the Forest Service facility. Immediately after you turn, you will see a sign for the Bill Williams Mtn. Trail. The road to the trailhead goes toward the camp and then turns left. At the 35.0 mile *56.0 km* point, you will see the trailhead parking area to your right.

TRAILHEAD: At the parking area. You will see a sign depicting the **Bill Williams Mountain Trail #21, Benham Trail #38,** and **Bixler Saddle #72** trails at the parking area. The sign does not show the Clover Spring trails. But don't worry, for they are well posted along the trail itself.

DESCRIPTION: You will hike along the Bill Williams Mountain Trail for a distance of 0.15 miles *0.24 km* to a trail junction, where you take the left fork for the Clover Spring Trail. We found the distances on this sign to be off a bit. At the 0.5 mile *0.8 km* point you come to a green gate with another trail junction beyond. The trail to the left is the City of Williams Link Trail #124. (It goes 1.0 mile *1.6 km* to meet Sheridan Ave. just west of 11th St.). Stay on the Clover Spring Trail. The trail has had a low pitch up to this point. Soon it gets steeper for a short distance before leveling off again. At

0.85 miles *1.36 km* you come to the third trail junction. Turn left. You will soon reach Clover Spring at the 1.0 mile *1.6 km* point.

The water from the spring flows from a concrete box on the hillside and crosses the trail, where a metal plate serves as a bridge. There is a sign to tell you that the place is Clover Spring. You will see the **Buckskinner Trail** taking off to the south from the spring.

The spring is the first part of the loop. Go back the way you came for 0.15 miles *0.24 km*, to the trail junction. From here, take the upper part of the loop. You will join the Bill Williams Mountain Trail at the 0.6 mile *1.0 km* point, where there are signs. Turn right and head downhill on the Bill Williams Mtn. Trail. You will return to the trailhead at the 1.5 mile *2.4 km* point, for a total loop of 2.5 miles *4.0 km.*

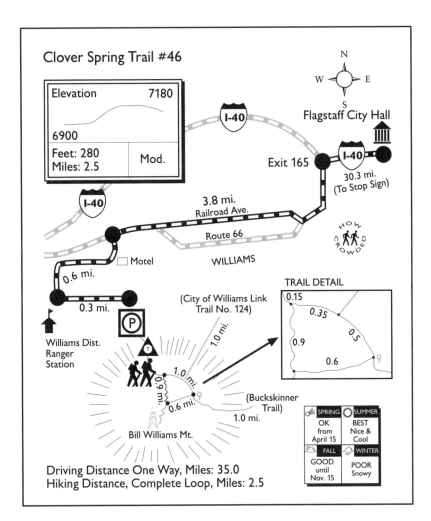

Coal Mine Canyon

General Information
Location Map C4
Coal Mine, Tuba City SE USGS Maps

Driving Distance One Way: 93.85 miles *150 km* (Time 2 hours)
Access Road: All cars, Last 0.75 miles *1.2 km* good dirt road
Hiking Distance One Way: 1.0 miles *1.6 km* (Time 1 hour)
How Strenuous: Moderate
Features: Gorgeous canyon

NUTSHELL: This requires a long drive but it is easy to reach on good roads. Though Coal Mine Canyon is incredibly beautiful, it is allowed to bask quietly in its splendor, host to the small number of people who know that it exists. It is home to the legendary Ghost of Coal Mine Canyon.

DIRECTIONS:
From Flagstaff City Hall Go:
   North on Highway 89 for 67.8 miles *108.5 km* (See Access Map, pages 10-11) to MP 480.8, where Highway 160 intersects 89 on the right. Turn right on Highway 160 and head east for to the 78.2 mile point *125.12 km*, the stoplight at Tuba City (MP 321.4). Turn right onto Highway 264. Drive past the Hopi village of Moenkopi, and enjoy looking down into Moenkopi Wash at the farms that line it. Soon you will climb a mesa. At the 93.1 mile point *148.96 km* (MP 336.8) take an unmarked unpaved road to your left. On this road, you will reach a junction at 93.4 miles *149.44 km*, where you go straight. At the next junction, 93.5 miles *149.6 km*, go right (NE). At the third junction, 93.65 miles *149.84 km*, take the middle road to the canyon: you will see that the right road goes to a windmill and the left road goes to a house. You will reach the rim at 93.85 miles *150.0 km*. Enjoy the view; then turn right and drive over and park at the picnic tables.

TRAILHEAD: WARNING: Do not try this hike if the ground is muddy! Walk through the gate into the picnic area and turn toward the canyon, where you will find a low ridge with a footpath on its top. Turn right on this and walk along it about 125 paces, to a point where you will see a faint path going downhill to your left. This is the trailhead.

DESCRIPTION: The trail is not marked, but it is distinct. The first portion is the most difficult, a very steep drop of about 100 feet, over which the trail goes straight down. This stretch may be too much for some hikers. After that, the trail is more level and is decent walking.
   You will be enthralled by the sights on this hike, as the canyon is a car-

nival of brilliant color, with lots of soft stone that has eroded into fascinating towers and sculptures. The color of the soil on the path changes continually. This place is heaven for photographers and geologists.

Keep watching the cliffs on your left (west). Where they end, you have reached the 0.66 mile *1.1 km* point. From here the trail dips down onto the canyon floor, where the canyon is much wider. Hikers can walk along the streambed for miles, but the best part is the first mile *1.6 km*.

The Coal Mine. Near the top of the canyon you can see a black layer. This is a low grade bituminous coal seam that was mined from about 1908-1915 and again from about 1947-1955.

The Ghost. We lack space for the legend here, but it is a wonderful story. Old accounts about how to see the Ghost are outdated, as it now impossible to drive to the east rim viewpoint that was used for ghost watching. There is no longer a campground. View it from the picnic area.

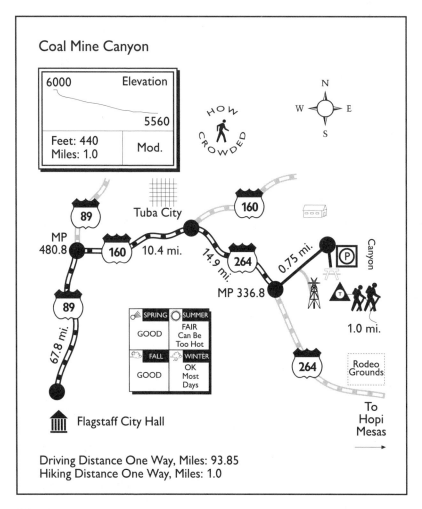

Coconino Rim Trail

Generai Information
Location Map C2
Grandview Point USGS Map
Kaibab (Tusayan) Forest Service Map

Driving Distance One Way: 87.8 miles *140.5 km* (Time 2 hours)
Access Road: All cars, Last 15.3 miles *24.5 km* good unpaved road
Hiking Distance One Way: 4.0 miles *6.4 km* (Time 1.75 hours)
How Strenuous: Easy
Features: Arizona Trail link, Mistletoe control exhibit

NUTSHELL: This trail goes along the crest of the Coconino Rim, a long arc-shaped ridge running southeasterly from Grandview Point at the Grand Canyon, 87.8 miles *140.5 km* from Flagstaff.

DIRECTIONS:
From Flagstaff City Hall Go:
North on Humphreys Street 0.60 miles *1.0 km* to a stoplight. See Access Map, page 10. Go left on Columbus and follow the curve north. Street signs will show the street first as Ft. Valley Road, then Highway 180. This is a major road to the Grand Canyon. At 50.4 miles *80.7 km* (MP 265.9), you will intersect Highway 64, coming out of Williams, at Valle. Go right and follow the highway to the 72.5 mile *116 km* point (MP 235.5), which you will find just as you come into Tusayan. Go right on FR 302 and follow it to the 87.7 mile *140.3 km* point, where there is a junction. Turn left on FR 310, where the sign says, "G.C.N.P. 1" and at 87.8 miles *140.48 km* you will see a sign for the Grandview Lookout (R). Turn right and park at the tower.

TRAILHEAD: At the parking area. There is a big sign. The trail is marked by posts placed every half mile *0.8 km*.

DESCRIPTION: The Arizona Trail is an ambitious project to create a linked series of trails that span Arizona from Utah to Mexico. Completion date is set for the year 2002. The Coconino Rim Trail is part of the system.
   The Coconino Rim is the uplifted portion of a large fault that created a crescent-shaped ridge about 500 feet high running southeasterly from the Grand Canyon. The Grand Canyon runs east-west in the area. The hiking trail takes advantage of the rim to bring the hiker into the Grand Canyon off of the main roads and above the desert.
   We recommend that you climb the fire tower before you hike. It provides great views, whereas the trail has few. Then, get underway. For the first 1.0 mile *1.6 km* of the trail the Forest Service has provided a series of signs

telling about the Dwarf Mistletoe, with examples pointed out in the forest. We were especially taken with the information that the mistletoe propagates by explosively shooting its sticky seeds as far as sixty feet.

You will pass through areas where the mistletoe was not eradicated and another where infected trees were removed. In the thinned area you are able to see into the Grand Canyon but it is only a glimpse.

The trail runs through an typical pine forest, so heavy that you can see into the distance in only a few places. We recommend hiking to the 4.0 mile *6.4 km* point, because you will encounter two viewpoints between the 3-mile and 4-mile markers. At the first you can see to the NNW, where the cliffs of the North Rim are in view. At the second you can see E, onto a vast plain, with the Painted Desert beyond. You can also see the shape of the Coconino Rim. We found a trail marker with a sign showing the Grandview TH to be 5.0 miles *8.0 km* along this part of the trail. We think it is way off.

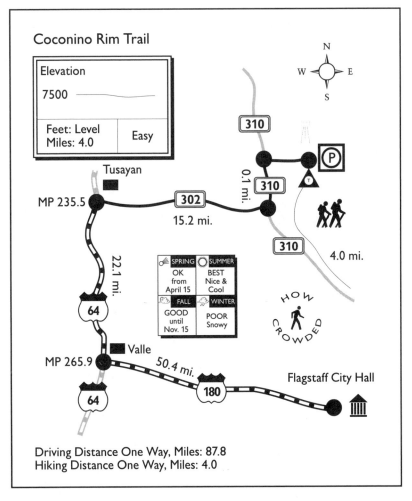

Coconino Rim Trail

Elevation	
7500 ———	
Feet: Level Miles: 4.0	Easy

N / W E / S

310

P

Tusayan

MP 235.5

310

302

15.2 mi.

0.1 mi.

310

4.0 mi.

22.1 mi.

🌱 SPRING	☀️ SUMMER
OK from April 15	BEST Nice & Cool
🍂 FALL	❄️ WINTER
GOOD until Nov. 15	POOR Snowy

HOW CROWDED

64

Valle

MP 265.9

50.4 mi.

64

180

Flagstaff City Hall

Driving Distance One Way, Miles: 87.8
Hiking Distance One Way, Miles: 4.0

Mangum

Connector Trail #80

General Information
Location Map E2
Kendrick Peak, Moritz Ridge and Wing Mt. USGS Maps
Kaibab Forest Service Map

Driving Distance One Way: 34.35 miles *54.96 km* (Time 1.25 hours)
Access Road: All cars, Last 20 miles *32 km* good gravel road
Hiking Distance One Way: 2.0 miles *3.2 km* (Time 1.0 hour)
How Strenuous: Moderate
Features: Nice forest, Views

NUTSHELL: This trail is located on Kendrick Mountain north of Flagstaff. After a brief climb it takes you from the **Bull Basin Trail** on the north side of the mountain to the **Pumpkin Trail** on the west side. Fire damage in 2000 has altered all these trails. Call 800-863-0546 for trail conditions.

DIRECTIONS:
From Flagstaff City Hall Go:
    North on Humphreys Street for 0.60 miles *1.0 km*. See Access Map, page 10. Turn left at the stoplight onto Columbus Avenue and follow it around a big curve to the north. You will see the street signs call this road Columbus at first, then Ft. Valley Road and then Highway 180. Stay on Highway 180 to the 14.4 miles *23.04 km* point (MP 230.1), where a gravel road takes off to the left. Turn left onto this road, FR 245, and follow it to the 17.4 mile *27.84 km* point where it intersects FR 171. Turn right on FR 171 and follow it to the 24.6 mile *39.36 km* point, where you will see a sign for the Pumpkin Trail. Go just beyond this, to the 24.7 mile *39.52 km* point and turn left on FR 171. Follow it to the 27.5 mile *44.0 km* point, where it meets FR 144 and turn right on FR 144, taking it to the 29.0 miles *46.4 km* point, where it intersects FR 90. Turn right on FR 90 and drive it to the 33.7 mile *53.92 km* point, where you will see FR 90A to the right. Take FR 90A to the 34.25 mile *54.8 km* point, where you will see a sign marking a road to the right to the Bull Basin trailhead. You can see the parking lot from this point. Turn right, downhill, and you will reach the parking area at 34.35 miles *54.96 km*.

TRAILHEAD: Use the Bull Basin Trailhead.

DESCRIPTION: From the parking area you walk a closed road along the west side of Bull Basin, a large grassy meadow. At 0.9 miles *1.4 km* you come to a trail junction where you see a trail to the right. A line of stones and poles indicate a trail junction mark the ground at this point. The **Bull Basin Trail** goes to the left, while the Connector Trail goes to the right.

The trail moves west along the base of Kendrick Mountain and then makes a gentle climb. After the climb, you will stay pretty much on the same level for the rest of the hike.

Because the trail is located on the north and west side of the mountain, the forest is more of a spruce and fir forest than a pine forest. It is quite attractive and is a pleasant walk. There are some aspens mixed in.

Along the trail there are some places where there are openings in the trees through which you can get views to the north. The landscape is one of wooded ridges below which a pastel desert begins abruptly and stretches to the Grand Canyon. About 0.1 mile *0.16 km* before the trail ends, you will enter a zone where the spruces stop and the pines begin.

The trail ends where it meets the Pumpkin Trail at a point 1.4 miles *2.25 km* from the Pumpkin Trailhead. There are signs at this junction. You could hike to the top of Kendrick on the Pumpkin Trail from here.

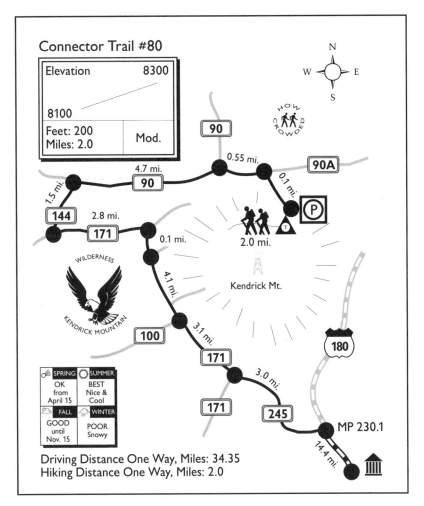

Crater Lake

General Information
Location Map E2
Kendrick Peak USGS Map
Coconino Forest Service Map

Driving Distance One Way: 21.7 miles *34.7 km* (Time 30 minutes)
Access Road: All cars, Last 1.0 miles *1.6 km* high clearance vehicle only
Hiking Distance One Way: 0.5 miles *0.8 km* (Time 15 minutes to the top)
How Strenuous: Moderate
Features: Charming hidden lake in a volcanic crater, Views

NUTSHELL: You can't see this little crater from the highway, but it is easy to reach and quite beautiful.

DIRECTIONS:
From Flagstaff City Hall Go:
    North on Humphreys Street for 0.60 miles *1.0 km*. See Access Map, page 10. Turn left at the stoplight onto Columbus Avenue and follow it around a big curve to the north. You will see the street signs call this road Columbus at first, then Ft. Valley Road and then Highway 180. Stay on Highway 180 to the 18.5 mile *29.6 km* point (MP 234.1), where a gravel road takes off to the left. Turn left onto this road, FR 760, and follow it to the 20.7 mile *33.1 km* point where a primitive unsurfaced road, FR 9009D appears to your left. Turn left on FR 9009D. This is a very rough road, with many large, exposed rocks. You may want to park at the junction and walk to the trailhead, which is 1.0 mile *1.6 km* from the fork. As you come near the trailhead, you will first see a sign announcing a travel restricted area. When you reach the trail-head, there is another sign saying "Official Notice." This is at a point where FR 9009D goes to the left, downhill. The hiking trail goes to your right, uphill.

TRAILHEAD: Not signed as a trail. Follow the old road, now closed.

DESCRIPTION: There are other hikes in the book that take the hiker up the north, west and south faces of Kendrick Peak, which is the tallest moun-tain in the region, save for the San Francisco Peaks. See the **Bull Basin**, **Connector**, **Kendrick Mountain** and **Pumpkin** trails. This is the only hike in the area of the east face of Kendrick, and it is on an adjacent volcanic crater. The Kendrick region was burned by a major forest fire in 2000. The fire swirled around Crater Lake, charring some trees but sparing others.
    The hiking trail is an old road, so it makes for an easy walk. You start on

the south face of the crater and move around, counterclockwise, to the east side, climbing about two hundred feet. As you climb, you have a few views into the surrounding area, but trees block your line of sight most of the time.

When you reach the bowl of the crater, you will find a fence with a maze-type gate. The road splits here. Take the right-hand road. It winds down to the floor of the crater, where you will find a charming lake with a horseshoe collar of aspens. This is a beautiful picturesque spot, perfect for a picnic. C. Hart Merriam saw this crater full to overflowing with rainwater in the summer of 1889.

After enjoying the lake, you might want to climb up to the rim of the crater and walk around it. There are some interesting red lava formations on the north end.

There are two Crater Lakes north of Flagstaff. The bigger and better known one is near the bottom of Hart Prairie, and is on private land that is posted with No Trespassing signs.

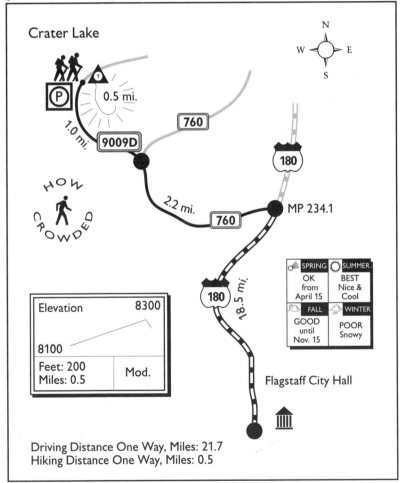

Crystal Point Trail

General Information
Location Map G3
Munds Park & Mormon Lake USGS Maps
Coconino Forest Service Map

Driving Distance One Way: 21.7 miles *34.72 km* (Time 35 minutes)
Access Road: All cars, Last 0.2 miles *0.32 km* good gravel road
Hiking Distance One Way: 1.25 miles *2.0 km* (Time 40 minutes)
How Strenuous: Easy
Features: Pleasant stroll through a pine forest to a lookout point

NUTSHELL: This hike is easy to reach on good roads.

DIRECTIONS:
From Flagstaff City Hall Go:
   West, then south on Route 66 to Milton Road. See Access Map, page 10.
Stay on Milton south and get onto Interstate-17 (toward Phoenix). Drive I-
17 south for 19.3 miles *31.0 km* to the Munds Park turn, Exit 322. You will
reach a stop sign at 19.5 miles *31.2 km*. At the stop sign, turn left. You will
drive into and through the Pinewood Subdivision, a well-developed area
complete with golf course. Stay on Pinewood Boulevard, which is the main
road through the area. At 21.5 miles *34.4 km* you will come up to the top of
a hill where the subdivision ends, the paved road ends, and a gravel road, FR
240, goes ahead into the forest. You will see a big brown sign here, showing the distance to Casner Park and other places. The Crystal Point trailhead
is just to the right (S) of this sign. The official parking area is another 0.2
miles *0.32 km* farther, a big, graveled lot to your left, at 21.7 miles *34. 72
km*.. (Usually you can find parking off the road at the trailhead sign as well).

TRAILHEAD: At the Forest Service road sign, just beyond the point where
the paving ends.

DESCRIPTION: The Crystal Point trail seems to be a collaboration of the
Forest Service and the residents of the subdivision. At the beginning it is
marked with typical Forest Service signs, but as you hike, you will notice a
number of informal signs that seem to have been put up by the people living
nearby.
   The trail moves along the top of a mesa in a southeasterly direction.
Every now and then you get a glimpse through the trees, showing you that
you are on a high ridge. The early going, up to the 1.0 mile *1.6 km* point is
quite level and easy, moving through a normal pine forest. This is a very
rocky area, but the rocks have been cleared from the trail, and the footing is

good.

The helpful signs installed by citizens inform you of significant distance points. There is even one for the halfway log, where you can sit and rest.

At 0.8 miles *1.28 km* you will come to the Lower Viewpoint. The name seems a bit optimistic, as the trees prevent open views. You can see the golf course and the walls of Oak Creek Canyon.

From this point the trail turns away from the edge and moves more steeply uphill to the top of a knob, which is Crystal Point (though the USGS map does not give any name to the knob). Even on this last leg, the steepest part of the trail, the hike is not difficult, and the distance is short.

At the top we found an ammo can with a number of log books dating back to 1992. As at the lower viewpoint, the views are somewhat disappointing because of the heavy tree cover. Even so, this is a delightful little hike.

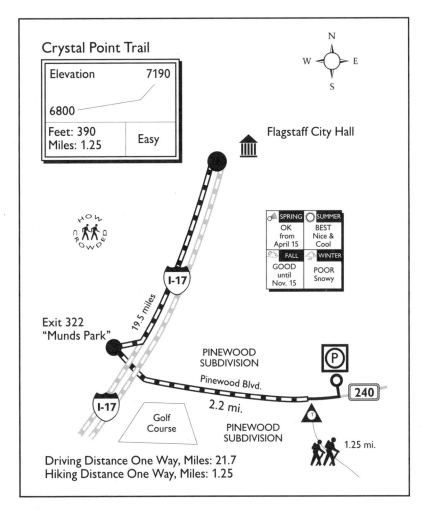

Davenport Hill Trail #63

General Information
Location Map F1
Williams South & Davenport Hill USGS Maps
Kaibab (Williams District) Forest Service Map

Driving Distance One Way: 40.7 miles *65.1 km* (Time 60 minutes)
Access Road: All cars, Last 4.0 miles *6.4 km* good gravel road
Hiking Distances: One way 2.5 mi. *4 km* (Time 1.25 hours) / Loop—1.0 mi.
     1.6 km (Time 30 min.) / Loop—1.8 mi. *2.9 km* (Time 1 hour)
How Strenuous: Moderate/Easy/Easy
Features: Beautiful forest, Nature trail, Lake

NUTSHELL: There are three hikes here: (1) Davenport Hill Trail, a 2.5 mile *4.0 km* trek to the top of a hill from which there are good views; (2) Ponderosa Nature Trail, an easy 1.0 mile *1.6 km* loop, (3) Dogtown Lake Trail, a 1.8 mile *2.9 km* loop around the lake.

DIRECTIONS:
From Flagstaff City Hall Go:
    South on Route 66 under the railroad overpass. Be sure to follow Route 66 when it turns right at the second stoplight. See Access Map, page 10. In about five miles *8.0 km* you will merge onto I-40 West and stay on it to the 30.3 miles *48.5 km* point, the Williams Exit, #165. Take that exit and at the stop sign go left to Williams. Go into town on Railroad Avenue to the 32.9 mile point *52.6 km* where you will find Fourth Street. Turn left on Fourth Street. As it leaves town its name changes to the Perkinsville Road (Highway 73). Stay on this road to the 36.7 miles *58.7 km* point, where you turn left onto FR 140. You will see a sign for "Dogtown Lake" here. Take FR 140 to the 39.5 mile *63.2 km* point, where you turn left on FR 132 into the campground, which you will reach at 40.7 miles *65.1 km*. Follow signs to the boat ramp for hikes 1 and 2. You park at the parking area by the boat ramp for hikes 1 and 2. For hike 3, go to the picnic area.

TRAILHEAD: At the Boat Ramp for hikes 1 and 2; at the Picnic Area for hike 3.

DESCRIPTION: Hike 1: At about a quarter of a mile *0.4 km*, just after you have passed over a bridge and the nature trail begins to loop back to camp, you will find the Davenport Hill Trail branching to the left. There is a sign. You will walk along a level bench to the 1.0 mile *1.6 km* point, where you cross a road. You are now at the foot of the hill and begin to climb. This involves winding around the hill, which gives you different viewpoints, though the forest is so thick that you only get glimpses toward Bill Williams Mountain and toward Davenport Lake. You reach an intermediate top at 1.5 miles *2.4 km*, a good resting point, then begin the final ascent. Toward the top you hike through a dense forest of oak, pine, fir and spruce. It is really lovely. The trail takes you north to the farthest point on the hill where it stops at a large cairn. There is a sign here reading, "Davenport Hill, Elevation 7805."

Hike 2: Dogtown Lake (named after a Prairie Dog colony) is a pretty lake in a scenic basin. You start on the nature trail, which takes you along the valley where a stream would flow if it hadn't been dammed to form the lake. The valley is marshy and lush. A brochure is keyed to numbered points along the trail, which loops back to the start.

Hike 3: From the picnic area, you make a loop around the lake. This hike is easy and quite level.

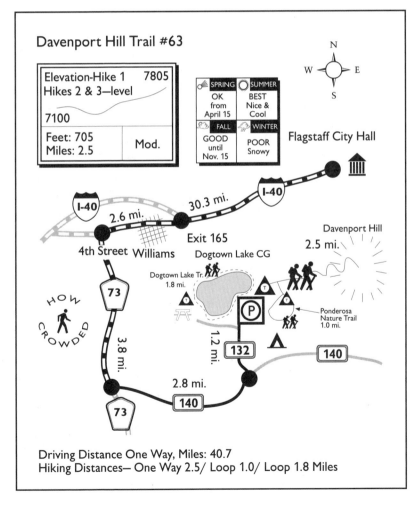

Davenport Hill Trail #63

Elevation-Hike 1	7805
Hikes 2 & 3—level	
7100	
Feet: 705	Mod.
Miles: 2.5	

SPRING	SUMMER
OK from April 15	BEST Nice & Cool
FALL	WINTER
GOOD until Nov. 15	POOR Snowy

Flagstaff City Hall

I-40   30.3 mi.   I-40

I-40   2.6 mi.

Exit 165

Davenport Hill 2.5 mi.

4th Street Williams   Dogtown Lake CG

HOW CROWDED

73

Dogtown Lake Tr. 1.8 mi.

Ponderosa Nature Trail 1.0 mi.

3.8 mi.   1.2 mi.   132

73   2.8 mi.   140

140

Driving Distance One Way, Miles: 40.7
Hiking Distances— One Way 2.5/ Loop 1.0/ Loop 1.8 Miles

Mangum

Deer Hill Trail

General Information
Location Map E3
Sunset Crater West USGS Map
Coconino Forest Service Map

Driving Distance One Way: 11.7 miles *18.7 km* (Time 30 minutes)
Access Road: All cars, Last 2.5 miles *4.0 km* good gravel road
Hiking Distance One Way: 5.3 miles *8.48 km* (Time 3.0 hours)
How Strenuous: Moderate except for the long distance
Features: Forests, Old logging railroad beds, Close to town

NUTSHELL: This trail takes you north from the Little Elden Springs Horse Camp through a fine forest, ending at a point on the Schultz Pass Road. In a couple of places the trail is atop old logging RR grades.

DIRECTIONS:
From Flagstaff City Hall Go:
East, then north on Highway 89. See Access Map, pages 10-11. Continue on Highway 89 to the 9.2 mile *14.72 km* point (MP 423.3) where you turn left on the gravel Elden Spring Road (FR 556). At the 11.3 mile *18.08 km* point pass by the turn to Horse Camp and drive to the 11.7 miles *18.7 km* point, where you turn into a parking lot with pole fence to your right. Park by the opening, where there is a big sign. (There is a toilet here). Do not drive directly into the Horse Camp, as that is for equestrians only.

TRAILHEAD: At the north end of the Horse Camp.

DESCRIPTION: From the parking area you hike 0.7 miles *1.12 km* to the Horse Camp following the signs. For the first 0.25 miles *0.4 km* the trail passes through what we call Goblin Garden. Then you keep moving on a gentle downhill grade to the Horse Camp.

When you get to the Horse Camp, pass through the gate and walk in, turning left at the first red gravel road and walking to the top (N) end of the camp, looking for Space #13. Northwest of this space you will see the trail going off into the woods. We zero our mileage here.

At 0.1 miles *0.16 km* you will pass through a yellow gate, the only place on this end where we found signs and markers. The sign says, "Schultz Pass Rd. 4.6 mi." You hike along a barbed wire fence to your right (W), then at 0.25 mi. *0.4 km* you turn right (N), still following the fence. This fence runs along the section lines due north and you will follow it all the way. At 0.4 miles *0.64 km* you will see two giant water tanks belonging to the Doney Park Water Company to your left.

At 0.5 miles *0.8 km* you come to a road and a pipeline. Go straight ahead across the road and the pipeline. Don't go through the blue fence or over the cattle guard. Soon the trail dips down into Weatherford Canyon, rises, then crosses an unnamed wash on the other side. At this point you are walking along the flank of Deer Hill, which rises above you to your left. You will hold the same contour line pretty steadily until the end. You will pass through two steel-pole gates, moving off Deer Hill at the second one. About 0.2 miles *0.32 km* from the farthest gate, where the path curves around a wash, you will be walking on the bed of the 1896-1925 Greenlaw logging railroad for a short distance. At the 3.0 mile *4.8 km* point you will be on another bit, easier to see because of the rock work.

At the end the trail opens a bit for views, then climbs to a point on the Schultz Pass Road 0.75 miles *1.2 km* from Highway 89. Our favorite way to do this hike is to use two cars and hike it one way.

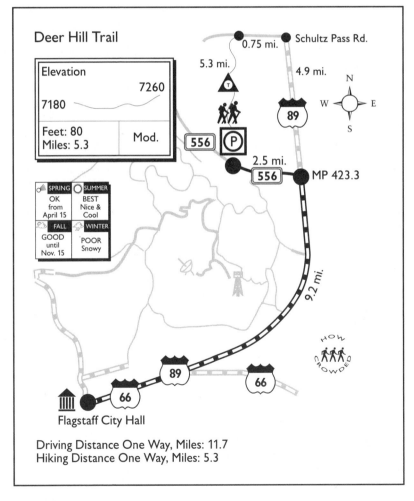

Doney Trail #39

General Information
Location Map D4
Wupatki SW USGS Map
Coconino Forest Service Map

Driving Distance One Way: 42 miles *67.2 km* (Time 60 minutes)
Access Road: All cars, All paved
Hiking Distance One Way: 0.50 miles *0.8 km* (Time 30 minutes)
How Strenuous: Moderate
Features: Views, Indian ruins

NUTSHELL: This is a short moderate trail located in the Wupatki National Monument northeast of Flagstaff. It takes you to the top of two cinder cones that give great unobstructed views of a fascinating volcanic field. You will also see some vestigial Indian ruins on this hike.

DIRECTIONS:
From Flagstaff City Hall Go:
    East, curving to north on Route 66-Hwy. 89. See Access Map, pages 10-11. Follow Highway 89 north out into the country. At 16.4 miles *26.24 km* (MP 430.3) you will reach the entrance to Sunset Crater National Monument. Turn right on the road into Sunset Crater. This road is also known as FR 545. At 18.4 miles *29.4 km* you will reach a ticket booth where you will have to pay admission. Just beyond that is the Sunset Crater Visitor Center, which is worth a look.
    At 26.0 miles *41.6 km* you reach the Painted Desert Vista. This is a look-out point where we recommend stopping to enjoy the view. Under the right lighting conditions it is superb. At 37.8 miles *60.5 km* you enter the Wupatki National Monument, which adjoins Sunset Crater, and you will see the road to the Wupatki Visitor Center to your left. This center is also worth a look.
    Keep following FR 545 to the 41.9 mile *67.0 km* point, where you will see a road to your left going to the Doney Picnic Ground. Take it. At 42.0 miles *67.2 km* you will reach the parking area, where you park.

TRAILHEAD: You will see a sign at the parking area.

DESCRIPTION: The trail is obvious when you start the hike. It climbs twin cinder cones, one higher than the other. The trail leads to a saddle between the two cones at 0.13 miles *0.2 km*. Here you can decide whether to go left to the lower cone or right to the higher one. We recommend that you go left first. It's less than 0.10 miles *0.16 km* to the left top and is a climb of only 100 feet. You will see some informative signs along the path. Just below the top you will see the smallest, crudest Indian ruin imaginable. There are good views from the top and a bench to sit on.

Then it's on to the higher cone. Each summit offers a different angle, so both are worthwhile. On the trail you will see a small partially excavated pit house. At the top you will find a bench where you can sit and enjoy the views. There is a nice sign there with a sketch identifying the mountains you see to the west.

Because these tops are bare cinder cones your view is unobstructed. Notice that a northeast-southwest line connecting the cinder cones also separates high ground on the southwest from lower ground to the northeast. This line marks the trace of a fault, or break, in the Earth's crust across which the rocks on the northeast have dropped down about 300 feet. Magma (molten rock) flowed up this fault from deep in the Earth to erupt and form the cinder cones.

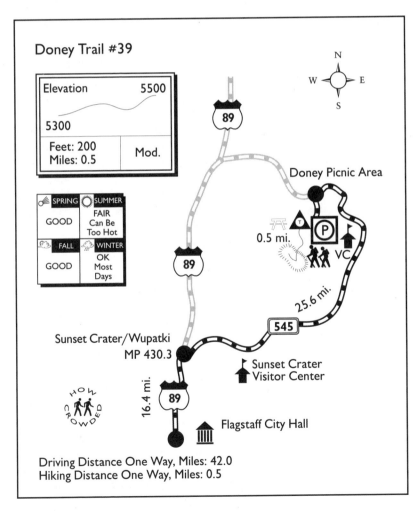

Dorsey Spring Trail

General Information
Location Map F2
Sycamore Point USGS Map
Coconino Forest Service Map

Driving Distance One Way: 22.95 miles *36.7 km* (Time 60 minutes)
Access Road: High clearance for last 0.65 miles *1.04 km*
Hiking Distance One Way: 2.3 miles *3.7 km* (Time 1.50 hours)
How Strenuous: Hard
Features: Hidden spring, Virgin forests

NUTSHELL: Located about 23 miles *36.8 km* southwest of Flagstaff, this trail takes you part of the way into Sycamore Canyon to a beautiful spring.

DIRECTIONS:
From Flagstaff City Hall Go:
    West a block on Route 66, then south, beneath the railroad overpass. See Access Map, page 10. At 0.5 miles *0.8 km* you will reach a Y intersection. The right fork is named Route 66. Take it. You will soon leave town. At 2.6 miles *4.2 km* you will reach a road going to the left. This is the Woody Mountain Road, FR 231. Take it. It is paved about a mile *1.6 km* and then turns into a cinder road. At 16.6 miles *26.6 km* you will intersect FR 538. Turn right onto FR 538 and follow it to the 22.3 mile *35.7 km* point, where it intersects the Kelsey Spring Road, FR 538E. Turn right on 538E. The roads to this point are good, but beyond it they are rough. At 22.7 miles *36.3 km* you hit another intersection where FR 538E forks to the left. This is the Dorsey Spring Road. Turn left onto it and follow it to its end at 22.95 miles *36.7 km*, where you will find a parking lot.

TRAILHEAD: You will see a big sign at the parking area.

DESCRIPTION: The Dorsey Spring Trail does not take you into the inner gorge of Sycamore Canyon like its nearby neighbors the **Kelsey Spring Trail** and the **Winter Cabin Trail** do. It stops at Dorsey Spring. Also unlike those trails, the parking lot is not located at the canyon's rim.
    From the parking area you will walk a closed jeep road. At 0.25 miles *0.4 km* you will see a closed road to the Hog Hill trailhead forking to the left. At 1.8 miles *2.9 km* you will reach the rim. From the rim area you will get a few views into the depths of the canyon, the only place on this trail where that is possible.
    You will hike down into Sycamore along a side canyon. It is fairly steep but the footing is decent and you only have to go half a mile *0.8 km*, to the

2.3 mile *3.7 km* point. The spring is on a small shelf to your left. The water has been channeled so it flows from a black plastic pipe. The spring is usually dependable but the Forest Service recommends purifying its water. From the place where the water comes out of the pipe you will see a thin river of green grass running down a long way, ultimately into Sycamore.

A few yards below the spring there is a large shelf of land, a beautiful idyllic spot.

You will also find markers for the **Kelsey-Winter Trail** coming through this large shelf of land. Dorsey Spring is located about midway between Kelsey Spring and Winter Cabin Spring on the Kelsey-Winter Trail. You can go north along Kelsey-Winter about 2.0 miles *3.2 km* to **Babe's Hole** and into the gorge of Sycamore Canyon via **Geronimo Spring** or you can go south about 2.0 miles *3.2 km* to **Winter Cabin** and into the Sycamore Canyon gorge via Ott Lake, so it is an ideal resting place in between.

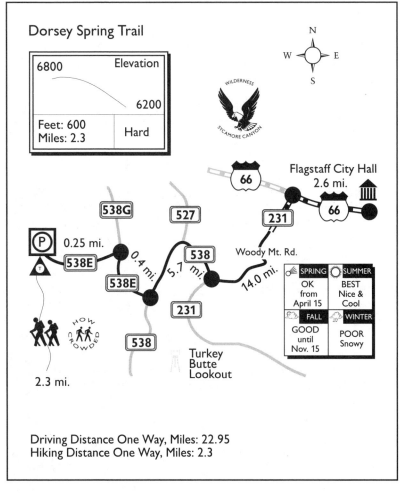

Elden Lookout Trail #4

General Information
Location Map E3
Flagstaff East USGS Map
Coconino Forest Service Map

Driving Distance One Way: 5.2 miles *8.3 km* (Time 10 minutes)
Access Road: All cars, All paved
Hiking Distance One Way: 3.0 miles *4.8 km* (Time 2 hours)
How Strenuous: Hard
Features: Views

NUTSHELL: This marked and maintained trail runs from the base of Mt. Elden in East Flagstaff to the top of the mountain where a fire lookout tower is located.

DIRECTIONS:
From Flagstaff City Hall Go:
    East on Highway 89. See Access Map, pages 10-11. At 5.2 miles *8.3 km* (MP 419.5), just beyond the Flagstaff Mall, you will see a sign for the "Mt. Elden Trailhead" and a paved driveway to your left into a parking lot bounded by a pole fence. Pull in there and park.

TRAILHEAD: There is a sign with map at the gate in the parking lot.

DESCRIPTION: You will meet the **Fat Man's Loop Trail** branching to the right shortly after you begin. After that you will come to two fences that have maze-type gates. Go through them. You will see clearly by now that you are walking directly toward Mt. Elden. In about a quarter mile *0.4 km* you will reach the junction with the **Pipeline Trail**, which goes left. For about the first mile *1.6 km* you will pass through a pine forest. The trail rises as it approaches the mountain. At the top of this approach, which is the apex of the Fat Man's Loop, you will see a sign showing the Elden Lookout Trail going uphill.
    From this point to the top, about two miles *3.2 km*, the trail is very steep. There is hardly a level stretch anywhere. You will note that a lot of work has been done on this trail, which was built in 1914. In some places "stairs" have been built and in others cribbing has been used to hang the trail out over space. Mt. Elden is so steep and so rocky that constant maintenance is needed to keep this trail open. Every year it must be cleared of fallen trees, rock slides, etc. We appreciate the work the Forest Service does on this trail.
    The forest through which you pass on your way to the top is not heavy. This is due to the terrain and a 1978 forest fire. Consequently there are many

open spaces for great views. You look out north and east into East Flagstaff, Doney Park, the Sunset Crater area, and the Painted Desert.

The three mile *4.8 km* point at the top where the sign indicating the end of the trail is located is not the absolute top of Mt. Elden. You will find a sign indicating that the tower is 0.25 miles *0.4 km* away. If you have enough energy, by all means, make this final ascent, because the views at the top are as good as any in the Flagstaff area. If a ranger is in the tower you may be invited up. Go. You won't regret it.

We like this hike much better going down, not only because it's easier on the heart, but because the views are before you, unfolding. Using two cars, you park the first one at the bottom. Then everyone rides the second car to the top. You hike down and then drive back to the top to retrieve the second car.

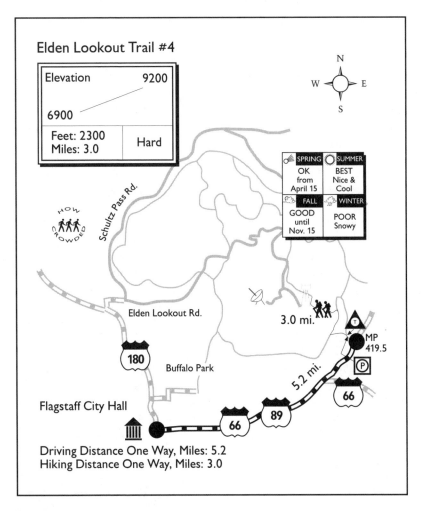

Mangum

Elden Pueblo

General Information
Location Map E3
Flagstaff East USGS Map
Coconino Forest Map

Driving Distance One Way: 6.4 miles *10.24 km* (Time 10 minutes)
Access Road: All cars, All paved
Hiking Distance One Way: 0.10 miles *0.16 km* (Time 30 minutes)
How Strenuous: Easy
Features: Indian ruins located inside Flagstaff city limits

NUTSHELL: Interesting Indian ruins, presently being excavated. Located just north of Flagstaff, this is more of a sightseeing excursion than a hike, as you do very little walking.

DIRECTIONS:
From Flagstaff City Hall Go:
    East, then north on Highway 89. See Access Map, pages 10-11. At 6.4 miles *10.24 km* (MP 420.7), you will see a sign, "Elden Pueblo Ruins" and a gravel drive going into the trees to your left just before the stoplight at the junction of Highway 89 and the Townsend-Winona Road. This is the entrance to the parking area for Elden Pueblo. Pull in there and park.

TRAILHEAD: There are no trail signs. A path starts at the west end of the parking lot. It is easy to find.

DESCRIPTION: From the parking lot there is a road going through a gate to your right (north). It does go to the ruin, but it is the long way around, intended for vehicles only, so that they can loop around and avoid driving right on the site of the ruins. You will find signs directing you to the pueblo site. The ruins are very near the highway and you will soon see them when you begin to walk the footpath. They are undergoing restoration but this is sporadic and there is no way of knowing on any particular day whether any-one will be there. If no one is present, you are welcome to help yourself and wander around. Unfortunately there are no self-guiding signs.
    At times the Forest Service sponsors amateur digs at Elden Pueblo, when the public is invited to come out and work for a day under the guidance of professional archaeologists. Look for announcements in the Flagstaff news-paper or call the Elden Pueblo Project Manager, Northern Arizona Natural History Association, (520) 523-9642 for recorded information on these digs. It's your chance to find out what archaeology is really like.
    Elden Pueblo was discovered in 1916 by Mary-Russell Ferrell Colton,

while horseback riding. The prominent federal archaeologist Jesse Fewkes conducted digs at the site in the early 1920s and sent carloads of artifacts from Elden Pueblo to the Smithsonian. The dismay of townspeople at seeing this wholesale loss of local relics was one of the main reasons that Mrs. Colton and her husband joined other townspeople and organized the Museum of Northern Arizona.

A look at this site shows you how much effort goes into excavation. You can appreciate better what has happened at some fully restored places such as Wupatki or Tuzigoot when you look at the work here. The more they dig at Elden Pueblo, the bigger the ruin seems and the present thought is that there may be an older ruin under the surface ruin.

In addition to the highly publicized Indian ruins such as Wupatki there are many smaller ruins like Elden Pueblo located northeast of Flagstaff.

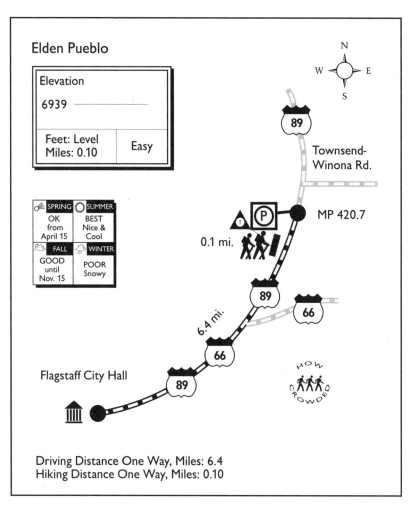

Elden Pueblo

Elevation	
6939	
Feet: Level Miles: 0.10	Easy

SPRING	SUMMER
OK from April 15	BEST Nice & Cool
FALL	WINTER
GOOD until Nov. 15	POOR Snowy

Townsend-Winona Rd.

MP 420.7

0.1 mi.

6.4 mi.

HOW CROWDED

Flagstaff City Hall

Driving Distance One Way, Miles: 6.4
Hiking Distance One Way, Miles: 0.10

Elden Skyline Trail

General Information
Location Map E3
Humphreys Peak & Sunset Crater West USGS Maps
Coconino Forest Service Map

Driving Distance One Way: 9.4 miles *15 km* (Time 40 minutes)
Access Road: All cars, Last 4.8 miles *7.7 km* winding gravel road
Hiking Distance One Way: 1.0 miles *1.6 km* (Time 35 minutes)
How Strenuous: Moderate
Features: Unsurpassed views of Flagstaff

NUTSHELL: This trail starts at Sunset Park near the top of Mt. Elden and goes to a point just below the lookout tower. It is also known as The Catwalk.

DIRECTIONS:
From Flagstaff City Hall Go:
  North on Humphreys Street for 0.6 miles *1.0 km.* See Access Map, page 10. Turn left at the light onto Columbus and follow it around a big curve. The street signs call this road Columbus Avenue at first, then Ft. Valley Road and then Highway 180. Stay on Highway 180 to the 3.1 miles *5.0 km* point (MP 218.6), where you turn right on the Schultz Pass Road, FR 420. At 3.6 miles *5.8 km* where the paving curves left take the paved Elden Lookout Road (FR 557) going straight. Follow FR 557 to the 9.4 mile *15 km* point, where you will park in an area off the right shoulder.

TRAILHEAD: Walk across the road, where you will see a footpath going uphill to the skyline. At the crest you will find signs.

DESCRIPTION: This trail is considered officially to be the last leg of the Sunset Trail. We feel that it is a much better experience to treat it as a separate trail, as the Sunset Trail is too long if you add this extension to it.
  The place where the trail starts is a junction of the **Sunset Trail** and the **Upper Oldham Trail** and you will find signs for each of them here. Go to the right, on the Sunset Trail.
  This whole area on top of Mt. Elden shows the results of what a forest fire can do. Hundreds of acres of prime forest were burned away in 1978 in the catastrophic Radio Fire. The area is just now beginning to heal.
  Your trail will take you along the crest of Mt. Elden, climbing uphill a bit a first and then dipping. Almost all the way you will have tremendous views. You look down on East Flagstaff, the Doney Park area, and off toward the Sunset Crater area. On a clear day you can see the Painted Desert.

One of the first trees to come back after a forest fire is the aspen and you will find groves of young aspens along this trail. They have replaced the spruce that predominated here before the fire.

At about the three-quarter mile *1.2 km* point, the trail comes very close to the road going to the fire lookout, but then it veers away from it. At the 1.0 mile *1.6 km* point you will reach the place where this trail meets the **Elden Lookout Trail** coming up from East Flagstaff.

This is the end of the trail, but at this point you have two options: one is to take the Elden Lookout Trail up to the fire tower, a quarter mile *0.4 km* hike. The views from the tower are superb. If a ranger is in the tower you may be invited up. Go up if you get the chance. You won't soon forget what you see from there. The other option is to bushwhack out to the end of a rocky knob that is to your left at the junction. This is only about one-tenth of a mile *0.16 km* and takes you to an excellent viewpoint.

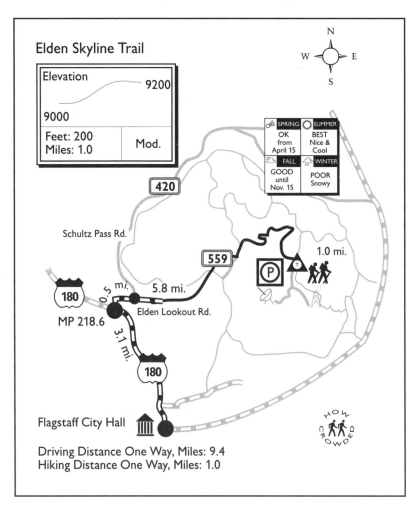

Mangum

Elden Spring Loop

General Information
Location Map E3
Flagstaff East USGS Map
Coconino Forest Service Map

Driving Distance One Way: 5.1 miles *8.16 km* (Time 15 minutes)
Access Road: All cars, All paved
Hiking Distance, Complete Loop: 2.0 miles *3.2 km* (Time 1.5 hours)
How Strenuous: Moderate
Features: Historic homesite, Historic grave, Fascinating lava cliffs and
boulders, Spring

NUTSHELL: A short drive takes you to this trail that packs many features into a two mile loop. This is a good one for kids.

DIRECTIONS:
From Flagstaff City Hall Go:
East, then north on Highway 89. See Access Map, pages 10-11. At 4.6 miles *7.36 km* (just before you arrive at the Flagstaff Mall) turn left on Cummings (Pizza Hut on the corner). Go up Cummings to its end, by Christensen School, and turn left on El Paso. Drive out El Paso for four blocks to Hamblin. Here you will see a wide unpaved apron to the right. Pull off on it and drive up to the pipeline fence, where you see a wide white gate flanked by two big H posts, at 5.1 miles *8.16 km*. Park at the gate.

TRAILHEAD: There are no trail signs where you park. Step over the criss-crossed logs that serve as a gate and walk up the pipeline road.

DESCRIPTION: Walk up to the top of the grade, where at 0.15 miles *0.24 km*, you will see a footpath to the right (N), and a big sign, "Welcome to the Mt. Elden Environmental Study Area...." The sign contains a confusing map. The trails on the map were made about 1980, and numbered posts were placed at interesting points. The project was not maintained.
There are many trails where you will hike. Stay on the main trail at all times. Soon you come to a trail junction. Go straight. At 0.6 miles *1.0 km*, you will come out into a clearing where you will see trail signs and an interpretive sign. At your right hand is a wooden sign, "Pipeline Road—Walk Through Time Tr." To the left of this signpost, going toward Mt. Elden (N) is a rough path down into a gully. This takes you to Elden Spring, a short walk. It is worth seeing. Come back up and walk out in the clearing to the interpretive sign, which tells you about the Elden Homesite. (We think the date is wrong: Elden came here in 1877).

Next, walk west on the main path. In about 0.1 mile *0.16 km* you will find the grave and another interpretive sign. After the grave site, go SW a short distance on the main trail to a trail junction. Here you find a sign pointing to the "Pipeline" to your left and to "Fire" on your right. Go right (NW).

You will soon come to a fork with a sign, "Elden Grave—Forces of Nature Trail." Go straight north toward the mountain on an unmarked trail. It takes you to a giant S-shaped crevice on the side of Mt. Elden. You will reach the crevice at the 1.0 mile *1.6 km* point. We think you will enjoy looking at the boulders and cliffs here and may want to do some exploring. Don't try to climb to the top of the crevice. An extremely fit, prepared hiker needs about four hours to get to the crest.

On the way back, retrace your path down to the "Pipeline-Fire" signpost, and follow the trail marked "Pipeline." You will reach the pipeline in only a few yards. Turn left and walk the pipeline road back down to your car.

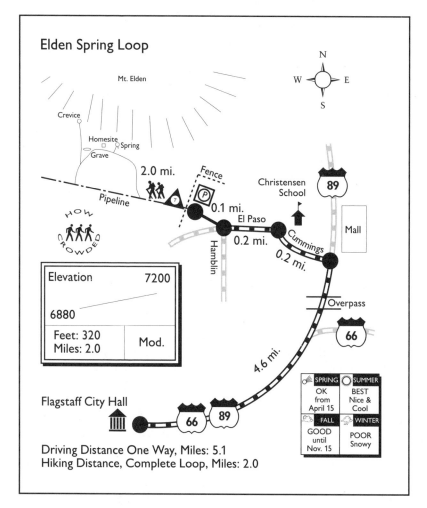

Mangum

Fat Man's Loop #25

General Information
Location Map E3
Flagstaff East USGS Map
Coconino Forest Service Map

Driving Distance One Way: 5.2 miles *8.3 km* (Time 10 minutes)
Access Road: All cars, All paved
Hiking Distance, Complete Loop: 2.4 miles *3.8 km* (Time 1.5 hours)
How Strenuous: Moderate
Features: Views

NUTSHELL: This maintained trail located in East Flagstaff at the base of Mt. Elden is designed to provide moderate exercise for a "fat man." It provides good scenery and views.

DIRECTIONS:
From Flagstaff City Hall Go:
    East, then north on Highway 89. See Access Map, pages 10-11. At 5.2 miles *8.3 km* (MP 419.5) just past the Flagstaff Mall, you will see a sign for the "Mt. Elden Trailhead" and a paved driveway to your left into a parking lot bounded by a pole fence. Pull in there and park.

TRAILHEAD: There are trail signs at the gate in the parking lot fence.

DESCRIPTION: The Forest Service has developed a trail system around the Mt. Elden-Dry Lake Hills areas in Flagstaff and this trail connects with others in that system. You will find trail information at the trailhead. Fat Man's Loop is a nice trail, well marked, The footing is good. As the name suggests, the trail makes a loop. It is not flat, as it climbs to a high point beyond midway and then descends.
    Start out on the main trail and watch for a fork at 0.15 miles *0.24 km*. There Fat Man's branches to the right. At 0.30 miles *0.48 km* you will come to a pole fence with a squeeze through opening designed to pass humans but not horses. At this point the trail, which up to now has been heading toward Mt. Elden, turns to the right and moves parallel to the base of the mountain. Just beyond this gate, a secondary trail intersects at right angles. Don't turn left or right here. Go straight. At 0.40 miles *0.64 km* you hit another trail junction. This is posted with a sign reading, "Fatman's Loop, Elden Lookout." You want to go left here, toward Mt. Elden. Soon after this, the trail winds around and under a giant old alligator-bark juniper tree, which is quite a sight. Since these trees live to be very old, this one must be ancient to have grown so large.

At 0.90 miles *1.44 km* you are high enough to get some views. To your right the open plain is Doney Park. To your left you see immense cliffs on Mt. Elden. These are made of columns of lava caused by huge volcanic outbursts two million years ago. All through this area you will see volcanic boulders, some of them big as a house and your trail will wind through a nifty crevice between boulders that is too narrow for a fat man.

You reach the high point of the trail at 1.5 miles *2.4 km*, where there is another trail junction. The path to the right is the **Elden Lookout Trail**, which is not for fat men as it is a very steep climb. You take the trail to the left, from where it is all downhill back to the starting point.

At 2.0 miles *3.2 km* you will reach another junction where there is a sign reading, "**Pipeline Trail No. 42**, **Oldham Trail No. 1**, Buffalo Park 4." Just beyond this point is another pole fence with a squeeze through. From there you saunter back to your car.

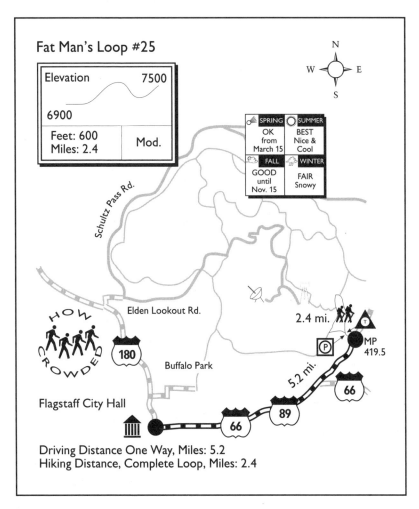

Flagstaff-North Trail

General Information
Location Map F3
Flagstaff West USGS Map
Coconino Forest Service Map

Driving Distance One Way: 1 Block (Time 5 minutes)
Access Road: All cars, All paved
Hiking Distance One Way: 2.0 miles *3.2 km* (Time 1 hour)
How Strenuous: Easy
Features: Urban trail, Available year-around, Historic site where Flagstaff
        got its name

NUTSHELL: This urban trail in north Flagstaff is very easy to reach, provides a pleasant stroll along a well-surfaced trail, and can be hiked almost
any day of the year. When the woods are muddy or snow-covered, this trail
can give you an opportunity to stretch your legs. We have enjoyed it even in
the depths of winter.

DIRECTIONS:
From Flagstaff City Hall Go:
   North one block on Humphreys Street, then turn left (W) on Aspen
Avenue and park along the street in the block between Humphreys and
Sitgreaves Streets. If hiking on a weekend or holiday, you can park in one
of the public parking lots you will find on Aspen Avenue.

TRAILHEAD: Look for a concrete walk on the east side of the Public
Library, along the river bank. You will see a little arched wooden bridge
there, which serves as a marker.

DESCRIPTION: Walk north along the concrete walk, past the bridge. In a
few steps you will come to a monument honoring Flagstaff men who died in
military service. Just beyond that you will cross Birch Avenue. Take a brief
jog to your left (W), then follow the trail north along the side of the Rio de
Flag, an intermittent stream. At Birch you will see the distinctive trail surface and the trail signs, which will guide you the rest of the way. At Cherry
you will dip down into the riverbed. (If the stream is in flood, you can detour
around to the west and north).
   You will come up out of the riverbed and cross Sitgreaves Street at Dale.
The trail forks at the bridge. Turn right, and continue north, along the east
bank of the riverbed near Flagstaff High School. In another couple of blocks,
you cross Bonito Street south of the Flagstaff Middle School. Beyond this
point you will soon reach the City Dam. There is an old log cabin here, built

by the Scouts in the 1930s. Views from the area of the dam are nice, as you have a sweeping vista of the San Francisco Peaks.

From the dam you will walk along the west side of the lake formed by the dam. At the trail fork, turn right, and you will soon approach Thorpe Road. Look to your left here and you will see the flag flying from a telephone pole set an a rock base. This is the Flagstaff Monument, the place there the flag staff that gave our town its name was raised on July 4, 1876. Take a little detour to see it. At this point you have hiked 0.75 miles *1.2 km*, so this is a good stopping point if you want a short walk.

North of Thorpe Road you follow the river as it skirts ball fields and homes. The path crosses Beal Road and Meade Lane. North of Meade Lane you pass a playground and a swimming pool. The path ends beyond the pool, where it reaches Crescent Drive. In the future this trail will extend several miles, out to Ft. Valley.

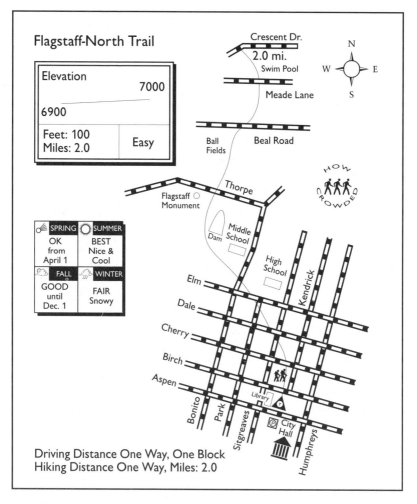

Mangum

Flagstaff Spring

General Information
Location Map E3
Humphreys Peak and Sunset Crater West USGS Maps
Coconino Forest Service Map

Driving Distance One Way: 21.6 miles *34.6 km* (Time 45 minutes)
Access Road: All cars, Last 4.5 miles *7.2 km* medium dirt road
Hiking Distance One Way: 3.5 miles *5.6 km* (Time 2.5 hours)
How Strenuous: Hard, Steep Climb, High elevations
Features: Highest mountain, Alpine forests, Great views

NUTSHELL: The San Francisco Peaks located north of Flagstaff are an extinct volcanic crater with an opening to the east. This trail takes you up the valley formed by that eastern opening into the heart of the crater.

DIRECTIONS:
From Flagstaff City Hall Go:
  East, then north on Highway 89. See Access Map, pages 10-11. At 17.1 miles *27.4 km* (MP 431.2)—just past the entrance to Sunset Crater—turn left onto FR 552 and take it to the 18.3 mile *29.3 km* point, where you will see a sign for Lockett Meadow. Go right. From here the road is a winding narrow gravel route which climbs up the face of the mountain. At 21.3 miles *34 km* you reach Lockett Meadow, where you will see a one-way road to your right into a campground. Take this and park in the Day Use Area at the 21.6 mile *34.6 km* point, just across from the campground toilet.

TRAILHEAD: The trailhead is posted with a big sign left of the toilet.

DESCRIPTION: This trail, like the highly recommended **Inner Basin Trail**, makes use of roads reserved for city vehicles to service the Flagstaff water supply. Hikers who are familiar with the Inner Basin Trail, will be surprised to see how different this trail is.
  Start by hiking the Inner Basin Trail. At the 1.5 mile *2.4 km* point you reach two green cabins at an elevation of 9,400 feet. At the cabins is a confusing three-way road junction. Look at the map for clarification. Take the middle road (WSW), the one marked "San Francisco Peaks, Inner Basin". The road to the left we call the **Tunnel Trail.** The road to the right is the **Abineau Pipeline Trail**, which goes uphill, then curves around to a point on the north face of Mt. Humphreys, along the way intersecting the **Bear Jaw Trail** and the **Abineau Canyon Trail #127**.
  After leaving the cabins, at the 1.6 mile *2.56 km* point you reach a fork in the road. To the left (S) you will see a pump house and may hear a loud

pump running. That is the fork to the Inner Basin Trail. You want to take the right fork here (WSW).

At the 2.3 mile *3.68 km* point there is another road junction, where you go right (NW). In this area you begin to see some of the huge colorful walls forming the Inner Basin of the Peaks. Also check behind you for grand vistas over the Sunset Crater and Painted Desert. At 2.8 miles *4.48 km* you will see a small sign marking Bear Paw Spring to your left in a valley. Keep going to the 3.0 mile *4.8 km* point, where you will be at the base of a curving red wall bordered by lush vegetation—a very scenic and awesome place. If you are tired, stop here, for you have seen the best part of this hike.

The road goes on, steeper than ever, to the 3.5 mile *5.6 km* point, where Flagstaff Spring is located, but all you see there a standpipe with a sign marked "Untreated Spring Water." There are no free flowing springs in the Inner Basin—all have been captured into pipes for the city's water supply.

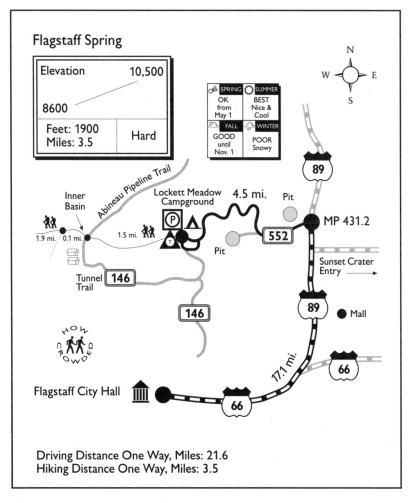

Flagstaff Spring

Elevation	10,500
8600	
Feet: 1900 Miles: 3.5	Hard

SPRING	SUMMER
OK from May 1	BEST Nice & Cool
FALL	WINTER
GOOD until Nov. 1	POOR Snowy

N
W — E
S

Abineau Pipeline Trail

Inner Basin

Lockett Meadow Campground

4.5 mi.   Pit

89

MP 431.2

1.9 mi.   0.1 mi.   1.5 mi.

P   △

552

Pit

Sunset Crater Entry ⟶

Tunnel Trail   146

146

89   ● Mall

HOW CROWDED

17.1 mi.

66

Flagstaff City Hall 🏛 ●————————   66

Driving Distance One Way, Miles: 21.6
Hiking Distance One Way, Miles: 3.5

Mangum

Fossil Springs Trail

General Information
Location Map G4
Strawberry USGS Map
Coconino Forest Service Map

Driving Distance One Way: 82 miles *131.2 km* (Time 2 hours)
Access Road: All cars, Last 3.2 miles *5.1 km* good unpaved road
Hiking Distance One Way: 3.8 miles *6.1 km* (Time 2 hours)
How Strenuous: Hard
Features: Beautiful canyon, Views, Perennial spring-fed stream

NUTSHELL: Starting at a point on the top of the Mogollon Rim near Strawberry, you hike an old road to the bottom, where you will find spring-fed Fossil Creek, a beautiful riparian environment.

DIRECTIONS:
From Flagstaff City Hall Go:
   West and then south on Route 66. See Access Map on page 10. At 0.5 miles *0.8 km* go straight on Milton Road, where there is a stoplight. At 1.7 miles *2.7 km* turn right at Forest Meadows. Then turn left on Beulah which will connect onto Highway 89A. At the 2.4 miles *3.8 km* point (MP 401.6) you will see the turnoff to the Lake Mary Road to your left (south). Take it and follow the Lake Mary Road (also known as FH3) to the 56.6 mile *90.6 km* point, the junction with Highway 87 at Clint's Well. Turn right on Highway 87 and drive it to the 76.3 miles *122 km* point, MP 271, where you reach the hamlet of Strawberry. Turn right (west) on Route 708 (also known as Fossil Creek Road). The road is paved for 2.5 miles *4 km*, then becomes unpaved. Stay on FR 708 to the 81.1 mile *130 km* point, where you will see the signed road to the trailhead to your right. Turn off on this access road, which has some washouts, but can be driven by any car that has reasonable clearance. You will reach the loop parking area at 82 miles *131 km.*

TRAILHEAD: At the parking place. There is a sign.

DESCRIPTION: For the first 3.0 miles *4.8 km* of this trail you follow an old road, now closed to vehicles, down to the bottom of the canyon. You can see this road from the top. Because the road was designed for motor vehicles, the grades are fairly moderate.
   At the bottom of the canyon, you will reach the streambed. Here the old road disappears and the trail turns into a footpath. You walk parallel to the creek and then cross it on stepping stones. Usually the creek is not deep here. On the other side, you walk the final 0.8 miles *1.28 km* down to the utility

hut. This is the most beautiful part of the hike, as the stream gets bigger and bigger as more springs feed into it. The vegetation is lush and there are many side trails taking you to the water's edge.

Fossil Creek is one of the most reliable, abundant water sources in northern Arizona, and was used from 1916-2000 to generate hydroelectric power. Originally the electric power went to Jerome, and was later expanded to go to Phoenix. The shutdown of the operation may mean removal of some of the works. Where the hike ends, was the beginning of the water works where water was channeled into a flume here and run seven miles down to the Verde River, passing through generating plants at Irving and Childs on its way.

The creek gets its name, not because it contains fossils, but because the water contains high levels of calcium, which encrusts objects in the water with a stony shell, like a fossil.

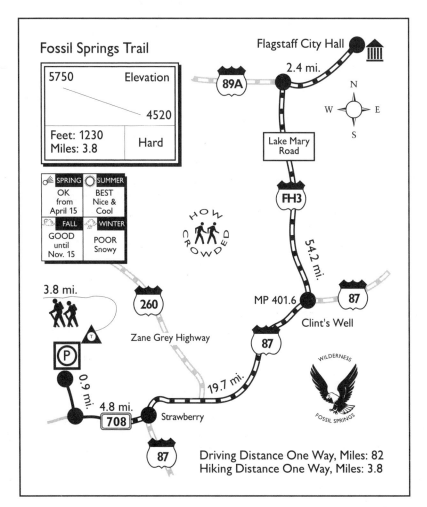

General Springs Trail

General Information
Location Map G4
Blue Ridge Reservoir & Dane Canyon USGS Maps
Coconino Forest Service Map

Driving Distance One Way: 78.4 miles *125.44 km* (Time 2 hours)
Access Road: All cars, Last 12.6 miles *20.2 km* good dirt roads
Hiking Distance One Way: 3.0 miles *4.8 km* (1.5 hours)
How Strenuous: Moderate
Features: Beautiful Mogollon Rim, Historic Indian war site, Arizona Trail

NUTSHELL: After enjoying a drive along the historic Crook Trail, you will take a refreshing hike.

DIRECTIONS:
From Flagstaff City Hall Go:
West, then south on Route 66, under the railroad overpass. At 0.5 miles *0.8 km*, go straight on Milton Road. See Access Map, page 10. At 1.7 miles *2.72 km* you will reach a stoplight at Forest Meadows Street. Turn right here onto Forest Meadows and go one block to Beulah. Turn left on Beulah and follow it south. Beulah merges onto Highway 89A. At 2.4 miles *3.84 km* (MP 401.6), turn left onto the Lake Mary Road. Follow the Lake Mary Road (also known as FH 3) to its end at the junction with State Route 87, 56.6 miles *90.6 km*. Turn right here on Highway 87, a paved road, and follow it to the 65.8 mile *105.3 km* point MP 280, where you turn left on FR 300, which is posted. FR 300 is surfaced with gravel and is a good road. Follow it to the 78 mile *125 km* point, where you will see a monument to the Battle of Big Dry Wash. Turn left here on FR 705 and proceed to the 78.3 mile *125.28 km* point, where you will find the General Springs Cabin. Enjoy looking at the cabin and reading the interpretive signs and then drive 0.1 mile *0.16 km* farther, where you will find a trail parking area bounded by a wooden pole fence.

TRAILHEAD: Beyond the opening in the fence you will see the trail sign sitting in the middle of a little meadow, where several cairns are also visible. The Fred Haught and Arizona Trails are combined here.

DESCRIPTION: The whole area involved in this hike is of historic interest. At the point where you turn from FR 300 onto FR 705, there is a monument to the Battle of Big Dry Wash, which was fought a few miles north on July 17, 1882. This battle was the last in the Apache Wars in Arizona although skirmishes continued for years afterward. On the south side of FR

300 is the **Railroad Tunnel Trail**, scene of a grandiose 1880s dream that failed. General Springs was named for General Crook, the famed Indian fighter, who led troops through this area on many occasions. The Apaches ambushed him and his men at the springs and nearly killed him. The cabin was built much later, about 1915, for a forest ranger.

The trail, which is a segment of the Arizona Trail, runs north, then northeast along the bottom of General Springs Canyon. It is a beautiful setting, a canyon in a lovely forest, with water running along the creekbed. The footing is mostly on soft sparkly sand, though you will cross the creek several times. Unless the water is really deep, you can just step across. At the 3.0 mile *4.8 km* point you will reach a trail junction where the Arizona Trail goes north and the Fred Haught Trail goes NE. This is a good place to stop for a day hike. The Arizona Trail runs for 5.0 more miles *8.0 km* to the Blue Ridge Reservoir from here, at the present time.

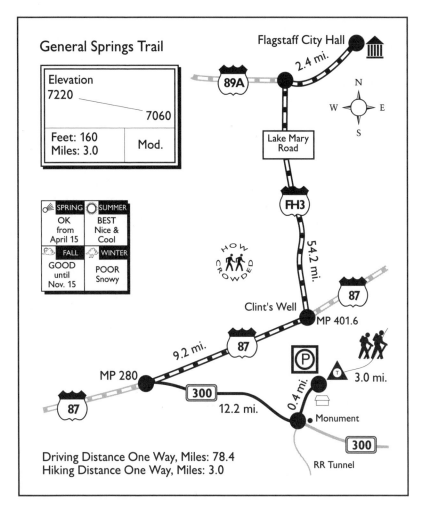

Mangum

Geronimo Spring

Driving Distance One Way: 24.1 miles *38.6 km* (Time 1 hour)
Access Road: High clearance needed for last 1.8 miles *2.9 km*
Hiking Distance One Way: 2.0 miles *3.2 km* (Time 1.5 hours)
How Strenuous: Hard, very steep
Features: Remote spring in the bottom of Sycamore Canyon

NUTSHELL: Located 24.1 miles *38.6 km* southwest of Flagstaff, this trail requires a strenuous descent to the bottom of Little LO Spring Canyon, a tributary of Sycamore Canyon. There are beautiful forests and cliffs, lots of good exploring at the bottom. **A personal favorite.**

DIRECTIONS:
From Flagstaff City Hall Go:
    West one block on Route 66, then left (S) beneath the railroad overpass. See Access Map, page 10. At 0.5 miles *0.8 km* you will reach a Y intersection where you turn right on Route 66. You will soon leave town. At 2.6 miles *4.2 km* you will reach a road going to the left. This is the Woody Mountain Road, FR 231. Take it. It is paved about a mile and then turns into a cinder road. At 16.6 miles *26.6 km* you will intersect FR 538. Turn right onto FR 538 and follow it to the 22.3 mile *35.7 km* point, where it intersects FR 538E. The road is rough beyond here. Turn right on 538E. At 22.7 miles *36.3 km* you hit another intersection, where FR 538E forks to the left, going to Dorsey Spring Road. Keep straight, now on FR 538G, and follow it to its end at 23.7 miles *37.9 km*, where it meets FR 527A. Turn left onto the Kelsey Trail road, going to the 24.1 mile *38.6 km* point, the parking area. This last 0.4 mile *0.64 km* stretch is terrible, a real tire-eater.

TRAILHEAD: You will see a sign at the parking area.

DESCRIPTION: This trail shares the same right of way with the **Kelsey Spring** and **Babe's Hole** trails and you have to pass through them to reach Geronimo Spring. So you get a three-hikes-in-one experience.
    The parking lot is located on the edge of the rim, so the trail immediately plunges down into the canyon. It passes through a beautiful forest, which gets more beautiful and interesting as you go. Kelsey Spring is reached in 0.5 miles *0.8 km*, on a shelf of level land. Enjoy it and then continue down the canyon until you reach Babe's Hole. At Babe's Hole several hill folds

come together to make a small protected pocket, with a spring bubbling out into a small pool

From Babe's Hole go downhill 0.1 miles *0.16 km*, to a junction. The **Kelsey-Winter Trail** goes left, to **Dorsey Spring** and then **Winter Cabin Spring**, and is marked. The trail to Geronimo Spring goes right and is unmarked.

From this point it is 0.75 miles *1.2 km* to the bottom. The trail becomes very steep about half way down. You will emerge at a trail junction, where Little LO Spring Canyon meets Sycamore Canyon. Take the left fork to Geronimo Spring, only a few feet away at a small flat area. The trail to the right takes you up Little LO Spring Canyon. You will find a trail to the west going into the big canyon.

This is a really remote wilderness spot, offering great opportunities for exploration.

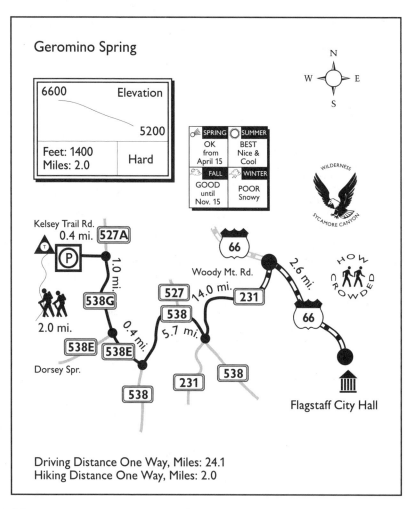

Government Knoll

General Information
Location Map E2
Parks and Wing Mt. USGS Maps
Kaibab (Williams) Forest Service Map

Driving Distance One Way: 25.9 miles *41.5 km* (Time 45 minutes)
Access Road: All cars, Last 11 miles *17.6 km* medium gravel road
Hiking Distance One Way: 0.5 miles *0.8 km* (Time 30 minutes)
How Strenuous: Moderate
Features: Views

NUTSHELL: This cinder cone at the north end of Government Prairie 25.9 miles *41.5 km* west of Flagstaff provides beautiful views of Kendrick Mountain and the San Francisco Peaks. It is easy to reach and climb.

DIRECTIONS:
From Flagstaff City Hall Go:
West a block on Route 66, then south, beneath the railroad overpass. See Access Map, page 10. At 0.5 miles *0.8 km* you will reach a Y intersection. The right fork is named Route 66. Take it. You will soon leave town, driving on a stretch of fabled Highway 66. At the 5.0 mile *8.0 km* point you will merge onto Interstate-40 West. Take Exit 185, "Transwestern Rd., Bellemont" at the 10.8 mile *17.3 km* point. From the exit turn right and go to the frontage road, where you turn left onto FR 146. You are now following another stretch of U.S. 66. Stay on this to the 18 mile *28.8 km* point, where you will see FR 107 fork right. Take FR 107 and follow it to the 23.2 mile *37.1 km* point, just beyond a bare hill we call Rain Tank Hill (unnamed on government maps). Here you will find FR 730 (formerly 793) to the right. It has no sign at the entrance and looks primitive but it is a decent road when it is dry. Turn right and follow FR 730. It will take you NE across the prairie. At 23.9 miles *38.3 km* you will see a sign marked 730 and 81. Take the left fork here. There is a gate at 24.1 miles *38.6 km*. Go through it. At 24.3 miles *38.9 km* you will pass the **Beale Road on Government Prairie**. Look for markers showing the right of way of this historic road as you pass. You can also see the old wagon tracks. At 25.4 miles *40.6 km* you will come to Horseshoe Tank at the base of Government Knoll. The road splits here. Take the left fork and drive along the north side of the hill. When you come to the 25.9 mile *41.5 km* point you will see a V-shaped notch in the hill with boulders at the bottom of the V. Park there.

TRAILHEAD: There is no trail. You walk up the hill through the notch.

DESCRIPTION: These cinder hills are all extinct volcanoes. From a distance they look symmetrical like a perfect cone or anthill. As you explore them you will find that most of them have a low side with a V-shaped opening gouged out by lava flow. Such is the case with Government Knoll.

Once you climb past the notch you are on the inside of the crater. Walk uphill to your left (north) on a gentle slope that is a natural ramp to the top. The highest point of the hill is the north side.

The hike is not long or overly hard. All you can see until you crest out are the sides of the crater. Then you break over the top and are presented with a genuine "*Aha!*" panorama.

This hill is located at the north end of Government Prairie, close to Kendrick Mountain and the San Francisco Peaks and you have superlative views of them. Government Prairie is a fragile environment, and is now closed to off-road vehicles.

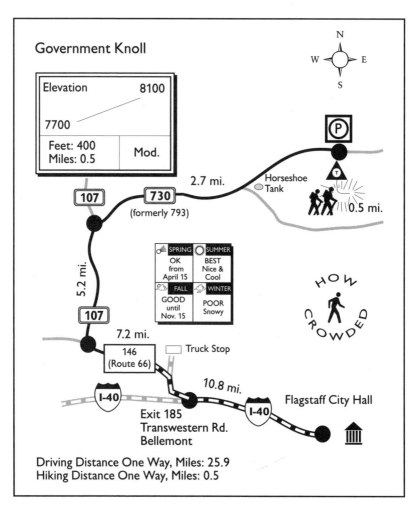

Mangum

Grand Falls

General Information
Location Map E4
Grand Falls USGS Map
Coconino Forest Service Map

Driving Distance One Way: 38.8 miles *62.1 km* (Time 1 hour)
Access Road: All cars, Last 9.1 miles *14.6 km* medium gravel road
Hiking Distance One Way: 0.75 miles *1.2 km* (Time 45 minutes)
How Strenuous: Moderate
Features: Waterfall, Painted Desert Views, Peaks views

NUTSHELL: Located 38.8 miles *62.1 km* east of Flagstaff, Grand Falls is Arizona's biggest waterfall, with a drop higher than Niagara's. Admire it from the top and then hike down to the water.

DIRECTIONS:
From Flagstaff City Hall Go:
   East, then north on Highway 89. See Access Map, pages 10-11. At 6.5 miles *10.4 km* (MP 420.5) you will reach the last stoplight in town at the junction of the Townsend-Winona Road. Turn right here onto the Townsend-Winona Road and follow it to the 14.7 miles *23.5 km* point (MP 428.8) where it intersects Leupp Road. Turn left on the Leupp Road and take it to the 29.7 miles *47.5 km* point (MP 443.5), where Navajo Route 70 joins it to the left. You will see a sign for the Grand Falls Bible Church at the turn. From here you follow Navajo Route 70 to the 38.3 miles *61.3 km* point. The road surface is of cinders. These sometimes cause loose pockets where traction is not good. The road is very dusty and washboardy. At 38.3 miles *61.3 km* there is an unmarked turn uphill to the left. Take it (it's rough) and you will top out at 38.8 miles *62.1 km* where you will see some picnic shelters. Park here near the rim. If you drive all the way to the river, you have missed the uphill turn.

TRAILHEAD: 375 feet from the last picnic shelter.

DESCRIPTION: Take this trip when the river, the Little Colorado, is carrying lots of water, which means during spring snow melt in March and April. When you reach the parking area, park at the first cluster of shelters. Some shelters are picnic tables and others are viewpoints. From this place you will see other shelters downstream. You can drive to the last one, but the road to that point is really rough. We prefer to park the car at the top and walk the rest of the way. When you reach the last shelter, you will see a jeep road that appears to go right to the rim. This is the trailhead. It is unmarked.

The trail is crude and goes abruptly to the river bottom. Once there you can walk along the shore toward the falls and—depending on how muddy it is—you can get quite close to the falls. If you get close enough to be hit by spray you will find that the water is almost as much soil as liquid and when it dries on you, it leaves a film of dirt. The high dirt content of the water accounts for the color and thickness of the falls, which look exactly like cocoa. The falls spill over two major levels. It is dangerous to hike behind the falls when water is running.

The wall that the falls spill over is Kaibab Limestone, whereas the wall on your side is basalt lava. An eruption from Merriam Crater (or a neighbor) seven miles to the west poured this lava into the canyon, damming the river and changing it to its present course. A thin finger of this lava, whose remnants you can see in the downstream direction, also flowed 15 miles along the riverbed before freezing into solid rock.

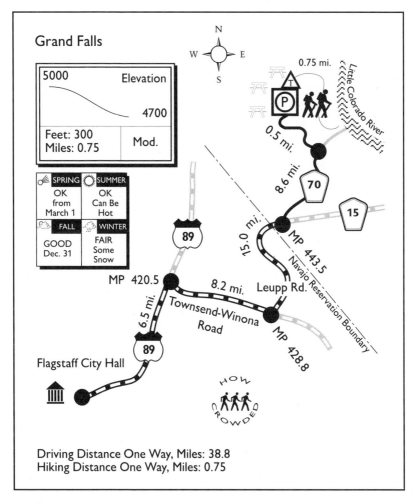

Mangum

Grandview Trail

General Information
Location Map B2
Cape Royal & Grandview Point USGS Maps
Kaibab (Tusayan) Forest Service Map

Driving Distance One Way: 89.1 miles *143 km* (Time 2 hours)
Access Road: All cars, All paved
Hiking Distance One Way: 3.5 miles 5.6 *km* (Time 6.5 hours)
How Strenuous: Hard
Features: Best views, Historic mine, Uncrowded

NUTSHELL: This trail is seldom maintained and is not as heavily used as Bright Angel or South Kaibab. It offers superior views (living up to its name), plus the exploration of old mine works.

DIRECTIONS:
From Flagstaff City Hall Go:
 North on Humphreys Street 0.60 miles *1.0 km* to a stoplight. See Access Map, page 10. Go left on Columbus Avenue and follow the curve north. Street signs will show the street first as Ft. Valley Road, then Highway 180, a major road to the Grand Canyon. At 50.4 miles *80.7 km* (MP 265.8), you will intersect Highway 64, coming out of Williams, at Valle. Go right at this junction and follow the highway to the south entrance to the Grand Canyon National Park. You will have to pay an entrance fee. Go on to the Rim Drive at 79.8 miles *127.7 km*, where you turn right, away from Grand Canyon Village. You will motor along the East Rim Drive to the 88.5 mile *141.6 km* point, the entrance to Grandview Point. Turn left here and go down to the parking areas, another 0.6 miles *1.0 km*, and park.

TRAILHEAD: At the NE end of the lower parking area. It is posted.

DESCRIPTION: The Grandview Trail was constructed in 1892 by Pete Berry, to serve his Last Chance copper mine, the richest in the Grand Canyon. Mules wrestled sacks of ore to the rim, from where the ore would be transported to Flagstaff, then to a smelter at El Paso.
 Berry was working on a shoestring and mostly with hand tools and a little dynamite. Constructing this trail under these conditions was a major feat that will cause you to marvel as you see it.
 The trail starts with a series of switchbacks as it descends sharply down the face of a cliff. Here you will find many "stairsteps" and "cobblestone" areas. The footing is difficult due to the steepness of the trail and the presence of loose rock underfoot. You must move slowly and cautiously. The

good news is that the scenery hits you—bam—right away and is constantly in view. After winding around a castle formation, the trail drops again very sharply. When it reaches the red rock, there are places where it was washed out and is now a mere thread, but you can always find the trail. As you move out toward Horseshoe Mesa, you think that the trail has leveled out, only to have it make the final drop to the mesa across a narrow ridge.

Some show the mileage on this hike as 2.0 miles *3.2 km*. We think this is inaccurate. If you go to Horseshoe Mesa and do some exploring there, you will hike at least 3.5 miles *5.6 km*. This hike is extremely steep and there is no water. This is a strenuous hike which should be undertaken only by those who are really fit and have adequate time and water.

A good hike is to go down 1.0 miles *1.6 km* (one hour) to the USGS marker, a disk set into a boulder at the right side of the trail. This gives a good taste of the trail without turning the hike into a death march.

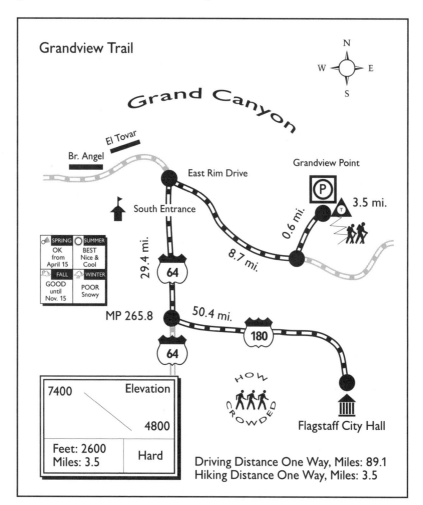

Griffiths Spring Canyon

Driving Distance One Way: 7.5 miles *12.0 km* (Time 20 minutes)
Access Road: All cars, All paved
Hiking Distance, Complete Loop: 1.2 miles *1.92 km* (Time 40 minutes)
How Strenuous: Easy
Features: Easy to reach trailhead, Near town

NUTSHELL: This is a short easy hike located just south of town on the road to Oak Creek Canyon. It is easy to reach, has parking, a toilet, a hard surface for universal access (wheelchairs), and will be developed as an interpretive site.

DIRECTIONS:
From Flagstaff City Hall Go:
West on Route 66 one block then left (south) on Route 66 under the railroad overpass. At 0.5 miles *0.8 km*, go straight on Milton Road. See Access Map, page 10. At 1.7 miles *2.7 km* you reach the stoplight at Forest Meadows, where you turn right. At the next corner turn left on Beulah and follow it out of town. Beulah will connect onto Highway 89A which is the road to Oak Creek Canyon and Sedona. At 7.5 miles *12.0 km* (MP 396.5) on Highway 89A turn to your left into the parking area. Look carefully as you approach the turnoff point, because it comes up suddenly.

TRAILHEAD: At the parking area. This is a developed trail, with map and a toilet.

DESCRIPTION: We formerly had a buskwhacking hike into Griffiths Spring Canyon, but in 2001 the Forest Service will open this new trail and facility in order to satisfy the demands for a system Griffith Springs hiking trail. In order to protect the fragile riparian habitat, they located their trail above the canyon itself. This is another trail that is designed for universal access, which means that it has a hard surface and can be traveled by people in wheelchairs. Again, we applaud this effort, making the woods available to all who want to enjoy them.
    The official trail makes a loop through the woods between the canyon and the highway, and there is nothing remarkable about it. There are a couple of points where hikers can see down into the canyon, but that is as much of the canyon experience as the trail now provides.

The trail takes you through a typical northern Arizona pine forest, following one contour so that the trail is not steep. You still have a chance to see the birds and other wildlife that come to the canyon for its water and grasses, which adds to the attraction of this trail.

Griffith Spring itself is located on the north, and you will not even see it on this trail. The planners hope that this trail will be used by Flagstaff school children as an interpretive site and study area and that the kids may erect markers and explanatory signs, etc. This is a great idea and should encourage children to love and respect their forests.

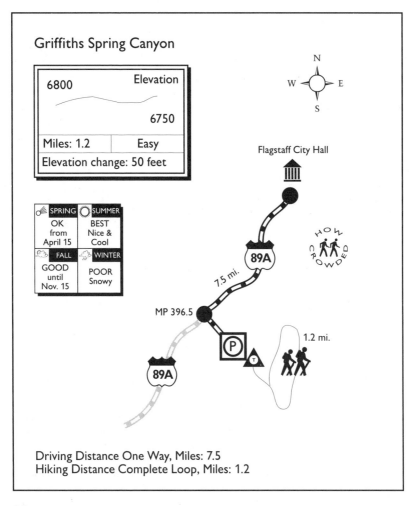

Griffiths Spring Canyon

Elevation	
6800	
	6750
Miles: 1.2	Easy
Elevation change: 50 feet	

SPRING	SUMMER
OK from April 15	BEST Nice & Cool
FALL	WINTER
GOOD until Nov. 15	POOR Snowy

Flagstaff City Hall

89A

7.5 mi.

MP 396.5

89A

1.2 mi.

Driving Distance One Way, Miles: 7.5
Hiking Distance Complete Loop, Miles: 1.2

Mangum

Heart Trail #103

General Information
Location Map E3
Flagstaff East & Sunset Crater West USGS Maps
Coconino Forest Service Map

Driving Distance One Way: 7.0 miles *11.2 km* (Time 15 minutes)
Access Road: All cars, Last 0.1 mile *0.16 km* good dirt road
Hiking Distance One Way: 3.85 miles *6.2 km* (Time 2.5 hours)
How Strenuous: Moderate to Hard
Features: Unusual red and white hills, Rock formations, Views

NUTSHELL: This trail, located just 7.0 miles *11.2 km* from City Hall, takes you up a red hill on the east face of Mt. Elden.

DIRECTIONS:
From Flagstaff City Hall Go:
  East, then north on Highway 89. See Access Map, pages 10-11. At 6.5 miles *10.4 km* (MP 420.7), you will see the stoplight at the junction of Highway 89 and the Townsend-Winona Road. Look for a dirt road (FR 9129) going into the trees to your left 0.40 miles *0.64 km* beyond the stoplight, at 6.9 miles *11.1 km* (MP 421.1). Take this dirt road to the parking area at the fence, at 7.0 miles *11.2 km*.

TRAILHEAD: There are lath-type trail signs. You will also see a sign through the fence saying, "Sandy Seep Vehicle Closure. This area closed to motor vehicles to protect the critical Sandy Seep deer winter range and to offer non-motorized recreation opportunities." Go through the opening in the fence and walk a few yards to your left, where you will pick up an old road. Follow the road.

DESCRIPTION: The road is easy to walk and makes a good hiking path because it has been closed to motor vehicles. At about one third of a mile *0.53 km* you will come to the back fence. The road turns right here. Keep following it. The road will wind through the forest and at about one mile *1.6 km* you will come to a hill. The road curves around it. At 1.5 miles *2.4 km* you will see a trail sign leave the road to the left. Get off the road and follow the footpath. Sandy Seep is to your right.
  You will walk into a ravine and then up to another closed road that leads to Mt. Elden. Note that the soil here is red. There are two redrock hills looking like importations from Sedona to your right and a red foothill projecting from the face of Mt. Elden. At 2.1 miles *3.4 km* you will reach the base of the red foothill, where there is a water tank. You will also see a plastic pipe

going up a canyon to tap a spring.

From this point the trail switchbacks up the red hill to the top of Mt. Elden. The trail is nicely laid out.

Sherry, with her photographer's eye, says this part of the trail is *visually exciting.* There are many bold and unusual lava dike formations, burnt trees like totems, vast views to the east, finger ridges running parallel to the hill you are climbing and other delights.

You will come to the top of Mt. Elden at a point on the **Sunset Trail** that is 0.56 miles *0.9 km* from its end, just above the Elden Lookout Road. If you are hardy, you could do the **Elden Skyline Trail** over to the lookout tower and then take the **Elden Lookout Trail** to the bottom.

This is a dandy two-car hike, parking one at the bottom and one at the top, then hiking down.

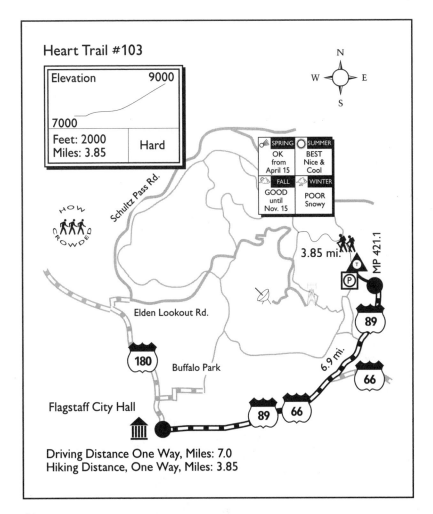

Hermit Trail

General Information
Location Map B2
Grand Canyon USGS Map
Kaibab (Tusayan) Forest Service Map

Driving Distance One Way: 90.6 miles *145 km* (Time 2.25 hours)
Access Road: All cars, All paved except last 0.2 mile *0.32 km*
Hiking Distance One Way: 2.0 miles 3.2 *km* (Time 2 hours)
How Strenuous: Hard
Features: Magnificent views, Historic trail

NUTSHELL: This trail at the west end of the south rim of the Grand Canyon is not as heavily used as Bright Angel or South Kaibab, and has less distractions. It is not maintained, but is still a good trail. You will hike 2.0 miles *3.2 km* to the rest house at Santa Maria Spring.

DIRECTIONS:
From Flagstaff City Hall Go:
   North on Humphreys Street 0.60 miles *1.0 km* to a stoplight. See Access Map, page 10. Go left on Highway 180, a major road to the Grand Canyon. At 50.4 miles *80.7 km* (MP 265.8), you will intersect Highway 64, coming out of Williams, at Valle. Go right at this junction and follow the highway to the south entrance to the Grand Canyon National Park at 75.1 miles *120 km*. You will have to pay an entrance fee. At 79.8 miles *127.7 km*, you reach the Rim Drive. Turn left, to Grand Canyon Village. You will reach the village area at the 82.1 mile *131.4 km* point. Keep going on the main road, past Bright Angel Lodge. In high season, you will have to park around here and take a shuttle bus to Hermit's Rest. Otherwise, you will drive there, to the 90.6 mile *145 km* point. You will see trail signs at Hermit's Rest.

TRAILHEAD: At the extreme end of the parking area. It is posted.

DESCRIPTION: The Santa Fe Railroad built the Hermit Trail in 1910 to avoid the tolls charged for the privately-owned Bright Angel Trail. The Santa Fe abandoned the trail in 1931 after the Bright Angel became public property, and the trail has been slightly maintained since.
   The Hermit is one of the few Grand Canyon trails created with professional engineering and with substantial capital. You will see examples of handwork all along the way, especially the "cobblestones."
   For a day hike, you do not need a permit nor do you need to advise the Park Rangers, but please be prepared. Take water (one quart per person), wear suitable shoes and clothing, and allow enough time.

Flagstaff Hikes

The footing—due to minimal maintenance—is so bad in most places that this trail is as slow going downhill as up, contrary to most Grand Canyon trails, which take twice as long to ascend as to descend. Views open up early and are a constant delight. At 1.2 miles *2 km*, you reach the Waldron Trailhead. The Dripping Springs Trailhead is next, at 1.5 miles *2.4 km.*

Down to this point, you have passed through white sandstones. From here, you enter the red Hermit Shale zone and will be in it to the end. The footing here is a mixture of good and bad, but it is very beautiful. As you round a bend, you will see the rest house in the distance.

At Santa Maria you will find a resting place built by the Santa Fe for its mule-ride guests decades ago. It makes a perfect stopping place for this day hike, with shade, a bench and water. The spring produces water year-around, but if you want to drink it, you should purify it.

The total trail length (to the river) is 8.9 miles *14.25 km.*

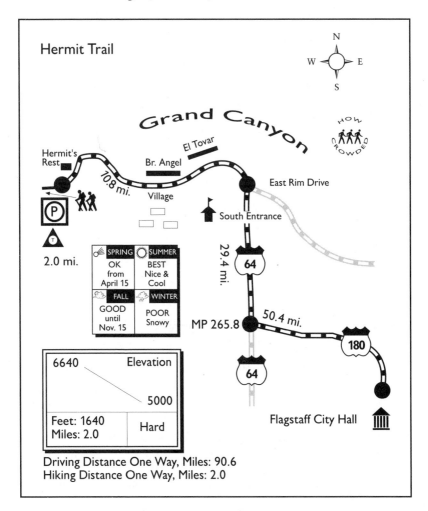

Mangum

Horse Crossing Trail #20

General Information
Location Map G4
Blue Ridge Reservoir USGS Map
Coconino Forest Service Map

Driving Distance One Way: 72.0 miles *115.2 km* (Time 1.5 hours)
Access Road: All cars, Last 2.0 miles *3.2 km* rough dirt road
Hiking Distance One Way: 1.5 miles *2.4 km* (Time 1 hour)
How Strenuous: Hard
Features: Views, Beautiful pristine stream, Remote canyon

NUTSHELL: This is one of the few trails into East Clear Creek, a remote canyon southeast of Flagstaff. The hike is steep but very beautiful.

DIRECTIONS:
From Flagstaff City Hall Go:
    West, then south on Route 66 under the railroad overpass. See Access Map, page 10. As you go south, take Milton Road, leaving Route 66. At 1.7 miles *2.72 km* you will reach a stoplight at Forest Meadows Street. Turn right here onto Forest Meadows and go one block to Beulah. Turn left on Beulah and follow it south. Beulah merges onto Highway 89A. At 2.4 miles *3.84 km* (MP 401.6), turn left onto the Lake Mary Road. Follow the Lake Mary Road (also known as FH 3) to its end at the junction with State Route 87, 56.6 miles *90.56 km*. Turn left here on Highway 87, a paved road, and follow it to the 66 mile *105.6 km* point MP 299.9, where you turn right on FR 95, which is well posted. FR 95 is surfaced with gravel and is an all-weather road. Follow it to the 70 mile *112 km* point, where you turn left on FR 513B, which is a fairly rough dirt road, with ruts and rocks. Drive to the 72 mile *115.2 km* point, where you will see a sign for the Horse Crossing Trailhead to your right. Pull in and park in the little loop.

TRAILHEAD: There is a sign at the parking area. The trail starts behind the sign.

DESCRIPTION: Although Flagstaff is a green oasis surrounded by deserts, there are very few year-round streams in the region. Streamside hikes can be very rewarding, and we wanted to include some of them in this book.
    From the trailhead, you have glimpses of the canyon. You will hike down 0.75 miles *1.2 km* to the bottom, a 500 foot drop. This descent is fairly mild and the trail is well laid out. There are cairns and blazes and the trail itself is distinct. At the bottom you will find East Clear Creek. You will see cairns here indicating a path to your left and to your right. The one to the

right is the trail. The one to the left is a detour to a nice pool with a sandy beach. A perfect place to wade or swim.

To follow the trail, take the cairn to the right. The bottom is overgrown with willows and other plants, and finding the path can be difficult. Look for cairns. You walk along the streambed for about 0.1 miles *0.16 km*, then cross over the creek, which is split here, on stepping stones. In a few more yards, you cross the creek again. Once across, you will walk 0.15 miles *0.24 km* along the south bank. When you have come 1.0 miles *1.6 km* from the beginning, the trail lifts up out of the canyon. This point was not well marked, so look carefully. The trail itself, once you are on it, is easy to follow.

The climb up to the other rim is harder than the first, as you go 500 feet in 0.5 mile *0.8 km*. You will pass through a beautiful forest, with lots of firs and oaks, to the top, where the trail ends at a cairn by the side of a primitive road.

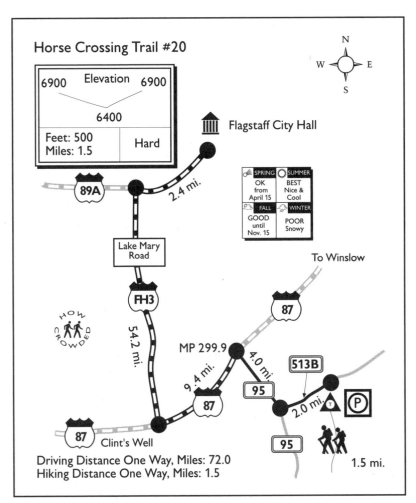

Houston Brothers Trail #18

General Information
Location Map G4
Blue Ridge Reservoir, Dane Canyon USGS Maps
Coconino Forest Service Map

Driving Distance One Way: 77.2 miles *123.5 km* (Time 1.5 hours)
Access Road: All cars, Last 11.2 miles *18 km* good dirt roads
Hiking Distance One Way: 1.5 miles *2.4 km* (Time 1 hour)
How Strenuous: Easy
Features: Beautiful pristine stream, Historic cabins

NUTSHELL: This charming little trail is located in "The Rim" country. It starts at the historic Pinchot Cabin and proceeds south along Houston Draw to Aspen Spring, another cabin site.

DIRECTIONS:
From Flagstaff City Hall Go:
West, then south on Route 66. The street name will change to Milton Road as you go south. See Access Map, page 10. At 1.7 miles *2.72 km* you will reach a stoplight at Forest Meadows Street. Turn right here onto Forest Meadows and go one block to Beulah. Turn left on Beulah and follow it south. Beulah merges onto Highway 89A. At 2.4 miles *3.84 km* (MP 401.6), turn left onto the Lake Mary Road. Follow the Lake Mary Road (also known as FH 3) to its end at the junction with State Route 87, 56.6 miles *90.56 km*. Turn left here on Highway 87, a paved road, and follow it to the 66 mile *105.6 km* point (MP 299.9), where you turn right on FR 95, which is well posted. FR 95 is surfaced with gravel and is an all-weather road. Follow it to the 72.5 mile point *116 km*, down into the bottom of the canyon, where you will find a little bridge across East Clear Creek. This is a road junction. Take the right-hand road, which is still FR 95, and climb uphill on a winding road. On the top, FR 95 curves frequently as it winds around the canyons that cut the area. At 77.0 miles *123.2 km*, you will see FR 139A going to the left. Take it. (Just before this, you will see a sign for Houston Draw to your left). At 77.2 miles *123.5 km* you will see a primitive road to your left going downhill into the bottom of Houston Draw. Stop here and park. We recommend that you not try to drive to the bottom. Begin the hike from here.

TRAILHEAD: The official trailhead is down in Houston Draw, about thirty yards south of Pinchot Cabin.

DESCRIPTION: You walk down the primitive road to the bottom of Houston Draw, a beautiful place, green because of its perennial stream. Turn south and in 0.2 miles *0.32 km*, you will see Pinchot Cabin. Go over and inspect it. There is an interpretive sign about the cabin. Gifford Pinchot, regarded as the father of the Forest Service, visited the site and remarked upon its beauty, and the cabin was named for him. This place is a trail intersection, with markers for the Arizona, U-Bar and Cabin Loop Trails.

Follow the canyon south, toward the Mogollon Rim. Since the rim is uplifted, you will be walking uphill, but it is a gradual easy climb. Look for tree blazes, which are plentiful. The map shows what a blaze looks like.

The little canyon is very pretty, the trail is soft, and it has no steep grades. There are some attractive rock outcrops, aspens and other interesting sights. The trail goes 7.0 miles *11.2 km* to the Rim Road, FR 300, but that makes a long hike. As a pleasant day hike, we recommend stopping at Aspen Spring, where you will find a corral and the ruins of an old log cabin. Aspen Spring is 1.5 miles *2.4 km* from where you parked.

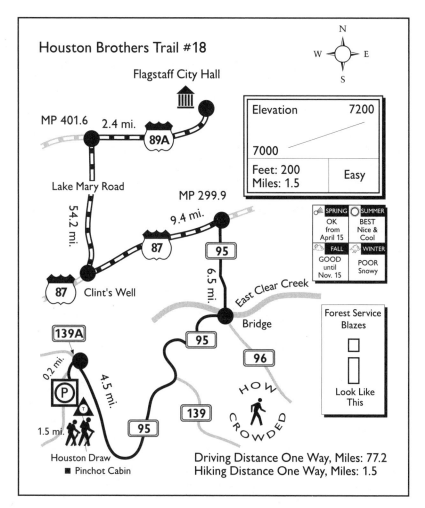

Mangum

Humphreys Trail #151

General Information
Location Map E3
Humphreys Peak USGS Map
Coconino Forest Service Map

Driving Distance One Way: 14.1 miles *22.56 km* (Time 30 minutes)
Access Road: All cars, All paved
Hiking Distance One Way: 4.5 miles *7.2 km* (Time 3 hours)
How Strenuous: Hard, Steep climb, High elevations
Features: Highest point in Arizona, Alpine forests, Unsurpassed views

NUTSHELL: Starting from a parking area below the Snow Bowl, north of Flagstaff, this strenuous climb takes you to the top of the San Francisco Peaks, the highest point in Arizona. This is the hardest hike in the book.

DIRECTIONS:
From Flagstaff City Hall Go:
   North on Humphreys Street for 0.60 miles *1.0 km*. See Access Map, page 10. Turn left at the stoplight onto Columbus Avenue and follow it around a curve to the north where it becomes Highway 180. Stay on Highway 180 to the 7.3 miles *11.7 km* point (MP 223), where you turn right onto the road to the Snow Bowl. Follow the Snow Bowl road to the top at 13.9 miles *22.2 km*. You will see a big sign for the trail as you approach. Just as you top out, turn left to get to the parking area. Drive out to the end of the loop, where there is a trail sign. Park near the sign, at the 14.1 miles *22.56 km* point.

TRAILHEAD: At the parking lot. You will see a sign

DESCRIPTION: Previously we used another trailhead, near the Sky Ride. Because of the risk of hikers getting cut off from their cars, we no longer recommend it. There are special concerns on the Humphreys Trail: lightning is a dangerous hazard—beware! Tundra and protected plant species above tree line are sensitive. Stay on the trail to protect them. There is no camping above tree line. You begin this hike by walking across an open meadow on Hart Prairie, headed toward a forest on the other side. This is a lateral move. Once in the trees, you will climb.
   The forest in the first couple of miles is a heavy one of fir, spruce and aspen. There are many fallen timbers, making a tangle on the floor. The trees are tall, shutting out most of the sun. It's dark and you have no views.
   As you go higher, the forest opens and you will encounter small meadows which permit views to the west. At about the 10,500 foot point the aspens begin to disappear. You can see from here into the Snow Bowl area.

What appear to be roads there are actually the ski runs cut through the trees. The major peak that you will see is Mt. Agassiz.

At 3.75 miles *6.0 km* the only trees are twisted and stunted bristlecone pines. There is no cover for the trail here and the footing is not very good. At 4.0 miles *6.4 km* you reach the rim where the Humphreys Trail joins the **Weatherford Trail** coming in from your right. You can look into the Inner Basin of the Peaks here and enjoy a splendid view. You can also see to the east for the first time on the hike.

The top will be different from what you imagined. You are above timberline. It is bare and almost always windy and cold. The footing is terrible, being a mixture of loose gravel and rough jagged lava. You can't really walk along the crest but must walk below it. To get to the top of Mt. Humphreys take the path to the left. The top is 0.50 miles *0.8 km* away. The elevation and the roughness of the trail make the crest hike hard. Allow a half hour.

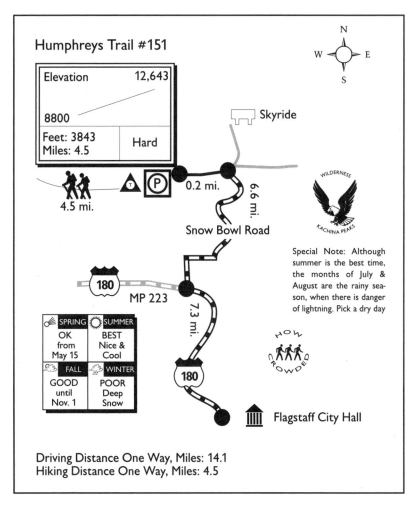

Mangum

Hutch Mountain

General Information
Location Map G3
Hutch Mountain USGS Map
Coconino Forest Service Map

Driving Distance One Way: 39.5 miles *63.2 km* (Time 1 hour)
Access Road: All cars, Good gravel roads for last 4.1 miles *6.6 km*
Hiking Distance One Way: 2.0 miles *3.2 km* (Time 1 hour)
How Strenuous: Moderate
Features: Beautiful heavy mixed forest, Views, Spring-fed mountain valley

NUTSHELL: This trail starts near the top of Hutch Mountain, southeast of Flagstaff, and winds part way down the mountain through a lush alpine forest ending in a scenic meadow.

DIRECTIONS:
From Flagstaff City Hall Go:

   West and then south (left) on Route 66 under the railroad overpass. At the 0.5 mile *0.8 km* point, go straight on Milton Road. At 1.7 miles *2.72 km* you reach the stoplight at Forest Meadows, where you turn right. At the next corner turn left on Beulah,which connects onto Highway 89A. At the 2.4 miles *3.84 km* point (MP 401.6) take the turnoff to the Lake Mary Road to your left. Follow the Lake Mary Road past Mormon Lake. At 35.4 miles *56.64 km* (MP 311) turn left onto FR 135. At the 38.0 mile *60.8 km* point, you will come to a junction. Go left and then immediately left again, on FR 135B, which is signed. This road climbs to a saddle near the top of Hutch Mountain. The last leg of the road, which goes up to the Fire Lookout Tower, is barred by a gate, as the tower is manned during the fire season. Park near the gate at the 39.5 mile *63.2 km* point.

TRAILHEAD: Unmarked. It is up the road beyond the gate 0.12 miles *0.2 km*. At the point where the road makes a big curve to the right, look down to your left and you will see the trail going into a stand of bushes.

DESCRIPTION: Although there are no signs, you will locate this trail easily and find it simple to follow. At first you will have a few views over Anderson Mesa and the desert beyond; then the trees close in and you are unable to see into the distance. The first 0.3 miles *0.48 km* of the trail is narrow, like a horse trail, and steep, dropping 450 feet. Thereafter the trail follows FR 92D and is fairly level.

   We love the Ponderosa pine forests surrounding Flagstaff, but we confess that there are times when we would like variety. This hike does the job.

Because of the elevation and the fact that you are hiking along the north face of Hutch Mountain, you will see a heavy forest of fir, spruce and aspen, punctuated by several clearings where there are many shrubs.

The trail drops down the mountain heading north and then turns west, running along the side of the mountain at the 8,000 foot level. From the 1.25 mile *2.0 km* point, the area on both sides of the road is clear, like a natural greenbelt, allowing you to look up at the mountain and enjoy the scenery.

At the 1.5 mile *2.4 km* point you will walk past a tank with high walls on your right. From here the road dips and you come to the NE edge of Gooseberry Spring, a lovely bowl-shaped mountain valley. Turn to your left, leaving the road, and walk down to the open grassy area, a scenic place to end the hike, at 2.0 miles *3.2 km*. The water of this reliable spring is captured in a concrete box topped by an iron cage, located to your left as you enter the open area. Treat the water before drinking.

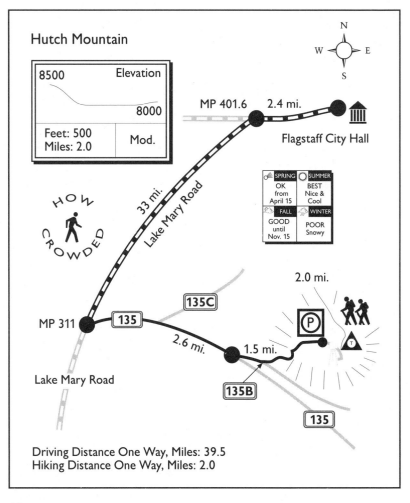

Inner Basin Trail #29

General Information
Location Map E3
Humphreys Peak and Sunset Crater West USGS Maps
Coconino Forest Service Map

Driving Distance One Way: 21.6 miles *34.6 km* (Time 45 minutes)
Access Road: All cars, Last 4.5 miles *7.2 km* medium dirt road
Hiking Distance One Way: 2.0 miles *3.2 km* (Time 1 hour)
How Strenuous: Hard, Steep Climb, High elevations
Features: High mountain, Alpine forests, Great views

NUTSHELL: The San Francisco Peaks located north of Flagstaff are an extinct volcanic crater with an opening to the east. This trail takes you up the valley formed by that eastern opening into the heart of the crater.

DIRECTIONS:
From Flagstaff City Hall Go:
    East, then north on Highway 89. See Access Map, pages 10-11. At 17.1 miles *27.4 km* (MP 431.2)—just past the entrance to Sunset Crater—turn left onto FR 552 and take it to the 18.3 mile *29.3 km* point, where you will see a sign for Lockett Meadow. Go right. From here the road is a winding narrow gravel route which climbs up the face of the mountain. At 21.3 miles *34 km* you reach Lockett Meadow. There you will see a one-way road to your right into a campground. Take this and park in the Day Use Area at the 21.6 mile *34.6 km* point.

TRAILHEAD: Drive all the way back into the trees among the campsites. The trailhead is posted with a big sign to the left of a toilet.

DESCRIPTION: The trail is a road that is used by the City of Flagstaff for maintenance vehicles, because the Inner Basin of the Peaks is the city's watershed. This makes the trail wide and easy to walk. Even so, at these high elevations, the hike will be more strenuous than you would think, given its relatively short distance. You will be climbing constantly.
    The Inner Basin of the Peaks has a tremendous amount of water because all the water from snow melting inside the crater gathers in the bowl. There are several springs in the basin. The early settlers of Flagstaff realized the importance of the basin as a water supply for the town and sewed up all the water rights. As a result most of the water is captured and channeled and you will see very little of it on the surface. The vegetation is lush, as the basin is moist, which makes a beautiful forest.
    At the 1.5 mile *2.4 km* point you will come to Jack Smith Spring where

there are two green cabins. There is a faucet outside the larger cabin from which you can *sometimes* drink delicious cold spring water. The elevation at Jack Smith is 9400 feet.

You will find a hiker's registration book here—please enter your name and other information. The spring is a crossroads and you will see a sign showing FR 146 going to the left to what we call the **Tunnel Trail** and ending at the Schultz Pass Road 8.5 miles *13.6 km* away. To the right FR 146 goes about 5.25 miles *8.4 km* to a point on the north face of Mt. Humphreys. Along the way it intersects the **Bear Jaw Trail** at 3 miles *4.8 km* and the **Abineau Canyon Trail #127** at 5 miles *8.0 km*.

Instead of taking a fork, go straight ahead. At 2 miles *3.2 km* you will break out of the timber into a bare area. This is the Inner Basin. We like to quit here, but the trail continues up the left side to the **Weatherford Trail.** Camping and horses are not allowed in the Inner Basin.

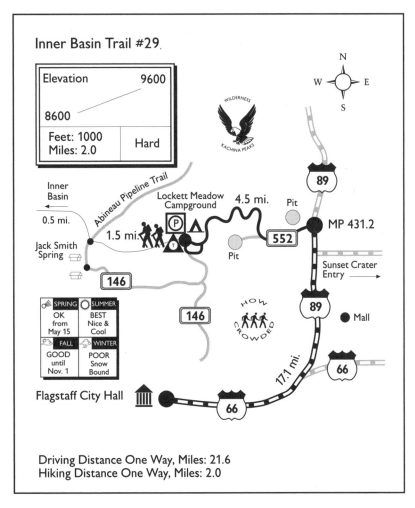

Mangum

James Canyon

General Information
Location Map F3
Mountainaire USGS Map
Coconino Forest Service Map

Driving Distance One Way: 11.9 miles *19.04 km* (Time 25 minutes)
Access Road: All cars
Hiking Distance One Way: 0.66 miles *1.056 km* (Time 30 minutes)
How Strenuous: Moderate
Features: Scenic canyon near town

NUTSHELL: This hidden canyon located close to Flagstaff provides a nice little hike to beautiful Keyhole Grotto.

DIRECTIONS:
From Flagstaff City Hall Go:
     West, then south on Route 66. See Access Map, page 10. Follow Route 66 beneath the underpass. At 0.5 miles *0.8 km*, go straight on Milton Road. Continue on Milton Road until you get on I-17 South. Drive I-17, looking for the Kelly Canyon Exit #331. Go past it but watch for MP 331 just south of Exit #331, and when you see it, slow down. You will drive over the James Canyon bridge just south of this MP. On the far side of the bridge, at MP 330.3, there is a wide clearing at the right side of the freeway. Pull to the right onto this clearing where you will find a road going through a gate in a barbed wire fence. Go through the gate just far enough to park securely.

TRAILHEAD: This is not a marked trail. There is no official trailhead. The hike begins from the parking place.

DESCRIPTION: At the place where you park, you will see a single-wire power line running along parallel to I-17. Walk over to this line, turn right and hike along under it going north, toward Flagstaff.
     The power line dips and crosses several washes, which meet to become James Canyon. The powerline rises and you climb to a point at 0.3 miles *0.48 km,* where you will find a barbed wire fence. The gate through the fence is just to the right (E) of the point where the power line meets the fence. Go through the gate and walk out into the bare area. Turn to your left and walk downhill. Look carefully, and you'll see that you are on an old dirt road. As you walk, you will see that you are approaching James Canyon. When you get near the rim, turn right and walk along the edge. Your objective is to pick up a foot path that runs along the rim. When you find this, follow it along the border of the canyon. This is not just a game trail, as you can see that

some rock work has been done on it.

The path soon begins to curve down, going to the canyon floor where there is a wide bench covered with pine needles, at about the 0.5 mile *0.8 km* point. This is the easy way into this steep canyon. Once on the canyon floor, turn right (N) and walk along the bottom. We hope you have picked a day when there isn't too much water running—usually not a problem.

Soon you will enter into a zone where you encounter buff colored sandstone. At the 0.6 mile *0.96 km* point, you will come to Keyhole Grotto (our name, don't look for it on maps). This is a beautiful place, with steep, vegetation-covered canyon walls, a water-carved gap in a sandstone bluff and a deep pool. You can climb up to the right to get on top of the sandstone and see down into the pool. A perfect place to meditate and enjoy the beauties of nature. We have hiked farther down, only to find our way blocked at 0.85 miles *1.36 km* by an impassable pour-over and gap.

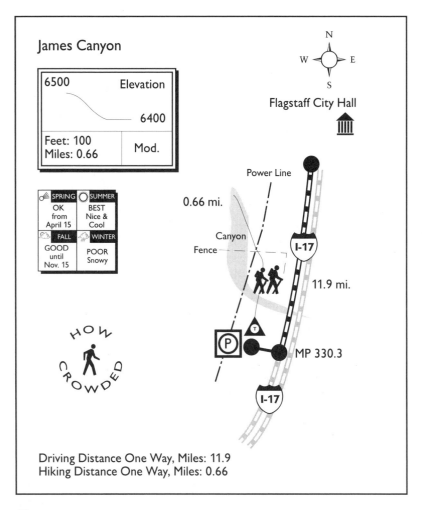

Johnson Crater & Johnson Canyon

General Information
Location Map F1
Ashfork and McLellan Reservoir USGS Maps
Kaibab Forest Service Map

Driving Distance One Way: 47.45 miles *76.0 km* (Time 1.5 hours)
Access Road: All cars, Last 2.75 miles *4.4 km* medium dirt road
Hiking Distance One Way: 2.0 miles *3.2 km* (Time 1 hour)
How Strenuous: Easy
Features: Interesting volcanic sinkhole, Disused railroad bed with historic
        tunnel

NUTSHELL: You stop at Johnson Crater—a volcanic sinkhole—and make a brief and easy walk to its lip, to enjoy a view into its depths. Then you drive on to the former Welch Station and park. You hike along the old railroad bed on the edge of a scenic canyon to a historic tunnel.

DIRECTIONS:
From Flagstaff City Hall Go:
    West on I-40, 44.7 miles *71.52 km* to the Welch Exit 151. From the exit, turn right (N). The paving ends immediately. Go across the cattle guard onto a gravel road, FR 6. At the 45.45 mile *72.72 km* point you will join a very old segment of Highway 66. At 45.8 miles *73.28 km* FR 6 turns left, leaving Old 66. Be sure to turn left on FR 6 here. At the 47.2 mile *75.52 km* point, you are at the top of a rise. You can see that the crater is to your left. Park and walk over to it. Then keep driving until you come to a cattle guard sign. Immediately beyond you will cross a gravel road. This gravel road is the old railroad bed. Park nearby. Before beginning the hike, you might want to look around the crossroads, which was the site of the old Welch station. Very little is left here, but you can see some concrete pads, etc.

TRAILHEAD: No trail. Hike along the old railroad grade to the north.

DESCRIPTION: This is an easy walk, like strolling along a level gravel road. It winds along the bank of Johnson Canyon, giving you some nice views. In places you can see where the railroad crews made cuts, and in others put in fills or trestles. High above you are thick cliffs of lava caprock. After passing through a gate and under a power line, you will make a big curve, where you will see steel reinforcing panels holding the hillside in place. After following a curve in the other direction, you will see the tunnel. It was nicely made, of local hand-cut stone. The tunnel is clean and dry and is only about 125 yards long, so light comes in at both ends. It is quite a

Grand Canyon-East Rim Drive

Sunset Crater-Winter

North of the San Francisco Peaks

Walnut Canyon-Island Trail

Government Knoll-Kendrick Peak

Grand Canyon-Autumn Sunset Clouds

Kendrick Park near Wildlife Trail

Lockett Meadow

San Francisco Peaks-Urban Trail

Northern Arizona Autumn

Lake Mary-Summer Storm at Sunset

sight, a pleasant place to visit.

The story behind the tunnel is this: in 1882 the Atlantic and Pacific Railroad built its line through Winslow, Flagstaff and Williams, with few difficulties except for some bridging. When the engineers got to Johnson Canyon, they decided to build this tunnel, a feat that took many weeks. It was the only tunnel on the line. The Santa Fe bought out the A&P in 1897.

There was a tragedy in the tunnel in January 1898 when the wooden support timbers then in use caught fire. Men were killed in the blaze. The heat was so intense that it took several days for the tunnel to cool off enough to allow repair crews to enter it. The smoke blackening of the walls is still visible. The wooden timbers were replaced with an impressive lining of steel boilerplate about halfway down the walls. During WWII, a guard house (ruins remain) was built near the top of the tunnel to prevent sabotage. The tunnel was last used in 1962 when the line was rerouted to avoid the canyon.

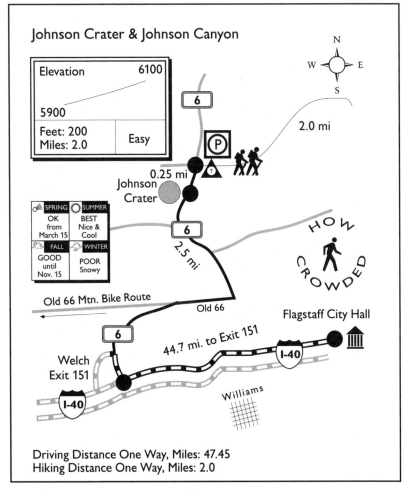

Driving Distance One Way, Miles: 47.45
Hiking Distance One Way, Miles: 2.0

Mangum

Kachina Trail #150

General Information
Location Map E3
Humphreys Peak USGS Map
Coconino Forest Service Map

Driving Distance One Way: 22.1 miles *35.35 km* (Time 1.5 hours)
Access Road: Two high clearance cars needed. Freidlein Prairie Road is
    rough
Hiking Distance One Way: 6.5 miles *10.4 km* (Time 3.5 hours)
How Strenuous: Hard
Features: High mountains, Alpine forests, Excellent views

NUTSHELL: This hike across the south face of the San Francisco Peaks displays the mountain forests at their best. **A personal favorite.**

DIRECTIONS:
From Flagstaff City Hall Go:
    North on Humphreys Street for 0.6 miles in two high-clearance cars. See Access Map, page 10. Turn left at the stoplight onto Columbus Avenue and follow it as it becomes Highway 180. Stay on Highway 180 to the 7.3 miles *11.7 km* point (MP 223), where you turn right on the well-posted road to the Snow Bowl. Drive both cars up the Snow Bowl Road 2.4 miles *3.8 km*. Turn right on FR 522, the Freidlein Prairie Road, which is very rough, rocky, and slow (20 minutes needed). The road soon forks. Go left. Drive to the 4.0 mile *6.4 km* point, where you find a parking area. Leave a car here and drive the other back out to the paved road. Turn right and drive 4.2 miles *6.72 km,* to a point where you see a sign for the Kachina Trail. Turn right and drive 0.2 miles *0.32 km,* parking near the trailhead.

TRAILHEAD: At the parking lot.

DESCRIPTION: This trail starts at 9400 feet and winds easterly across the south face (Flagstaff side) of the Peaks. Most of the hike holds to a band between the 9200 and 8800 foot levels, rising and falling within this contour. This is a very gradual hike for the Peaks, where trails tend to be very steep.
    The trail passes through a lovely forest of fir, spruce and aspen. This is a good trail to take in the fall to see the changing aspen leaves.
    You will pass interesting lava boulders and cliffs. In places you will find clearings that give you views out over the countryside.
    At the 4.0 mile *6.4 km* point is a signed trail junction. One sign points right, to the "Freidlein Road." Do not turn right here. Keep going straight.
    Just beyond this junction you will enter Friedlein Prairie, a beautiful

open area, visible from Flagstaff. You will walk near the foot of the prairie, enjoying breathtaking views up the mountain, with Fremont and Doyle Peaks on the skyline.

The trail continues for 2.1 miles *3.4 km*, dropping more steeply at the end, to meet an old road. This is the historic Weatherford Road, now part of the **Weatherford Trail**. (Please note that we do not use the Schultz Pass access to the Weatherford Trail. We prefer to follow the old road.) Turn right here and walk 0.4 miles *0.64 km* down to your car, for a total hike of 6.5 miles *10.4 km*.

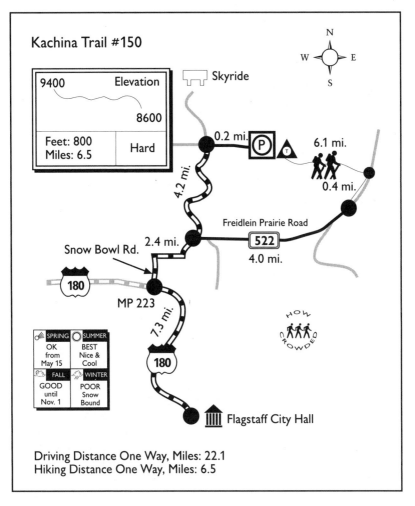

Kelsey Spring Trail

General Information
Location Map F2
Sycamore Point USGS Map
Coconino Forest Service Map

Driving Distance One Way: 24.1 miles *38.6 km* (Time 1 hour)
Access Road: High clearance needed for last 1.8 miles *2.9 km*
Hiking Distance One Way: 0.50 miles *0.8 km* (Time 30 minutes)
How Strenuous: Moderate
Features: Views, Sycamore Canyon access

NUTSHELL: Located about 25 miles *40 km* southwest of Flagstaff, this is a scenic trail in its own right as well as being an access trail into Sycamore Canyon.

DIRECTIONS:
From Flagstaff City Hall Go:
　West, then south on Route 66 beneath the railroad overpass. See Access Map, page 10. At 0.50 miles *0.8 km* you will reach a Y intersection. The right fork is Route 66. Take it. You will soon leave town. At 2.6 miles *4.2 km* you will reach a road going to the left. This is the Woody Mountain Road, FR 231. Take it. It is paved about a mile *1.6 km* and then turns into a cinder road. At 16.6 miles *26.6 km* you will intersect FR 538. Turn right onto FR 538 and follow it to the 22.3 mile *35.7 km* point, where it intersects FR 538E. Turn right on 538E. The road is rough beyond here. At 22.7 miles *36.3 km* you hit another intersection, where FR 538E forks to the left, going to Dorsey Spring Road. Keep straight, now on FR 538G, and follow it to its end at 23.7 miles *38 km*, where it meets FR 527A. Turn left onto the Kelsey Trail road, going to the 24.1 mile *38.6 km* point, the parking area. This last 0.4 mile *0.64 km* stretch is terrible, a real tire-eater.

TRAILHEAD: You will see a big sign at the parking area.

DESCRIPTION: The Kelsey Spring Trail is marked and maintained by the Forest Service and is in good condition. Start this hike by going to the rim of Sycamore Canyon rather than taking the main trail down into the canyon. You will see an unmarked but distinct footpath going to the rim to the left of the main trail. The main trail goes down into the canyon, whereas the rim trail stays on top. Sycamore Canyon deserves the overworked adjective "awesome" and the rim here is a great vantage point from which to see it. After you fill your eyes then go back to the main trail and make your descent.

The trail down is fairly steep but the footing is good and it passes through a beautiful forest. At 0.50 miles *0.8 km* you will reach a meadow onto which Kelsey Spring flows after running out of a concrete box. Take a look around and you will find the remains of an old cabin. There isn't much left, no standing walls, just some lumber and rubble. If you want to see an interesting cabin, try the nearby **Winter Cabin Trail.**

The shelf of land on which the spring is located is a veritable Shangri-La, a tranquil remote haven away from the cares of the world. Visit this place on a fine summer day when the spring is flowing, flowers are blooming and birds are singing and you won't want to come back out. It is idyllic.

From Kelsey Spring the trail goes on down another 0.7 miles *1.1 km* to **Babe's Hole**, then down another 0.8 miles *1.28 km* to **Geronimo Spring**, in the inner gorge of Sycamore Canyon.

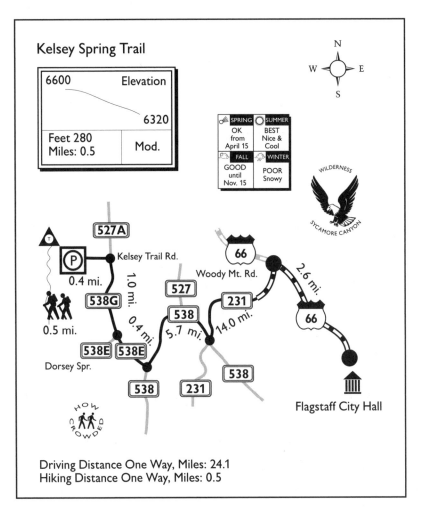

Kelsey-Winter Cabin Trail

General Information
Location Map F2
Sycamore Point USGS Map
Coconino Forest Service Map

Driving Distance One Way: 24.1 miles *38.6 km* (Time 1 hour)
Access Road: High clearance needed for last 1.8 miles *2.9 km*
Hiking Distance One Way: 5.5 miles *8.8 km* (Time 3 hours)
How Strenuous: Hard
Features: Springs, Pristine forests, Views

NUTSHELL: This trail is located in Sycamore Canyon, 24.1 miles *38.6 km* southwest of Flagstaff. It takes you along the side of the canyon between Kelsey Spring and Winter Cabin.

DIRECTIONS:
From Flagstaff City Hall Go:
    West, then south on Route 66 beneath the railroad overpass. See Access Map, page 10. At 0.50 miles *0.8 km* you will reach a Y intersection. The right fork is Route 66. Take it. You will soon leave town. At 2.6 miles *4.2 km* you will reach a road going to the left. This is the Woody Mountain Road, FR 231. Take it. It is paved about a mile and then turns into a cinder road. At 16.6 miles *26.6 km* you will intersect FR 538. Turn right onto FR 538 and follow it to the 22.3 mile *35.7 km* point, where it intersects FR 538E. Turn right on 538E. The road is rough beyond here. At 22.7 miles *36.3 km* you hit another intersection, where FR 538E forks to the left, going to Dorsey Spring Road. Keep straight, now on FR 538G, and follow it to its end at 23.7 miles *37.9 km*, where it meets FR 527A. Turn left onto the Kelsey Trail road, going to the 24.1 mile *38.6 km* point, the parking area. This last 0.4 mile *0.64 km* stretch is terrible, a real tire-eater.

TRAILHEAD: You will see a big sign at the parking area.

DESCRIPTION: From the parking area you hike down the **Kelsey Spring Trail**. You will reach Kelsey Spring at 0.5 miles *0.8 km*. Then go down the trail to **Babe's Hole** at 1.2 miles *2.0 km*. Go on down the trail to 1.3 miles *2.1 km*, where you reach a trail junction. The Kelsey-Winter Trail goes left, while the trail to **Geronimo Spring** goes right.
    From this point, the trail moves along the side of the canyon within a one hundred foot band, with minor ups and downs. The first portion of the trail is in a forest, but at about the 1.7 mile *2.7 km* point you will reach a clear area. This is nice for variety and gives good views of Sycamore Canyon.

Then you enter into a wooded area again.

You will reach Dorsey Spring at 2.9 miles *4.6 km*. The trail turns left and goes uphill to the actual spring, getting there at 3.10 miles *5.0 km*. Before the spring, in a flat area, there is a sign showing the way to Winter Cabin.

The second leg of the trail from **Dorsey Spring** to **Winter Cabin** follows the same lateral course but is more interesting. There are more open spots, high cliffs on your left, a Thumb Butte on your right. There is about a half mile where you pass narrowly through scrub oak and locust, meaning thorns and sharp edged leaves. Bare arms and legs will be scratched here. You will reach Winter Cabin at 5.5 miles *8.8 km*.

You can reverse your course when you reach Winter Cabin and go back to the Kelsey Spring trailhead or you can hike 1.1 miles *1.76 km* up to the Winter Cabin trailhead (where you have thoughtfully parked a second car).

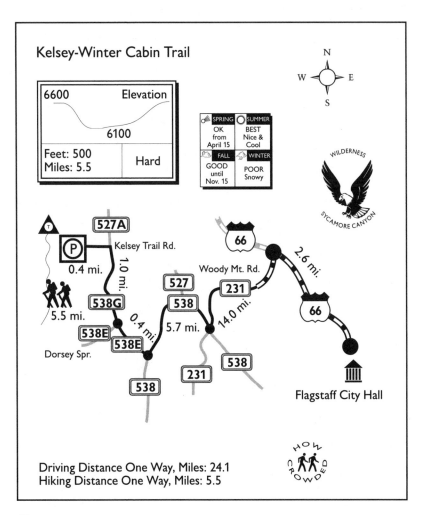

Mangum

Kendrick Mountain Trail #22

General Information
Location Map E2
Kendrick Peak and Wing Mt. USGS Maps
Kaibab Forest Service Map

Driving Distance One Way: 21.0 miles *33.6 km* (Time 45 minutes)
Access Road: All cars, Last 6.6 miles *10.6 km* good gravel road
Hiking Distance One Way: 4.6 miles *7.36 km* (Time 3.0 hours)
How Strenuous: Hard
Features: Ten thousand foot peak, Views

NUTSHELL: Kendrick Peak is next tallest to the San Francisco Peaks in the area of this book. This trail winds to the summit for great views. Terrible fire damage in 2000 altered it. Call 800-863-0546 for trail conditions.

DIRECTIONS:
From Flagstaff City Hall Go:
North on Humphreys Street for 0.6 miles *1.0 km*. See Access Map, page 10. Turn left at the stoplight onto Columbus Avenue, which becomes Highway 180. Stay on Highway 180 to the 14.4 miles *23.04 km* point (MP 230.1), where you turn left on FR 245, and follow it to the 17.4 mile *27.84 km* point where it intersects FR 171. Turn right on FR 171 and follow it to the 20.5 mile *32.8 km* point, where you will see a sign for the Kendrick Mountain Trail. Turn right on FR 190, the drive to the Kendrick Mountain trailhead, and follow it into the parking lot, which you will reach at 21.0 miles *33.6 km*. There is a toilet at the lot.

TRAILHEAD: Well marked with a sign at the parking area.

DESCRIPTION: The Forest Service has developed nice facilities at the trailhead, with a good parking lot, trash dump and toilet.

You will walk along a footpath to the 0.7 mile *1.12 km* point, where you join an old road, now closed. Hiking an old road is good news, for yesterday's road builders had to hold a gentle grade so that the engines of the old cars could make the grade.

As you go higher, you rise above a logged area and get into very attractive woods of mixed conifers and large aspen groves. From here the trail follows an unending series of steep switchbacks. Stay on the trail. Cutting switchbacks causes erosion. There are several open spaces from which to enjoy views across Government Prairie.

At 2.0 miles *3.2 km* the road ends and you follow a footpath. This is a good path, following the contours of the mountain intelligently and providing good footing. It was built as a working trail so that rangers could reach the fire lookout tower by horseback.

From a distance you will notice that Kendrick Peak has one definite sharp point, not a series of peaks like its neighbor, the San Francisco Peaks. You will reach a flat area just below the absolute peak at about 4.1 miles *6.56 km.* Here you will find the Old Lookout Cabin. It was built in the years 1911-1912 and is remarkably preserved considering the harsh winters it endures. The **Bull Basin Trail** terminates just behind the cabin.

From this flat there is one last climb to the tower, reached at 4.6 miles *7.36 km.* One nice thing about the Kendrick hike is that you never rise above timber line. At the base of the tower you can see over the trees, but when you climb it, you get tremendous views, some of the best in the region.

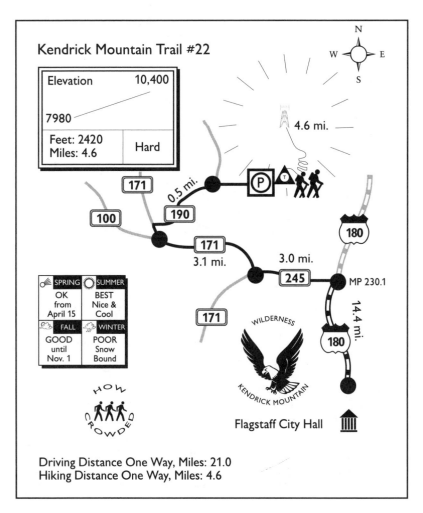

Mangum

Keyhole Sink #114

General Information
Location Map E2
Sitgreaves Mtn. USGS Map
Kaibab Forest Service Map

Driving Distance One Way: 22.6 miles *36.2 km* (Time 40 minutes)
Access Road: All cars, All paved
Hiking Distance One Way: 0.6 miles *1.0 km* (Time 20 minutes)
How Strenuous: Easy
Features: Hidden pond, Cliffs with Indian rock art

NUTSHELL: This easy hike is located in the Parks area, 22.6 miles *36.2 km* west of Flagstaff. It follows a little canyon into a picturesque rounded box. Water is dammed there by cliffs on which are scratched Indian rock art.

DIRECTIONS:
From Flagstaff City Hall Go:
   West a block on Route 66, then south, beneath the railroad overpass. See the Access Map on page 10. At 0.5 miles *0.8 km* you will reach a Y intersection. Take the right fork here, staying on Route 66. You will soon leave town. At the 5.0 mile *8.0 km* point you will merge onto Interstate-40 West. Continue west on I-40, to the 18.0 mile *28.8 km* point, where you take Exit 178, Parks Road. Turn right at the stop sign and travel to the 18.4 mile *29.4 km* point, where there is a second stop sign. Turn left here. You are now on a portion of an older alignment of Route 66 heading west. At the 19.0 mile *30.4 km* point you will see the Parks Store to your right. Keep going west to the 22.6 mile *36.2 km* point where you will see the entrance to the Oak Hill Snow Play Area to your left. Pull into the parking lot for the Oak Hill Snow Play Area and park there.

TRAILHEAD: Across Route 66, directly in line with the Oak Hill entrance.

DESCRIPTION: The Keyhole Sink Trail was opened in the summer of 1992. Across the highway from the parking lot, you will see a pole fence with a green metal gate. This is the start of the trail, and it is posted. The trail will follow a small canyon that winds around into a bottom, where you will see a stand of young aspen trees lining the floor of the canyon.
   You will walk a short distance along the canyon bottom until you come to a fence made of aspen logs. An interpretive sign is located at the gate, along with a Guest Register. Sign in and then go through the fence. Here the aspen grove stops and you will be looking into a charming little bowl where the canyon ends against basalt cliffs some thirty to forty feet high. The floor

of the bowl is covered with grass.

Walk toward the farthest, blackest cliff. In wet years there will be a pond of water at the base of the cliffs, because the cliff acts as a natural dam for all the water flowing into the canyon. We have visited this place when there was quite a lot of water in the pond, and we have also seen it bone dry.

As you face the cliff, look for rock art on the cliff faces to the left of the blackest face. There are two major panels of rock art. If you look carefully, you will see a few more figures scattered here and there. The panel shown on the interpretive sign is to your left as you face the end cliff.

This is a natural waterhole for game and you will see elk and deer sign around it. It would also be a trap for any game cornered against the cliffs.

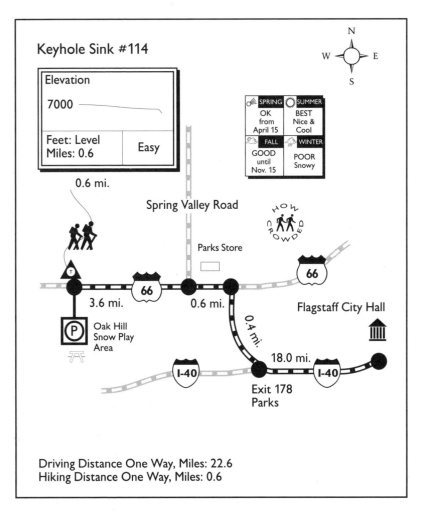

Keyhole Sink #114

Elevation

7000

Feet: Level
Miles: 0.6

Easy

SPRING	SUMMER
OK from April 15	BEST Nice & Cool
FALL	WINTER
GOOD until Nov. 15	POOR Snowy

0.6 mi.

Spring Valley Road

HOW CROWDED

Parks Store

66

66

3.6 mi.

0.6 mi.

0.4 mi.

Flagstaff City Hall

Oak Hill Snow Play Area

I-40

18.0 mi.

I-40

Exit 178 Parks

Driving Distance One Way, Miles: 22.6
Hiking Distance One Way, Miles: 0.6

Mangum

Kinder Crossing Trail #19

General Information
Location Map G4
Blue Ridge Reservoir USGS Map
Coconino Forest Service Map

Driving Distance One Way: 71.0 miles *113.6 km* (Time 1.5 hours)
Access Road: All cars, Last 0.75 miles *1.2 km* rough dirt road
Hiking Distance One Way: 0.67 miles *1.1 km* (Time 1 hour)
How Strenuous: Moderate
Features: Beautiful pristine stream, Remote canyon

NUTSHELL: This is one of the few trails into East Clear Creek, a perennial stream in a remote canyon southeast of Flagstaff in the Mogollon Rim country.

DIRECTIONS:
From Flagstaff City Hall Go:
    West, then south on Route 66 under the railroad overpass. See Access Map, page 10. At 0.5 miles *0.8 km*, go straight, on Milton Road. At 1.7 miles *2.72 km* you will reach a stoplight at Forest Meadows Street. Turn right here onto Forest Meadows and go one block to Beulah. Turn left on Beulah and follow it south. Beulah merges onto Highway 89A. At 2.4 miles *3.84 km* (MP 401.6), turn left onto the Lake Mary Road. Follow the Lake Mary Road (also known as FH 3) to its end at the junction with State Route 87, 56.6 miles *90.6 km.* Turn left on Highway 87, a paved road, and follow it to the 66.0 mile *105.6 km* point MP 299.9, where you turn right on FR 95. FR 95 is surfaced with gravel and is an all-weather road. Follow it to the 70.25 mile *112.4 km* point, where you turn left on the access road. There is a sign for Kinder Crossing Trail here, but the road is not numbered. The road is easy to follow and is decent for about the first half mile *0.8 km*, but after that, it gets very rough. At 71.0 miles *113.6 km*, the road forward is blocked by a berm and the road swings downhill to the right to a parking loop. This last 0.1 miles *0.16 km* is almost impossibly rough and we recommend that you park at the berm and walk to the trailhead.

TRAILHEAD: We found no sign, but the trail was distinct and obvious. It is to your right as you face the canyon. Look for a couple of cut logs.

DESCRIPTION: The first 0.5 miles *0.8 km* is a gentle gradual descent into the canyon. At first, you walk along a nice soft path covered with pine needles. Then, as you get about half way down, you hike across exposed sandstone ledges. These are a little harder to walk on, but are not difficult. The last leg of the hike is a little steeper, but not bad.

The trail comes down to the water at a scenic pool at the foot of some impressive and colorful cliffs, where there is a nice gravel beach. This is a great spot for some photographs. If the water is high enough, you might even try a swim in the pool.

If you want to take the entire hike, you turn left (west) at the water and follow a path that is up some distance, away from the stream. Look for blazes in the trees. In 0.15 miles *0.24 km*, the trail crosses the stream on stepping stones on either side of a little sand bar, then goes up a side canyon, to reach the top at 1.5 miles *2.4 km*. Unless you are simply keen on hiking the entire trail in order to say that you have done it, we think you will be happier staying at the creek and doing some exploring in this very pretty canyon with its perennial stream.

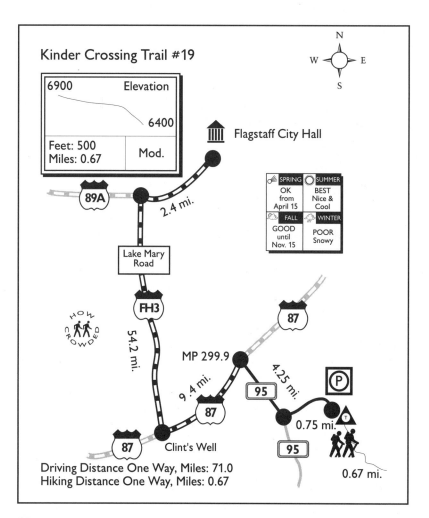

Mangum

Lakeview Trail #132

General Information
Location Map G3
Mormon Lake USGS Map
Coconino Forest Service Map

Driving Distance One Way: 28.2 miles *45.1 km* (Time 35 minutes)
Access Road: All cars, Last 0.2 miles *0.32 km* good gravel road
Hiking Distance One Way: 1.25 miles *2.0 km* (Time 40 minutes)
How Strenuous: Moderate
Features: Beautiful forest, Excellent views

NUTSHELL: This hike gently climbs a ridge radiating south from Mormon Mountain. At the ridge top you are treated to sweeping views of Mormon Lake and the surrounding countryside.

DIRECTIONS:
From Flagstaff City Hall Go:
    West, then south on Route 66 under the railroad overpass. At 0.5 miles *0.8 km*, get onto Milton Road. See Access Map, page 10. At 1.7 miles *2.72 km* you will reach a stoplight at Forest Meadows Street. Turn right here onto Forest Meadows and go one block to Beulah. Turn left on Beulah and follow it south. Beulah merges onto Highway 89A. At 2.4 miles *3.84 km* (MP 401.6), turn left onto the Lake Mary Road. Follow the Lake Mary Road to the 23.0 mile *36.8 km* point (MP 323.6), where you turn right onto the Mormon Lake Road. At 28 miles *44.8 km*, on the Mormon Lake Road, you will see a sign for the Lakeview Trail. Turn right here and follow the gravel road and signs to the 28.2 miles *45.1 km* point near the toilet at the campground.

TRAILHEAD: You will see a sign marking the trail to your left as you enter the campground.

DESCRIPTION: At the beginning of the trail you will encounter a little stream, a rarity in northern Arizona. There is a line of stepping stones across the stream, making it easy to cross. Once across, you will see the trail heading uphill to your right. In 0.1 miles *0.16 km* you will see the official trailhead sign for the Lakeview Trail. The trail is narrow but in good condition. It is well maintained. This is rocky soil, but the footing is pretty comfortable.
    The forest around Mormon Mountain is particularly beautiful. In addition to the ubiquitous Ponderosa pine, there is much oak and you will also see some aspen. Flowers and shrubs grow in profusion. Benches have been thoughtfully placed at the beginning, halfway and top of the trail. Since this

is a moderately easy hike, you can take your time. No need to hustle. Stop at the benches to catch your breath and enjoy the experience.

For nine-tenths of the hike, you cannot understand why the trail has been given the name Lakeview. Then, as you near the top, you can see why. The trail has been climbing gradually up a ridge. As you come to the top of the ridge, you find that its top is a lava cliff. Around the perimeter no pine trees grow, so you have unobstructed views.

You can walk around the ridge top and enjoy great views. As the name suggests, Mormon Lake is fully in view. Depending upon the wetness of the preceding winter, Mormon Lake will either be a substantial body of water or a great big pasture with a small pond in its center.

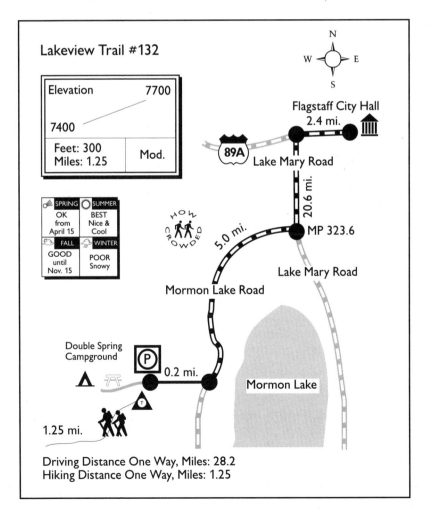

Driving Distance One Way, Miles: 28.2
Hiking Distance One Way, Miles: 1.25

Mangum

Lava Flow Trail

General Information
Location Map E4
Wupatki SW USGS Map
Coconino Forest Service Map

Driving Distance One Way: 22.1 miles *35.36 km* (Time 30 minutes)
Access Road: All cars, All paved
Hiking Distance, Complete Loop: 1.0 mile *1.6 km* (Time 45 minutes)
How Strenuous: Easy
Features: Views, Extinct volcanoes, Self-guided nature trail

NUTSHELL: This is an easy trail located in the Sunset Crater National Monument 22.1 miles *35.36 km* northeast of Flagstaff. It takes you on a fascinating self-guided nature walk through a volcanic field.

DIRECTIONS:
From Flagstaff City Hall Go:
East, then north on Highway 89. See Access Map, pages 10-11. At 16.4 miles *26.24 km* (MP 430.3) you will reach the entrance to Sunset Crater National Monument. Turn right on the road into Sunset Crater. This road is also known as FR 545. At 18.4 miles *29.44 km* you will reach a ticket booth where you will have to pay admission. Just beyond that is the Visitor Center, which is worth a look. At 21.9 miles *35.0 km* you will see a road branching off to your right marked Lava Flow Trail Drive. Take it. It leads to a parking area at 22.1 miles *35.36 km.*

TRAILHEAD: You will see a sign at the parking area.

DESCRIPTION: This trail is designed as a self-guided walk with points of interest keyed to a guide booklet that is available from the dispenser located at the beginning of the trail. You can take a booklet free. If you decide to keep it, then you put fifty cents into the dispenser at the end of the trail. If you don't want to keep the booklet, then you return it to the dispenser.

The trail is paved for a short distance. In fact the Forest Service has created a paved short version of the trail for wheelchair bound visitors—a nice gesture. On the main trail, once the paving ends, the trail surface is composed of black cinders. You would have no trouble walking the trail in street shoes but you would scuff them up plenty if you did. Jogging shoes or light trail shoes are excellent footgear for this hike.

A hiker could hurry around the trail in thirty minutes but we recommend that you take your time. Use the booklet and read it at the stopping points that are described in the booklet. These points really are interesting and even people who don't like museums or educational walks should find something to enjoy. These black cinder locations have a special feeling that some people respond to very positively. In winter you can sometimes see some startling special effects when white drifts of snow form stark contrasting patterns against the black cinders.

Until 1973 visitors could hike to the top of Sunset Crater. Because of the severe erosion that the multitudes of hikers were causing to the face of the crater, hiking Sunset Crater is now forbidden. The sides of the crater are covered with deep loose black cinders and are therefore unstable. They kept sloughing away from the trails. It is too bad people can't enjoy the experience anymore as we did when we were kids, but the closure was necessary.

One of the features of this trail is an ice cave, a lava tube such as you encounter on the **Lava River Cave** hike, but it was closed in 1992 because it was collapsing.

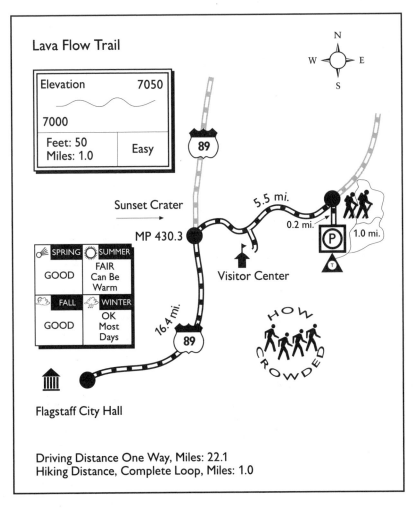

Lava Flow Trail

Elevation 7050

7000

Feet: 50
Miles: 1.0 — Easy

Sunset Crater

MP 430.3

5.5 mi.

0.2 mi.

1.0 mi.

16.4 mi.

Visitor Center

SPRING SUMMER
GOOD — FAIR Can Be Warm

FALL WINTER
GOOD — OK Most Days

HOW CROWDED

Flagstaff City Hall

Driving Distance One Way, Miles: 22.1
Hiking Distance, Complete Loop, Miles: 1.0

Lava River Cave

General Information
Location Map E2
Wing Mountain USGS Map
Coconino Forest Service Map

Driving Distance One Way: 18.75 miles *30. 0 km* (Time 40 minutes)
Access Road: All cars, Last 4.35 miles *6.96 km* good gravel road
Hiking Distance One Way: 0.75 miles *1.2 km* (Time 40 minutes)
How Strenuous: Moderate
Features: Unusual underground lava tube

NUTSHELL: This underground lava tube located northwest of Flagstaff is a unique experience.

DIRECTIONS:
From Flagstaff City Hall Go:
   North on Humphreys Street for 0.60 miles *1.0 km*. See Access Map, page 10. Turn left at the stoplight onto Columbus Avenue, which becomes Highway 180. Stay on Highway 180 to the 14.4 miles *23.04 km* point (MP 230.1), where you turn left on FR 245, and follow it to the 17.4 mile *27.84 km* point where it intersects FR 171. Turn left onto FR 171 and follow it to the 18.5 mile *29.6 km* point, where it intersects FR 171B. Turn left on 171B and take it to the 18.75 mile *30.0 km* point where you will find parking.

TRAILHEAD: You will see a blocked road at the parking area. Walk up this road 0.25 miles *0.4 km* to the opening of the cave.

DESCRIPTION: Even if you know nothing about volcanoes it is obvious that the area where this cave is located is an ancient volcanic field. Craters and cinder cones dot the landscape everywhere. The mighty San Francisco Peaks themselves are a huge volcanic crater.
   Lava tubes are formed when the outer portion of a river of lava cools while the interior is still hot and flowing. Under the right conditions the outer skin will form a hard shell and the inner core will flow right on through like water going through a straw, leaving an empty tube.
   That's what you will find on this trip. The Forest Service has made an attractive entrance down into the tube using native stone to form a natural stairway. You have to duck to get into the opening and crawl over fallen stone, but then the tube deepens so that you can stand upright. The height of the tube is not uniform, however, and there are low and high places along the way. The tube goes on for about 0.75 mile *1.2 km*. Temperatures in the cave are from 32-40°F year around. The coldest spot is near the entrance and

you may find ice there in the spring. The cave was discovered in 1915 by lumberjacks who were logging nearby.

You must come properly prepared for this hike. It can be dangerous if you are unprepared. Once you get a short way past the daylight coming in from the entrance you are in absolute darkness. The floor, ceiling and walls are all extremely rough and uneven and you have to watch every step. Every member of your party should dress warmly, carry lights and have good hiking shoes. We recommend that each person have two good flashlights equipped with fresh batteries.

About halfway you will enter a thirty foot high vault with a side tunnel going off to your right. Keep looking at the floor and you will observe different flows of the lava. At the end, the tube pinches closed, like the crimp on the end of a toothpaste tube.

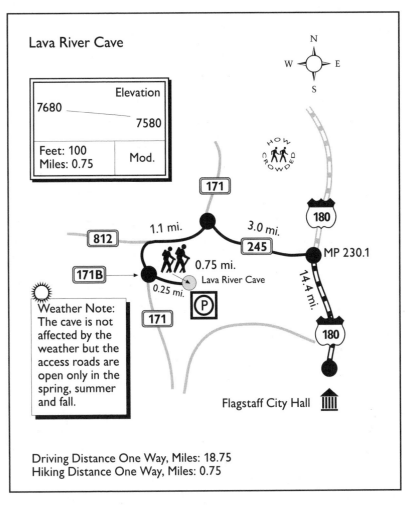

Ledges Trail #138

General Information
Location Map G3
Mormon Lake USGS Map
Coconino Forest Service Map

Driving Distance One Way: 27.0 miles *43.2 km* (Time 30 minutes)
Access Road: All cars, All paved except last 0.3 miles *0.48 km*
Hiking Distance, Complete Loop: 1.5 miles *2.4 km* (Time 45 minutes)
How Strenuous: Moderate
Features: Views

NUTSHELL: This is a nice trail at the base of Mormon Mountain, 27.0 miles *43.2 km* southeast of Flagstaff. It takes you through a pine forest to The Ledges, a ragged basalt cliff, from where you have fine views of Mormon Lake.

DIRECTIONS:
From Flagstaff City Hall Go:
    West, then south on Route 66 under the railroad overpass. See Access Map, page 10. At 0.5 miles *0.8 km*, get onto Milton Road. At 1.7 miles *2.72 km* you will reach a stoplight at Forest Meadows Street. Turn right here onto Forest Meadows and go one block to Beulah. Turn left on Beulah and follow it south. Beulah merges onto Highway 89A. At 2.4 miles *3.84 km* (MP 401.6), turn left onto the Lake Mary Road. Follow the Lake Mary Road to the 23.0 mile *36.8 km* point (MP 323.6), where you turn right onto the Mormon Lake Road. At 26.7 miles *42.7 km*, on the Mormon Lake Road, you will see a sign marked "Dairy Springs Amphitheater." Turn right here and follow the gravel road and signs to the 27.0 miles *43.2 km* point, at the back of the Dairy Springs Campground.

TRAILHEAD: There is a large sign at the parking lot.

DESCRIPTION: This area is used for cross-country skiing in the winter and you will see signs and triangles nailed to trees along the way marking the various ski trails. The triangles for the Ledges Trail are silver.
    From its start the trail gradually ascends a hill. The sides of the trail here are lined with rocks. You will see some houses below you toward Mormon Lake. At about 0.25 miles *0.4 km* you begin to see the lake and it will be in sight most of the way from this point.
    Mormon Lake is a natural lake. It was originally called Mormon Dairy Lake because of the Mormon pioneers who ran a dairy here for several years. Later, the name of the lake was shortened to Mormon Lake. Dairy

Springs is another legacy from that time.

The trail goes through a forest of pine, oak and spruce. It reaches its apex at 0.75 miles *1.2 km* and then begins to descend. At 0.90 miles *1.44 km* you come onto the ledges for which the trail is named. Few things grow in this bare rock, so this is a good viewpoint. After the ledges the trail goes downhill toward the Mormon Lake Road.

At about 1.0 miles *1.6 km* you will come to a group of homes. These are summer homes and if you are making the hike in the summer you may be greeted by inquisitive dogs or children. Many paths through this area make following the main trail difficult. No worries. Just keep working your way downhill toward the highway, which you can see plainly. When you reach the highway, go right (west) and you will return to the driveway entrance in about 0.20 miles *0.32 km*, from where it is about 0.1 mile *0.16 km* back to your car.

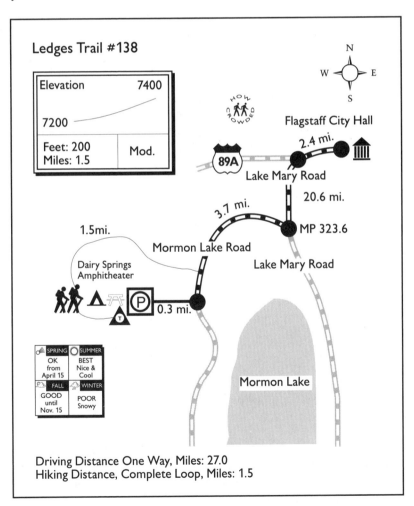

Ledges Trail #138

Elevation 7400

7200

Feet: 200
Miles: 1.5

Mod.

HOW CROWDED

N
W E
S

Flagstaff City Hall

89A

2.4 mi.

Lake Mary Road

20.6 mi.

3.7 mi.

MP 323.6

1.5mi.

Mormon Lake Road

Lake Mary Road

Dairy Springs
Amphitheater

0.3 mi.

SPRING
OK
from
April 15

SUMMER
BEST
Nice &
Cool

FALL
GOOD
until
Nov. 15

WINTER
POOR
Snowy

Mormon Lake

Driving Distance One Way, Miles: 27.0
Hiking Distance, Complete Loop, Miles: 1.5

Mangum

Little Bear Trail

General Information
Location Map E3
Sunset Crater West USGS Map
Coconino Forest Service Map

Driving Distance One Way: 11.7 miles *18.7 km* (Time 30 minutes)
Access Road: All cars, Last 2.5 miles *4.0 km* good gravel road
Hiking Distance One Way: 4.4 miles *7.0 km* (Time 2.5 hours)
How Strenuous: Hard
Features: Alpine forests, Views

NUTSHELL: This trail, built in 1996-7, takes you from a point on the Little Elden Trail to a saddle between the Dry Lake Hills and Little Elden. Along the way you will enjoy tremendous views. **A personal favorite.**

DIRECTIONS:
From Flagstaff City Hall Go:
East, then north on Highway 89. See Access Map, pages 10-11. At 6.5 miles *10.4 km* you will pass the last stoplight in town at the Townsend-Winona Road. Continue on Highway 89 to the 9.2 mile *14.72 km* point (MP 423.3) where a gravel road (FR 556) takes off to the left. Turn in on this. You will see a sign identifying it as Elden Spring Road. Drive up this road. At the 11.3 mile *18.08 km* point you will see the turn to Horsecamp. Pass this by and keep going to the 11.7 miles *18.7 km* point, where you will see a parking apron and pole fence to your right. Pull in and park by the opening, where there is a big sign. (You will also find a toilet at this parking area.)

TRAILHEAD: Behind the sign (N) a few yards you will see the trail marker. Turn left and walk uphill.

DESCRIPTION: You will start this hike by walking a short (0.3 mile *0.48 km*) segment of the Horsecamp Trail, to the point where it joins the Little Elden Trail. The length of the Little Bear Trail by itself is 3.5 miles *5.6 km* but you must hike 0.9 miles *1.44 km* to get to it.
Where the two trails join, turn to the right and follow the Little Elden Trail for 0.6 miles *1.0 km*, where the Little Bear Trail takes off to the left. From this point it is 3.5 miles *5.6 km* to the top.
The trail is designed so that it climbs gently, making wide swings as it goes up the grade. At a point about 1.5 miles *2.4 km* up the trail you will come to a lookout point. Here there is a short detour to a rock knob from where you can enjoy views to the north, out over Doney Park and the cinder

hill area. Sunset Crater shows up clearly.

Throughout the trail you will be hiking on one of the colder spots on the mountain, as a result of which the forest is composed of more firs than pines. In places there are pockets of aspens, and we even saw a few willows. This would be a pretty place in the fall when the leaves are changing color.

In a couple of other places higher up the trail, you pass under the foot of some beautiful rock cliffs, not too high but very picturesque. Higher still you will come to an even finer lookout point, again on a bare knob. The last leg of the trail takes you onto a saddle where you intersect the **Sunset Trail** at a point about 1.5 miles *2.4 km* from its Mt. Elden trailhead. This makes it possible to connect onto other trails in the Mt. Elden system (see map).

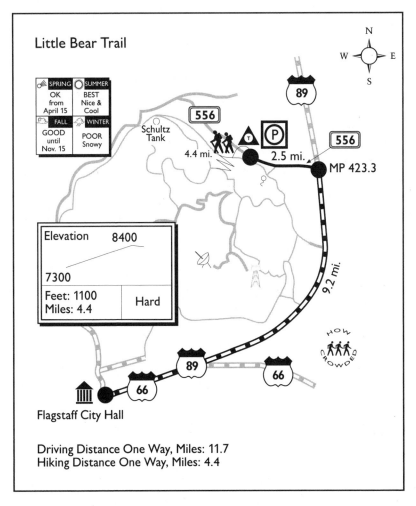

Little Bear Trail

	SPRING	SUMMER
	OK from April 15	BEST Nice & Cool
	FALL	WINTER
	GOOD until Nov. 15	POOR Snowy

556

Schultz Tank

4.4 mi.

T P

2.5 mi.

89

556

MP 423.3

Elevation   8400

7300

Feet: 1100
Miles: 4.4   Hard

9.2 mi.

HOW CROWDED

89   66

66

Flagstaff City Hall

Driving Distance One Way, Miles: 11.7
Hiking Distance One Way, Miles: 4.4

Mangum

Little Elden—Heart

Driving Distance One Way: 11.7 miles *18.7 km* (Time 30 minutes)
Access Road: All cars, Last 2.5 miles *4.0 km* good gravel road
Hiking Distance One Way: 2.9 miles *4.64 km* (Time 2.0 hours)
How Strenuous: Moderate
Features: Beautiful spring, Cliffs, Views

NUTSHELL: Starting near Little Elden Spring north of Flagstaff, this trail takes you south around the base of Little Elden Mt. into a scenic bowl.

DIRECTIONS:
From Flagstaff City Hall Go:
East, then north on Highway 89. See Access Map, pages 10-11. At 6.5 miles *10.4 km* you pass the last stoplight in town at the Townsend-Winona Road. Stay on Highway 89 to the 9.2 mile *14.72 km* point (MP 423.3) where you turn left on a gravel road (FR 556). You will see a sign identifying it as Elden Spring Road. Drive this to the 11.7 miles *18.7 km* point, where you will see a parking apron and pole fence to your right. (Do not turn off into the Horsecamp itself. Stay on the Elden Springs Road, FR 556).

TRAILHEAD: There is a trail sign at the parking lot. Behind the sign (N) a few yards you will see the trail marker. Turn left and walk uphill.

DESCRIPTION: The Forest Service designates the trail you will use as the Little Elden Trail, which is almost 6.0 miles *9.6 km* long, starting at Schultz Tank and ending at its connection with the Heart Trail, . We have divided the Little Elden Trail into two segments for this book. One we call Little Elden—Heart Trail and the other we call the **Little Elden Springs— Schultz Tank Trail.**
After hiking 0.3 miles *0.48 km* you will meet the Little Elden Trail. Turn left here. At the 0.9 mile *1.44 km* point you will reach Little Elden Spring. Surrounded by a fence, it is located uphill against a rock face to your right. Soon afterwards the trail turns around the toe of the mountain. Here the forest becomes different, the aspens disappear, the pines thin out, and junipers and oak predominate. You will have some nice views.
The face of Little Elden itself is very interesting in this stretch. It looks like a huge rock pile full of eye-catching formations, lines, crevices and mystery. Is that a cave you see or only a seam? The rock is a light rust color.

For about the first mile you will walk along close to the base of the mountain, then swing away from it.

The trail serpentines to its high point at about 2.0 miles *3.2 km*. From there you will go downwards and approach several low hills that are not made of volcanic rock, but instead are composed of white sedimentary stone. Soon after you pass the first hill, you will come to the base of a higher hill with a sharp peak. Here you will walk into a patch of deep sand. There is an open park here, a lovely place. To your left is a depression with willows growing at its bottom. This is Sandy Seep.

You will leave the park and at 2.9 miles *4.64 km*, you will intersect the **Heart Trail**. It comes in from your right at an acute angle and goes uphill. This junction is the beginning of the **Sandy Seep Trail**. If you walk a little farther you will reach the trail junction where the **Christmas Tree Trail** comes in. This gives you a selection of choices. (See map).

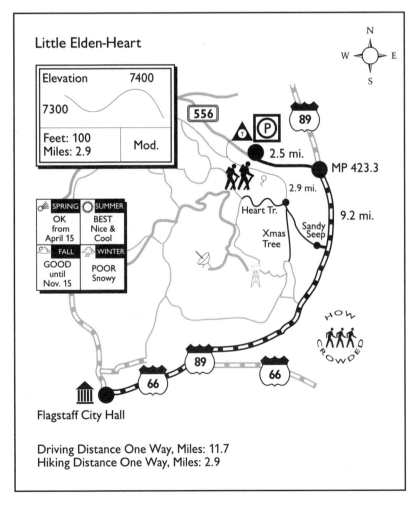

Little Elden-Heart

Elevation	7400	
7300		
Feet: 100 Miles: 2.9	Mod.	

	SPRING	SUMMER
OK from April 15		BEST Nice & Cool
	FALL	WINTER
GOOD until Nov. 15		POOR Snowy

556

89

2.5 mi.

MP 423.3

2.9 mi.

Heart Tr.

9.2 mi.

Xmas Tree

Sandy Seep

HOW CROWDED

89

66

66

Flagstaff City Hall

Driving Distance One Way, Miles: 11.7
Hiking Distance One Way, Miles: 2.9

Mangum

Little Elden—Schultz Tank

General Information
Location Map E3
Humphreys Peak & Sunset Crater West USGS Maps
Coconino Forest Service Map

Driving Distance One Way: 11.7 miles *18.7 km* (Time 30 minutes)
Access Road: All cars, Last 2.5 miles *4.0 km* good gravel road
Hiking Distance One Way: 3.0 miles *4.8 km* (Time 1.5 hours)
How Strenuous: Moderate
Features: Alpine forests, Views

NUTSHELL: Starting above Little Elden Spring 11.7 miles *18.7 km* north of Flagstaff, this trail takes you northwest around the base of Little Elden Mountain and the Dry Lake Hills to Schultz Tank, a large pond.

DIRECTIONS:
From Flagstaff City Hall Go:
    East, then north on Highway 89. See Access Map, pages 10-11. At 6.5 miles *10.4 km* you pass the last stoplight in town at the Townsend-Winona Road. Stay on Highway 89 to the 9.2 mile *14.72 km* point (MP 423.3) where you turn left on a gravel road (FR 556). You will see a sign identifying it as Elden Spring Road. Drive this to the 11.7 miles *18.7 km* point, where you will see a parking apron and pole fence to your right. (Do not turn off into the Horsecamp itself. Stay on the Elden Springs Road, FR 556).

TRAILHEAD: You will see a small gap in the middle of the pole fence at the parking area. Go through there, away from the road, and you will find the trail marker. Turn left and walk uphill.

DESCRIPTION: The Little Elden Trail was designed to open up more of the fabulous Mt. Elden recreation area and to take some of the pressure off of the heavily used parts of the system that are closer to town. It is a very nice trail. The trail officially starts at Schultz Tank and ends where it meets the **Heart Trail**, for a total length of about 6.0 miles *9.6 km*. We like to divide it into two segments, which is the way we are presenting it in this book, so that you can take advantage of the mid-entry point.
    You will first hike across the road and uphill for a distance of 0.3 miles *0.48 km* to intersect the Little Elden Trail. You will see a signpost here. Turn right. The first leg of this hike takes you through a pine forest that has been recently logged. This means that the forest is thin and not pretty, but you get some views. You walk along following the base of Little Elden for a short distance. You can see clearly the saddle between Mt. Elden and the Dry

Lake Hills. Thereafter you hike along the base of the Dry Lake Hills. You will meet the new **Little Bear Trail** soon.

You are never very far from FR 556 and there are times when you can see it plainly—and hear traffic on it.

At 7800 feet you leave the bare pines and enter a more interesting forest of pines, firs and aspens. This has not been logged and is much more attractive. At about 7900 feet you will come into a small canyon on the north face of a hill that seems to get lots of moisture. The growth is heavy here and very attractive. Where the trail crosses the bottom a spring (sometimes) flows.

About a half mile from the end, the trail winds around Schultz Tank and winds up at the **Sunset Trail** parking area.

TIP: Take two cars. Park the first one at the trailhead. Drive the second one 2.1 miles *3.36 km* to intersect FR 420, then go left 0.75 miles *1.2 km* to the Sunset Trailhead. Park, and hike back from there.

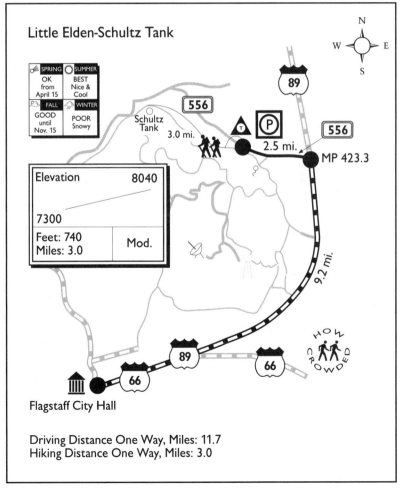

Little Spring to Bismarck Lake

General Information
Location Map E3
Humphreys Peak and White Horse Hills USGS Maps
Coconino Forest Service Map

Driving Distance One Way: 22.0 miles *35.2 km* (Time 40 minutes)
Access Road: All cars, but high clearance suggested.
Hiking Distance One Way: 1.15 miles *1.84 km* (Time 1.0 hours)
How Strenuous: Moderate
Features: Beautiful alpine forest, Meadow with lake, Peak views

NUTSHELL: A steep climb through lovely alpine forests takes you to an aspen ringed lake.

DIRECTIONS:
From Flagstaff City Hall Go:
    North on Humphreys Street for 0.6 miles *1.0 km*. See Access Map, page 10. Turn left at the stoplight onto Columbus Avenue and follow it around a big curve to the north. You will see the street signs call this road Columbus at first, then Ft. Valley Road and then Highway 180. Stay on Highway 180 to the 19.4 miles *31.04 km* point (MP 235.1), where the unpaved upper Hart Prairie Road branches off to the right. Turn right onto this road, which is also identified as FR 151, and follow it to the 21.8 miles *34.88 km* point. There FR 418B branches to the left going to Little Spring. Take FR 418B and follow it for about 0.2 miles *0.32 km* to a roadblock. There is a small parking place to your left here. it is no longer possible to drive all the way to Little Spring on this road.

TRAILHEAD: From the parking spot hike the old road 0.4 miles *0.64 km* to the spring, which is marked by the greenery that thrives on its water. Behind the spring you will see an old road going uphill with a barricade across it. This is the trail. You will hike 0.3 miles *0.48 km* to the spring.

DESCRIPTION: The water at Little Spring made the land valuable for ranching, and the clearing was a natural place to set up a ranch house. For many years there were a couple of cabins at Little Spring, but now you can see only faint remnants of them.
    Little Spring played an important role in Flagstaff's early days, as it was a stop on the famous Flagstaff-Grand Canyon Stage Coach line because of its dependable water.
    The clearing is a beautiful place to bring the family for a picnic. The spring itself isn't much. It has been captured and pours through a metal pipe

into a small pool always swarming with gnats. On the uphill side of the spring you will see a barricade with signs for the Bismarck Lake Elk Preserve. Hike up the road blocked by the barricade.

You will walk up through a beautiful forest of aspen and spruce. This north slope of the mountain seems to get plenty of water. The forest floor is covered with ferns, and on a hike in August we saw mushrooms everywhere.

The first 0.35 miles *0.56 km* of the trail is a bit of a struggle because it is so steep. At this point you will come across an old road. Go to the right (south) here. Soon you will enter a more level area where there is a narrow open park leading toward a large park. From the 0.5 mile *0.8 km* point you will be in sight of the San Francisco Peaks, which look enormous from here.

The trail ends at Bismarck Lake. Calling this small pond a lake seems like a misnomer, but remember, this is dry Arizona.

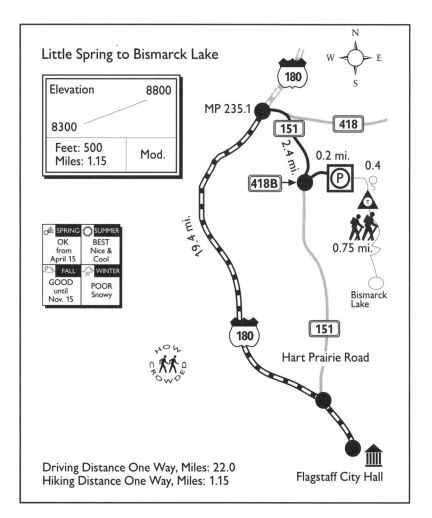

Lonesome Pocket Trail #61

Driving Distance One Way: 52.6 miles *84.2 km* (Time 1.75 hours)
Access Road: All cars, Last 10.5 miles *17 km* decent gravel roads
Hiking Distance One Way: 5.0 miles *8.0 km* (Time 3.0 hours)
How Strenuous: Hard
Features: Views

NUTSHELL: A long drive through remote country takes you to seldom seen viewpoints on the Mogollon Rim west of Sycamore Canyon. You descend an old livestock trail to the bottom of the Rim.

DIRECTIONS:
From Flagstaff City Hall Go:
    West, then south on Route 66 under the railroad overpass. See Access Map, page 10. Turn right at 0.5 miles *0.8 km* and follow Route 66 out of town. It merges with I-40 west in 5.0 miles *8.0 km*. Stay on I-40 West to the 30.3 mile *48.5 km* point, Williams Exit #165. Take that exit and at the stop sign go left to Williams. Go into downtown Williams on Route 66 (Railroad Avenue) and turn left at Fourth Street, 32.9 miles *52.6 km*, which will take you out of town. Beyond town, the road is called County 73 (the Perkinsville Road). At 42.1 miles *67.4 km* turn left (east) onto unpaved FR 354. Take FR 354 to the 49.3 mile *78.9 km* point, where you will see FR 354 turn to your right (west). FR 105 starts here. Take FR 105 to the 50.9 mile *81.4 km* point, where it intersects FR 125. Turn right (south) on FR 125 and follow it to its end at 52.6 miles *84.2 km*, where you park.

TRAILHEAD: From the parking place, FR 7125 goes south. A lath-type marker limits road usage to hikers, bikers and horse riders.

DESCRIPTION: You will hike an old jeep road. To your right (west) is Wagner Hill. Starting in a thick pinon-juniper forest, the road goes along terrain that is fairly flat, with a few ups and downs, in a southerly direction. The forest thins as you come out onto a mesa where you begin to see canyons all around you. You are walking toward the outer edge of the Mogollon Rim.
    At 1.4 miles *2.3 km* you reach the rim. The road curves to the left (east) here. There is a great lookout at this place, to which you may want to detour.
    You will pass through a gate at 2.3 miles *3.7 km*. At 2.4 miles *3.8 km* the road forks. Take the right fork, which brings you right to the rim. At 2.6

miles *4.2 km*, look for a triple-trunk juniper with a blaze. This is the start of the trail to the bottom of the rim. You will see a footpath plunging steeply between two barbed wire fences. You will now descend 1660 feet in 2.4 miles *3.8 km* to a ranch house (clearly visible from the start down) at Henderson Flat. The trail is very rocky and not maintained. All the way down, you will enjoy sweeping views across the Verde Valley to the Black Hills and beyond.

We recommend using two cars. From 4th Street in Williams, take both cars to the end of the paving on the Perkinsville Road, 24.5 miles *39.2 km*. Follow the unpaved Perkinsville Road to the 29.8 miles *47.7 km*, point where you will see a sign for Henderson Flat pointing to your left. This is FR 181. Drive FR 181 to the 37.55 mile *60 km* point, and park at the ranch house, where you will see trailhead signs. Then take one of the cars back up to the top. You'll need 2.5 hours to drive this shuttle.

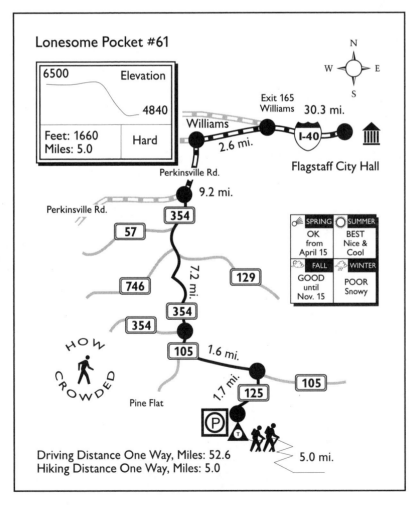

Lonesome Pocket #61

6500	Elevation
	4840
Feet: 1660 Miles: 5.0	Hard

Williams

Perkinsville Rd.

Exit 165 Williams **30.3 mi.**

I-40

Flagstaff City Hall

2.6 mi.

Perkinsville Rd. **9.2 mi.**

354

57

746

129

7.2 mi.

354

354

105 **1.6 mi.**

1.7 mi. 125

105

Pine Flat

HOW CROWDED

❄ SPRING	☀ SUMMER
OK from April 15	BEST Nice & Cool
☁ FALL	☁ WINTER
GOOD until Nov. 15	POOR Snowy

P

5.0 mi.

Driving Distance One Way, Miles: 52.6
Hiking Distance One Way, Miles: 5.0

Mangum

Lookout Trail at Snow Bowl

General Information
Location Map E3
Humphreys Peak USGS Map
Coconino Forest Service Map

Driving Distance One Way: 14.4 miles *23.0 km* (Time 40 minutes)
Access Road: All cars, All paved
Hiking Distance, Complete Loop: 0.38 miles *0.6 km* (30 minutes plus ride time)
How Strenuous: Moderate (Short, but elevation affects many hikers)
Features: High mountains, Alpine forests, Excellent views

NUTSHELL: To make this hike, you drive to the Snow Bowl and take the Sky Ride. Around the area where you exit the ride, a hiking trail has been created in order to provide views and a taste of the high alpine terrain.

DIRECTIONS:
From Flagstaff City Hall Go:

North on Humphreys Street for 0.6 miles *1.0 km*. See Access Map, page 10. Turn left at the stoplight onto Columbus Avenue and follow it around a big curve to the north. You will see that the street signs call this road Columbus at first, then Ft. Valley Road and then Highway 180. Stay on Highway 180 to the 7.3 miles point *11.7 km* (MP 223), where the road to the Snow Bowl branches off to the right. It is well posted. Follow the Snow Bowl road to the Sky Ride parking area at 14.4 miles *23.0 km*. Park there.

TRAILHEAD: You must buy a ticket and take the Sky Ride to the top. This means, of course, that you can only take this hike in the months when the Sky Ride is open.

DESCRIPTION: The Snow Bowl is a delightful place in summer, especially after there have been a few rains, when it smells fresh and alpine and everything is green and lovely. We like to take a leisurely half day, and our favorite time is in mid-October, when the aspen leaves are turning gold. We will often drive up, have lunch on the patio, then take the ride to the top, enjoying the superb views all along the way. We think that this is the best way to see the changing leaves in the fall, as you are treated to views that are simply unavailable any other way.

You will see the ski runs carved out of the forest as you travel on the lift, and you can imagine what the ski conditions are like here in the winter.

To make the hike, one gets off the ride and follows the signs there. The trail loops around from observation point to observation point and comes back to the lift. The trail is short and there is very little climb, but we have observed that many people find the trail a bit difficult because of the high elevation.

The Forest Service is making every effort to protect the San Francisco Peaks. Because the Peaks are so beautiful and so accessible, they are being loved to death. The **Humphreys Trail** and the Lookout Trail are the only legal trails on this part of the mountain. There is no access to Agassiz Peak or Humphreys Peak from the Lookout Trail and there is no camping allowed in the area.

Hours for the Skyride: Mid-June to Labor Day it runs 7 days a week, from 10:00 a.m. to 4:00 p.m. From Labor Day to Mid-October, it runs Friday, Saturday & Sunday only, from 10:00 a.m. to 4:00 p.m. The ride takes 25 minutes each way. Every rider must get off at the top.

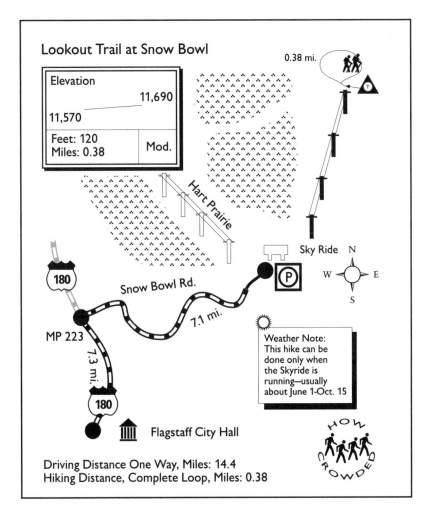

Mangum

Mack's Crossing

General Information
Location Map G4
Quayle Hill, Leonard Canyon USGS Maps
Coconino Forest Service Map

Driving Distance One Way: 71.4 miles *114.24 km* (Time 1.5 hours)
Access Road: All cars, Last 0.8 miles *1.28 km* good gravel roads
Hiking Distance One Way: 2.0 miles *3.2 km* (Time 1.5 hours)
How Strenuous: Moderate
Features: Beautiful pristine stream, Remote canyon, Historic road

NUTSHELL: This hike provides the easiest access to East Clear Creek, a perennial stream located in a deep, scenic canyon. It's a long drive, but there's a big payoff.

DIRECTIONS:
From Flagstaff City Hall Go:
     West, then south on Route 66 under the railroad overpass. See Access Map, page 10. At 0.5 miles *0.8 km*, go straight, on Milton Road. At 1.7 miles *2.72 km* you will reach a stoplight at Forest Meadows Street. Turn right here onto Forest Meadows and go one block to Beulah. Turn left on Beulah and follow it south. Beulah merges onto Highway 89A. At 2.4 miles *3.84 km* (MP 401.6), turn left onto the Lake Mary Road. Follow the Lake Mary Road (also known as FH 3) to its end at the junction with State Route 87, at 56.6 miles *90.6 km*. Turn left on Highway 87, a paved road, and follow it to the 70.6 mile *112.96 km* point (MP 304.5), where you turn right on FR 319. The USGS maps are misleading from this point, because the area which you will now travel has been subdivided since the maps were prepared. FR 319 is also known as Enchanted Lane. Drive in to the 70.8 mile *113.28 km* point, where you turn right on Green Ridge Drive. Take this to the 71.3 mile *114.08 km* point, where there is a stop sign. Turn right on Juniper Drive and then take an immediate left on Cedar Drive. At the 71.4 mile *114.24 km* point you will see Primitive Road FR 317. Park here. Warning: Do not try to drive FR 317. It is dangerous and impassable.

TRAILHEAD: The sign marking the beginning of FR 317. Although FR 317 cannot be driven, it makes a fine hiking trail.

DESCRIPTION: The road you will hike was built by pioneer John T. McMenamin, date unknown. You will see old culvert boxes made of hand-cut stone in places. The road was in use until W.W.II, but has been impassable for years. Even a good 4 x 4 could not drive it now. Don't drive it!

For its day, the road was a major project, requiring lots of blasting. The road makes two major curves as it descends into the canyon. The top half is not very interesting, but as you get nearer the bottom, you can see East Clear Creek and the lovely green riparian vegetation that lines it. From this point you will be enchanted.

When you reach the bottom, at the 1.75 mile *2.8 km* point, you will see a primitive road going off to your left just above creek level. Follow it another 0.25 miles *0.4 km* to an old campground area, where the trail will drop down to a nice sandy beach where there is a long deep swimming hole. There are tall, beautiful cliffs here, a very pleasant spot to cool your tootsies or go for a plunge. If you want to walk along the bottom of the creek, you must come prepared. It requires wading, and you will need a pair of shoes that you don't mind getting wet.

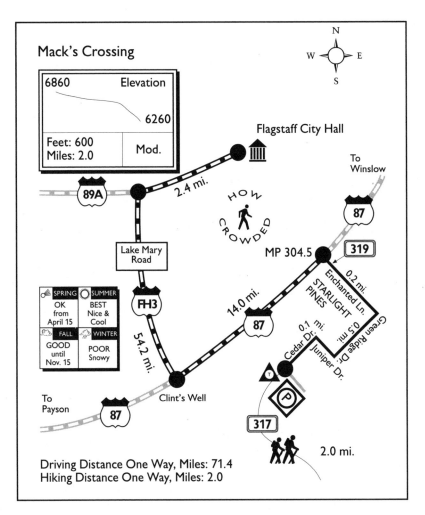

Mangum

Marshall Lake

General Information
Location Map F3
Flagstaff East, Lower Lake Mary USGS Maps
Coconino Forest Service Map

Driving Distance One Way: 14.45 miles *23.2 km* (Time 25 minutes)
Access Road: All cars, Last 1.2 miles *1.9 km* good unpaved road
Hiking Distance One Way: 5.8 miles *9.28 km* (Time 3 hours)
How Strenuous: Moderate
Features: Easy to reach, Beautiful canyon with cliffs and caves

NUTSHELL: Best as a two-car shuttle. This trail is a leg of The Arizona Trail. It starts on Anderson Mesa at scenic Marshall Lake, then crosses the mesa to descend into Walnut Canyon where you have good views, climbing out at Sandys Canyon to your second car.

DIRECTIONS:
From Flagstaff City Hall Go:
    West, then south on Route 66 under the railroad overpass. See Access Map, page 10. At 0.50 miles *0.8 km* you will reach a stoplight at a Y inter-section. Leave Route 66 here and go straight on Milton Road. At 1.70 miles *2.72 km* you reach the stoplight at Forest Meadows, where you turn right. At the next corner turn left on Beulah and follow it out of town. Beulah will connect onto Highway 89A. At the 2.4 miles *3.84 km* point (MP 401.6) you will see the turnoff to the Lake Mary Road to your left at the last stoplight in town. Turn and follow the Lake Mary Road to the 7.9 mile point *12.6 km* (MP 338.4)—just across a cattle guard—where you will see an unpaved road to your left with a big steel gate. Turn in here and go about 0.2 miles *0.32 km* to the parking lot for the **Sandys Canyon** Trailhead. Leave your second car here and have all hikers get into the first car. Back out on the Lake Mary Road, reset your odometer, turn left, and drive 4.1 miles *6.56 km* (MP 334.3) where you will see the paved Marshall Lake road to your left going uphill. Turn left and take it to the 5.35 mile *8.6 km* point, where you will see a gravel road to your left, FR 128. Turn left and take FR 128 to the 6.35 miles *10.2 km* point, where the road forks at Marshall Lake. Take the left fork and follow it to the 6.55 mile *10.5 km* point and park.

TRAILHEAD: At the parking place. Look sharp, for the road in this area goes on past the trailhead. All you have to guide you is a small wooden sign.

DESCRIPTION: The trail heads west across Anderson Mesa through a typ-ical pine forest. You will be on fairly level ground for the first part of the hike. At the 3.0 mile *4.8 km* point you cross two jeep roads and begin to descend into a canyon. At 3.5 miles *5.6 km* you will catch views of the San Francisco Peaks. Walnut Canyon will come into view, and you will walk along its rim northerly. There is a good viewpoint at the top of the canyon. At this place you are just about due south of your second car, but in order to get down into the canyon and back up the other side, you must loop around to the north. Walnut Canyon is quite impressive from here.

At 4.0 miles *6.4 km,* you begin a steep hike to the canyon bottom, passing beautiful cliffs. These have strong crossbedding lines and a rosy hue that shows in late afternoon light. You reach the bottom at 4.5 miles *7.2 km* where you meet the Sandys Canyon Trail. Turn left (S) on the Sandys Canyon Trail. In 0.50 miles *0.8 km* you come to a side canyon where you climb 200 feet to the top in 0.2 miles *0.32 km*. From the top, walk south along the rim to the second car, which is 0.6 miles *1.0 km* away.

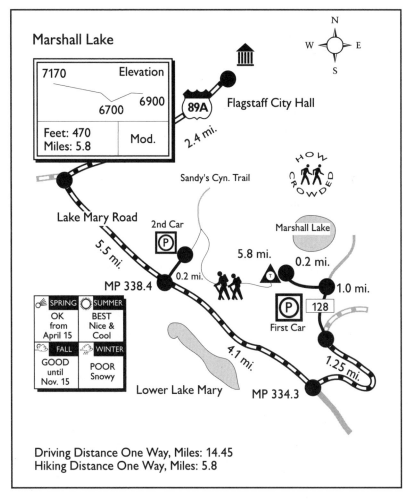

Mangum

Maxwell Trail #37

General Information
Location Map G4
Calloway Butte USGS Map
Coconino Forest Service Map

Driving Distance One Way: 57.8 miles *92.5 km* (Time 1.5 hours)
Access Road: All cars, Last 8.9 miles *14.24 km* good gravel road
Hiking Distance One Way: 0.80 miles *1.3 km* (Time 45 minutes)
How Strenuous: Hard
Features: Views, Beautiful pristine stream, Remote canyon

NUTSHELL: This is one of the few trails into West Clear Creek, a remote canyon 57.8 miles *92.5 km* southeast of Flagstaff. The hike is short but steep and very beautiful.

DIRECTIONS:
From Flagstaff City Hall Go:
    West, then south on Route 66 under the railroad overpass. See Access Map, pages 10-11. At 0.5 miles *0.8 km*, leave Route 66 and go straight on Milton Road. At 1.7 miles *2.72 km* you will reach a stoplight at Forest Meadows Street. Turn right onto Forest Meadows and go one block to Beulah. Turn left on Beulah and follow it south. Beulah merges onto Highway 89A. At 2.4 miles *3.84 km* (MP 401.6), turn left onto the Lake Mary Road. Follow the Lake Mary Road to the 48.9 mile *78.2 km* point (MP 297.7), where you turn right onto a gravel road, FR 81. Follow FR 81 to the 52.0 mile *83.2 km* point, where you reach a fork. Take the left fork, on FR 81E. Drive to the 55.8 mile *89.28 km* point, another fork. You will see a sign for the Maxwell Trail at the fork. Go left, to the 57.8 mile *92.5 km* point. Here you will find some campsites and a parking area. The road goes another 0.25 miles *0.4 km* but the last stretch is very rough. You may want to park at 57.8 miles *92.5 km* and walk the rest of the road.

TRAILHEAD: There is a sign at the parking area at the end of the road.

DESCRIPTION: West Clear Creek is a tributary of the Verde River. Its headwaters are on the uplands of the Mogollon Rim, where this hike takes place. Located in a remote area, West Clear Creek canyon cuts a course running from east to west. At its low end it joins the Verde River near Camp Verde.
    Getting to the trailhead you will drive through a pine forest that has plenty of open parks. These make good grazing areas for cattle and have been used for ranching ever since settlement of the country began in the late

1800s. The area has been thoroughly logged too, including some of the wild back country along FR 81.

When you get to the trailhead you can get glimpses into the canyon. These tell you that it is very steep. The walls of the canyon are a buff colored sandstone with pink tints. It looks a lot like **Walnut Canyon** near Flagstaff.

The trail takes you by a serpentine route to the canyon bottom where there is an unspoiled stream, living up to its name, Clear Creek. Along the way you walk right in the shadow of enormous cliffs.

The canyon at the bottom is rather narrow and there appear to be no developed trails along the streambed. It is possible to do some hiking at the bottom but this means boulder hopping and wading.

You will be enthralled by the quiet beauty of this canyon, especially at creekside, but look out for poison ivy and keep an eye out for snakes.

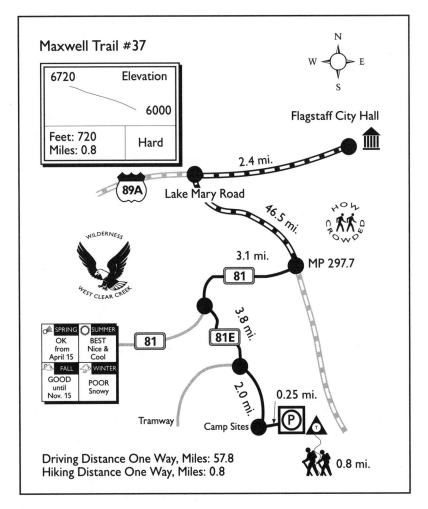

McMillan Mesa Trail

General Information
Location Map F3
Flagstaff East, Flagstaff West USGS Maps
Coconino Forest Service Map

Driving Distance One Way: 2.7 miles *4.32 km* (Time 10 minutes)
Access Road: All cars, All paved
Hiking Distance One Way: 1.75 miles *2.8 km* (Time 50 minutes)
How Strenuous: Easy
Features: Flagstaff Urban Trail System hike, Easy to reach, Nice mesa
with views over town

NUTSHELL: McMillan Mesa is an island between east and west Flagstaff. This trail takes you across the top of the mesa from west to east.

DIRECTIONS:
From Flagstaff City Hall Go:
East on Route 66 for 1.0 miles *1.6 km* to Switzer Canyon Road. Turn left (N) on Switzer Canyon Road and drive it to the 1.6 mile *2.56 km* point, where you turn right onto N. Turquoise Drive. Follow N. Turquoise Drive to the 1.9 mile *3.04 km* point, where you turn right onto E. Ponderosa Parkway. Follow E. Ponderosa Parkway to the 2.4 mile *3.84 km* point, where you turn left on N. Locust. At the 2.5 mile *4.0 km* point turn right on E. Apple. Follow E. Apple to the 2.6 mile *4.16 km* point, where you turn left on N. Hemlock. Take Hemlock to the 2.7 mile *4.32 km* point, where you will find a gravel parking place surrounded by boulders.

TRAILHEAD: At the parking place.

DESCRIPTION: From the parking place you will make a gradual easy climb to the top of the mesa, heading east.

The top of the mesa is a pleasant surprise. Although the town has built up around it, the city has owned McMillan Mesa for several years and most of it has been kept in pristine condition, with open grassy space in the middle of the mesa and trees around its perimeter.

You will hike over to the eastern rim of the mesa and then turn north and walk along the rim. From here there are nice views of the San Francisco Peaks, the Dry Lake Hills and Mount Elden. You can look down onto sections of East Flagstaff.

The trail proceeds northerly and is quite level, making an easy walk. As it approaches the place where Forest Drive cuts across the mesa near Buffalo Park, the trail turns east again and comes down off of the mesa. The last short leg of the hike is a fairly steep descent down to Coconino High School, and is very close to the road. Some hikers (like us) prefer to turn back at the head of the descent so that we can enjoy the peace and quiet of the mesa undistracted by the cars speeding up and down Cedar Hill.

The Flagstaff Urban Trails do a good job of providing a respite from the city, getting the hiker into the countryside to enjoy contact with nature. This trail is one of the best for a quick, relaxing stroll in the quiet of the grassland and forest.

Side Trail: Go past the first jeep road to your right, then take the second jeep trail, which you will come to at 0.3 miles *0.48 km*. After a rocky beginning, this road smooths out and takes you onto an unsurfaced trail that loops around a point on the mesa, from which you have good views over town. Total distance 1.5 miles *2.4 km*.

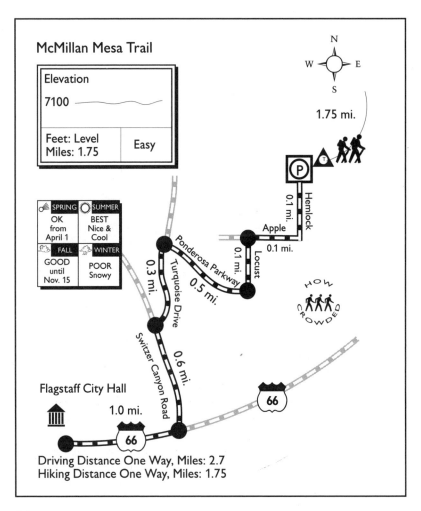

Mangum

Mormon Mountain Trail #58

General Information
Location Map G3
Mormon Lake & Mormon Mountain USGS Maps
Coconino Forest Service Map

Driving Distance One Way: 27.0 miles *43.2 km* (Time 30 minutes)
Access Road: All cars, Last 0.3 miles *0.48 km* good gravel road
Hiking Distance One Way: 2.25 miles *3.6 km* (Time 75 minutes)
How Strenuous: Moderate
Features: Beautiful forest

NUTSHELL: This hike takes you to the top of the dominant mountain on the landscape 27.0 miles *43.2 km* southeast of Flagstaff.

DIRECTIONS:
From Flagstaff City Hall Go:
    West, then south on Route 66 under the railroad overpass. At 0.5 miles *0.8 km*, leave Route 66 and go straight on Milton Road. See Access Map, page 10. At 1.7 miles *2.72 km* you will reach a stoplight at Forest Meadows Street. Turn right here onto Forest Meadows and go one block to Beulah. Turn left on Beulah and follow it south. Beulah merges onto Highway 89A. At 2.4 miles *3.84 km* (MP 401.6), turn left onto the Lake Mary Road. Follow the Lake Mary Road to the 23.0 mile *36.8 km* point (MP 323.6), where you turn right onto the Mormon Lake Road. At 26.7 miles *42.7 km*, on the Mormon Lake Road, you will see a sign marked "Dairy Springs Amphitheater". Turn right here and follow the gravel road and signs to the 27.0 miles *43.2 km* point, at the back of the Dairy Springs Campground.

TRAILHEAD: There is a large sign at the parking lot marking the trailhead.

DESCRIPTION: This area is used for cross-country skiing in the winter and you will see signs and triangles nailed to trees along the way marking the various ski trails. This is also the trailhead for **The Ledges** hike, which you will find described in this book.
    This trail is gentle and wide at the start. The path of the ski trail is marked by graphics and metal triangles nailed to trees. White triangles mark the path you want to follow on this hike. The trail climbs through a lovely forest of pine, oak and fir, with some aspen located near the top. From the 0.5 mile *0.8 km* point to the 1.0 mile *1.6 km* point the grade is very steep but the rest of the trail is not particularly steep for a mountain trail.
    Just before you reach the top, you pass through a very attractive old

growth forest, but the top is disappointing, as it has been logged. As with many mountains, reaching the top is deceptive. You come to a point where you clearly stop climbing and level out on what appears to be a crest only to find that it is merely a fold or a bench. This happens on this hike. You will not reach a point where you can definitely say to yourself, *"This is the top."*

One of the attractions of a mountain hike is being rewarded with great views at the summit of the mountain. Unfortunately that does not happen here because the trees are so tall and thick that they block your view. We stopped at the 2.25 mile *3.6 km* point but the path goes on, to a trailhead on FR 9466L, about 0.5 miles *0.8 km* from several transmission towers. These towers are eyesores and are out of sight if you stop at the 2.25 mile *3.6 km* point.

You will see a sign at the area where we recommend stopping that is marked *1.5 miles* to the start. The sign is short by 0.75 miles *1.2 km*.

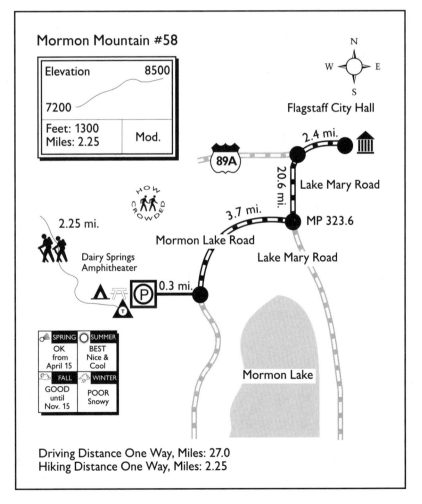

Mangum

Museum Nature Trail

General Information
Location Map F3
Flagstaff West USGS Map
Coconino Forest Service Map

Driving Distance One Way: 2.9 miles *4.64 km* (Time 15 minutes)
Access Road: All cars, All paved
Hiking Distance, Complete Loop: 0.5 miles *0.8 km* (Time 30 minutes)
How Strenuous: Easy
Features: Beautiful and informative nature trail

NUTSHELL: This nature trail is located adjacent to the Museum of Northern Arizona, 2.9 miles *4.64 km* north of Flagstaff. It takes you down into a pretty canyon and along a streambed where many plants of the area grow and are identified.

DIRECTIONS:
From Flagstaff City Hall Go:
   North on Humphreys Street a distance of 0.6 miles *1.0 km* to the stop sign at Columbus. See Access Map, page 10. Turn left here onto Columbus, which becomes Ft. Valley Road and Highway 180 as it goes north. At the 2.9 mile *4.64 km* point (MP 218.5) you will be at the entrance to The Museum of Northern Arizona. Turn left into its lot.

TRAILHEAD: To the left of the main entrance to the museum. It is marked as the *Rio de Flag Nature Trail*.

DESCRIPTION: If you have not visited The Museum of Northern Arizona, then by all means do so, as it is well worth seeing. These people really know their business and have a number of fascinating displays. It is a very good place to learn about northern Arizona. You will have to pay an admission fee at the door. This is the place to ask for a copy of the *Rio de Flag Nature Trail Guide*, a free booklet identifying the sights along the nature trail.
   At the beginning, you walk along the rim of a canyon. Below is the Rio de Flag, an intermittent stream that comes from the San Francisco Peaks, courses through Flagstaff and joins the Little Colorado River. The walls of the canyon here are about fifty feet high.
   At various points along the trail you will find numbered markers. These are keyed into the brochure. Plants and other objects of interest are identified. You might want to pay attention, because point #14 is poison ivy. At 0.1 mile *0.16 km* the trail dips down into the canyon and follows the streambed.

The streambed is overgrown with Arroyo Willows through most of the area. There is a little spring hidden in the willows, which flows in wet years and causes a stream to run along the bottom, an attractive feature.

You hike along the north bank; then the trail meanders across the stream, crosses it on a plank bridge, and loops back to the south. At point # 24, a fallen tree, the trail splits. You can go to your left across the creek and climb back to the top, returning to the starting point the way you came along the rim portion of the trail. Taken this way the trail is about 0.4 miles *0.64 km* long. It is more interesting to take the right fork instead, on a short spur called The Aspen Trail. This takes you up a flight of semi-steps to the top and over to a side canyon where a stand of aspens grows, a lovely spot.

From here the trail returns to the canyon floor and loops back to the trail junction, from where you go back to the trailhead on the first leg of the trail. Done this way, the hike is about 0.5 miles *0.8 km* long.

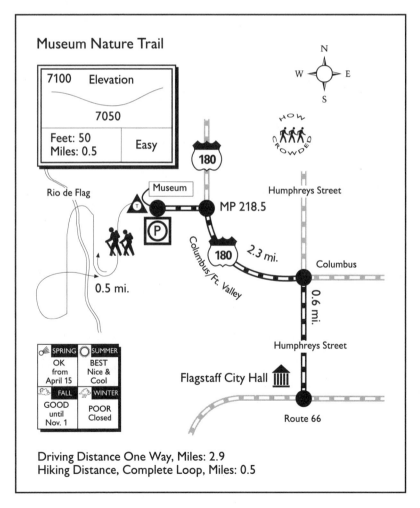

Mangum

O'Leary Peak

General Information
Location Map E4
O'Leary Peak & Sunset Crater West USGS Maps
Coconino Forest Service Map

Driving Distance One Way: 22.0 miles *35.2 km* (Time 30 minutes)
Access Road: All cars, Last 3.9 miles *6.24 km* medium condition dirt road
Hiking Distance One Way: 1.5 miles *2.4 km* (Time 1 hour)
How Strenuous: Hard
Features: Views, Volcanic field

NUTSHELL: This trail takes you to the top of a peak located about 22.0 miles *35.2 km* northeast of Flagstaff. The peak dominates the Sunset Crater area and gives great views as a reward for a fairly strenuous climb.

DIRECTIONS:
From Flagstaff City Hall Go:
East, then north on Highway 89. See Access Map, pages 10-11. At 16.4 miles *26.24 km* (MP 430.3) you will reach the entrance to Sunset Crater National Monument. Turn right on the road into Sunset Crater. This road is also known as FR 545. At 18.1 miles *29 km* you will reach a dirt road going to your left marked FR 545A. Turn onto FR 545A and follow it. You will soon come to O'Leary Peak and begin to climb it. The road was built to service a fire lookout tower located on the top, so it is wide and in good condition. At the 22.0 miles *35.2 km* point you will reach a gate. Park there.

TRAILHEAD: You will not see any trail signs. Walk up the road to the top.

DESCRIPTION: The gate is located at a saddle and is a good place to stop and begin this hike. You could drive all the way to the top if the gate is open, but what's the fun of that? The gate is open when a fire ranger is in the lookout tower. This means, roughly speaking, during the summer when fire danger is high. Except in bad weather the road may be driveable any time of year.

As you walk up the road you will find that it winds around the mountain. Because of this you get to see out in all directions as you go. You will have great views. At first you will see into the Sunset Crater National Monument and then into the Bonito Lava Flow, which is part of the monument. Both of these are very interesting.

At the top you will find the fire lookout tower. If the ranger is present, ask to go up. Most of these people are very cordial and enjoy a bit of company as a break from their lonely vigils. The views from the tower are truly splendid. If you are interested in volcanoes, this is a must. O'Leary Peak itself is an extinct volcano. You will see out over a huge volcanic field running for many miles north and east of the San Francisco Peaks. You will also have grand views of the Painted Desert.

The walkway to the fire tower is a strange one. Corrugated metal sections looking something like treads for a giant Caterpillar tractor have been joined together to make a deckway. This gives good footing when it is dry but we wouldn't want to walk it while it is wet. We certainly wouldn't want to be on it when lightning was flashing. The metal plates would be a powerful attractor of thunderbolts. Fire towers themselves are well grounded and you need not fear being struck while you are in one, though their metal skin will glow and sizzle and scare the hell out of you.

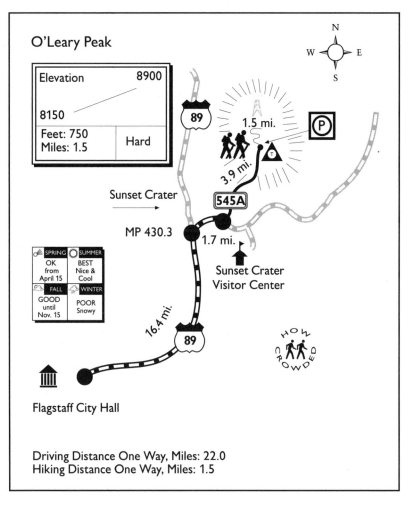

Mangum

Oak Creek Vista

General Information
Location Map F3
Mountainaire USGS Map
Coconino Forest Service Map

Driving Distance One Way: 13.7 miles *21.92 km* (Time 20 minutes)
Access Road: All cars, All paved
Hiking Distance, Complete Loop: 0.20 miles *0.32 km* (Time 30 minutes)
How Strenuous: Easy
Features: Sightseeing spot, Signs explaining flora and fauna

NUTSHELL: More of a stroll than a hike, this easy trail is located 13.7 miles *21.92 km* south of Flagstaff on the rim of Oak Creek Canyon.

DIRECTIONS:
From Flagstaff City Hall Go:
West, then south on Route 66 under the railroad overpass. At 0.5 miles *0.8 km*, leave Route 66 and go straight ahead on Milton Road. See Access Map, page 10. At 1.7 miles *2.72 km* you reach the intersection of Forest Meadows, where there is a traffic light. Here you turn right. You will see a sign for Highway 89A, which is the road you want. At the next corner turn left on Beulah and follow it out of town. Beulah will connect onto Highway 89A which is the road to Oak Creek Canyon and Sedona. At 13.7 miles *21.92 km* (MP 390) you will see the road to Oak Creek Vista to your left. Pull in on that road and park. It is paved and there are many parking spaces.

TRAILHEAD: The trail is paved. Pick it up from the parking lot at any point. It makes a loop, so you can join it anywhere you like and come back to where you started.

DESCRIPTION: The Forest Service has made an attractive viewpoint out of the old highway alignment, which used to go through here. On a busy weekend when the weather is good, you will find Native Americans selling jewelry on blankets they have laid out along the sides of the path.

The path follows around a bend in the canyon rim. Several standpoints have been established along the rim with signs at each point. The signs explain the history, biology, zoology and geology of the area. You will get some impressive views into the canyon depths from these standpoints.

The canyon is very deep below this part of the rim, probably one thousand feet or more. The area directly below the viewpoints is actually Pumphouse Wash, a tributary of Oak Creek Canyon, rather than Oak Creek Canyon itself. You will pass over Pumphouse Wash when you drive down through Oak Creek Canyon. It is spanned by the first big bridge you come to, just below the Sterling Springs Fish Hatchery.

At the canyon rim, the rock you see is a thick cap of gray basalt (lava) at the top with white or buff sandstone cliffs below the gray. The redrock for which Sedona is famous occurs in lower strata. The basalt cliff faces here are favorite spots for rope climbers. Look for them on the cliff faces to the east (on your left) on the same wall of the canyon you are standing on.

An interesting sight is Highway 89A corkscrewing around the toe of a fin as it works its way downhill and comes out onto the floor of Oak Creek Canyon.

This is a very gentle and satisfying walk, an easy stroll for Aunt Maude or other visiting relatives. Kids even seem to like it. It gives an appreciation of the size and depth of Oak Creek Canyon.

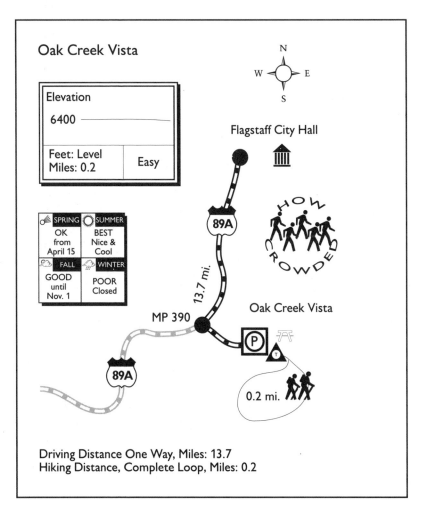

Oak Creek Vista

Elevation	
6400 ————	
Feet: Level Miles: 0.2	Easy

SPRING	SUMMER
OK from April 15	BEST Nice & Cool
FALL	WINTER
GOOD until Nov. 1	POOR Closed

N
W — E
S

Flagstaff City Hall

HOW CROWDED

89A

13.7 mi.

MP 390

Oak Creek Vista

P

89A

0.2 mi.

Driving Distance One Way, Miles: 13.7
Hiking Distance, Complete Loop, Miles: 0.2

Mangum

Old Caves Crater

General Information
Location Map E3
Sunset Crater West USGS Map
Coconino Forest Map

Driving Distance One Way: 9.6 miles *15.4 km* (Time 20 minutes)
Access Road: All cars, Last 0.5 miles *0.8 km* medium cinder road
Hiking Distance One Way: 0.5 miles *0.8 km* to top (Time 30 minutes)
How Strenuous: Moderate
Features: Indian ruins, Strange volcanic caves

NUTSHELL: Old Caves Crater is a cinder hill located east of Flagstaff. On top of the crater are a fascinating series of natural caves that were used as dwellings by the ancient Native Americans whom we call the Sinaguans. Note: As we write this in late 2000, this trail is still being planned and final decisions have not been made. By the time you make this hike, the official trail may be in place, in which case you can follow the signs. Until then, these directions should get you to the site.

DIRECTIONS:
From Flagstaff City Hall Go:
East on Route 66. Highway 89 runs concurrently with Route 66 as the highway goes through Flagstaff, so you will see road signs with both designations until 66 veers off in East Flagstaff. At 8.6 miles *13.76 km* (MP 422.9) you will be well out into the country. There you will see the Silver Saddle Road coming in from the right. Take this road (it is paved) to the 9.1 mile *14.56 km* point, where you will see unpaved FR 9148R taking off to the left toward a hill. Turn left on FR 9148R and take it to the 9.3 mile *14.88 km* point, where you will find a V fork. Take the right fork. At 9.5 miles *15.2 km* you will come to a small black cinder pit that has been used as a dump. Go past it uphill, bypassing the road to the left you will see. You will come to a place at about 9.6 miles *15.4 km* where the road splits into a V where it meets a cross road. Take the left fork and park just beyond the crossroads, where you will see a road going uphill. Park at the crossroads and do not try to drive farther, as the road is deep, loose black cinders beyond.

TRAILHEAD: There are no trail signs. The road becomes difficult to drive after the 9.6 mile *15.4 km* point, so you park and then walk the road.

DESCRIPTION: Old Caves Crater has been known since the first Anglo settlers came into Flagstaff, but it has not received much publicity. This is hard to understand, because it is a fascinating site.

You will walk up a road that has been closed to vehicular travel to the top of the hill, emerging on the south face of the crater. On top you will find a number of caves that appear to have been formed by gas bubbles passing through red lava. These bubbles formed hollows and then burst in such a way that openings to the caves were created.

The site has been thoroughly pothunted and rockfalls have closed the entrances to several of the caves. This was a major Sinagua pueblo, occupied about 1200 A.D. One wonders where these people got their water, as there is none visible. Maybe conditions have changed over the centuries or there is a hidden spring or natural tank nearby.

You will find a footpath over to the higher north knob of the crater. It is an easy 0.2 mile *0.32 km* walk, worth doing to enjoy the views. The total hike, allowing for exploring both knobs, is about 1.5 miles *2.4 km*.

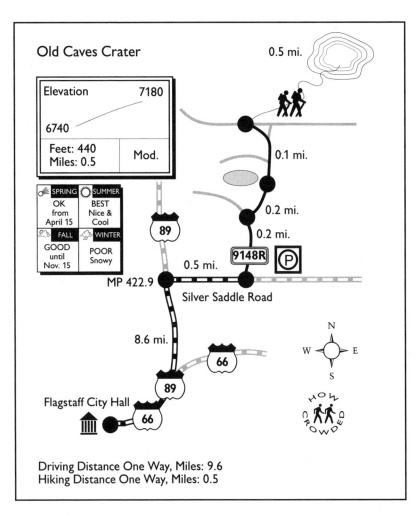

Mangum

Old Lowell Observatory Road

Driving Distance One Way: 1.0 mile *1.6 km* (Time 5 minutes)
Access Road: All cars, All paved
Hiking Distance One Way: 1.5 miles *2.4 km* (Time 45 minutes)
How Strenuous: Moderate
Features: Beautiful forest, Nicely maintained trail, Extremely easy access

NUTSHELL: This urban trail located in west Flagstaff is a moderate, pleasant walk to the top of Observatory Mesa, a long ridge that forms the western boundary of the town.

DIRECTIONS:
From Flagstaff City Hall Go:
    West on Route 66 a block, where Route 66 curves left. See Access Map, page 10. Go straight on Santa Fe Avenue—do not turn left under the overpass. At 0.50 miles *0.8 km*, turn right on Toltec Street. At 1.0 miles *1.6 km* you will see the trail by a stone hut to your left. There is no parking to the left. Turn right into a paved parking lot near the ball fields. Park there.

TRAILHEAD: The trail is unmistakable. It is a graded and graveled path marked by boulders and signs.

DESCRIPTION: This trail is part of the City of Flagstaff Urban Trail System.
    As you walk the trail, look to your left at the last line of boulders just before you start up a small side canyon. The dirt road that you will see there is the original road. Then you will walk up a little canyon that is pleasant and peaceful with a nice stand of big old pine trees, then top out on the mesa.
    At 0.50 miles *0.8 km* you will reach a fence marking private property. The trail turns left at the fence and goes up the shoulder of Mars Hill. At 0.7 miles *1.12 km* you reach a point where the old road to Lowell Observatory turns left. There are signs here. Go straight ahead. You will climb some more, to the 0.8 mile *1.28 km* point, where you top out. From there the trail is level to the end. The trail terminates at a road junction at 1.5 miles *2.4 km*, on top of Observatory Mesa.
    The old road you follow for the first 0.7 miles *1.12 km* was built by the Town of Flagstaff about 1894 as part of the town's inducements to get Dr. Percival Lowell to locate his observatory in Flagstaff. Lowell was checking

out several sites and had narrowed the list to a few contenders. Tucson was another hot prospect. Lowell sent scientist A. E. Douglass, who later was famed for developing the science of dendrochronology (tree ring dating), to investigate Flagstaff. The town fathers wined and dined Douglass and made such a favorable impression on him that he told Lowell Flagstaff was the place. The boosters promised Lowell that he could have his choice of ten acres of land free anywhere in the town and that the town would also build a road to the site for him. Lowell picked land at the top of the hill and the town obligingly built this road. The road has been relocated twice since then.

Lowell Observatory has been a magnificent asset for Flagstaff, crowned by the discovery there of the planet Pluto in 1930 by Clyde Tombaugh, who was working out some of Lowell's old theories. Lowell died in 1916 in his mansion (since torn down) at the observatory.

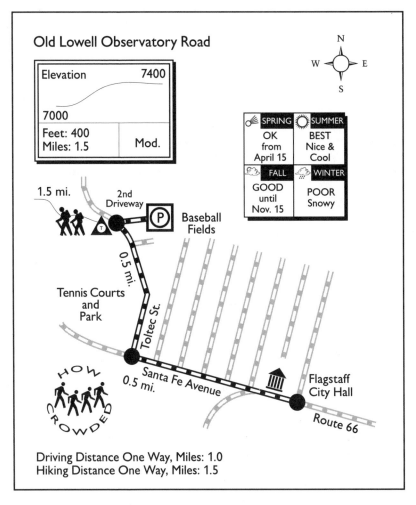

Mangum

Oldham Trail #1

General Information
Location Map E3
Flagstaff East & West, Humphreys Peak & Sunset Crater W. USGS Maps
Coconino Forest Service Map

Driving Distance One Way: 2.3 miles *3.7 km* (Time 10 minutes)
Access Road: All cars, All paved
Hiking Distance One Way: 3.3 miles *5.28 km* (Time 1 hour 45 minutes)
How Strenuous: Moderate
Features: Views

NUTSHELL: This trail is part of the Mt. Elden trail system, taking you from Buffalo Park through a beautiful forest.

DIRECTIONS:
From Flagstaff City Hall Go:
   North on Humphreys Street to the stoplight at 0.60 miles *1.0 km*. See Access Map, page 10. Turn right here onto Columbus Avenue and go one block east to the next stop sign, at Beaver Street. Turn left onto Beaver Street and go up the hill. At the 1.0 mile *1.6 km* point you will reach Forest Avenue. Turn right on Forest and follow it over a hill. On top of the hill, at 1.9 miles *3.04 km*, you will find Gemini Drive. Turn left onto it and at 2.3 miles *3.7 km* you will come to Buffalo Park. Park at Buffalo Park.

TRAILHEAD: There are trail signs and a map at the gate.

DESCRIPTION: This popular trail is easy to reach, scenic and fun, so many people use it.
   Buffalo Park is an open plain extending back 0.5 miles *0.8 km* from the gate. In the 1960s it was run as a sort of living zoo but failed due to lack of funds. You can see some vestiges of this operation near the entrance, where a welcoming arch and buffalo statue survive. Lately the City of Flagstaff has turned the area into a public park for joggers and walkers.
   Oldham Trail No. 1 starts at the fence at the rear of the park. To reach it, walk straight back on the main footpath from the gate, which is wide and graveled, until you reach the natural gas substation and the back fence, at 0.5 miles *0.8 km*. Here the footpath goes through the fence, narrows and becomes the Oldham Trail.
   The trail was originally developed by an old timer named Earl Oldham, who worked as a ranger for the Forest Service, was a member of the Coconino County Board of Supervisors and did sheep ranching on the side.

At. 1.25 miles *2.0 km* you will reach the junction of the Oldham Trail and the **Pipeline Trail**. The two trails are marked. If you just want a simple leisurely stroll, this is a good place to turn back. Up to this point the trail is gentle with little change in elevation. From here, the trail begins to climb.

After you pass through Buffalo Park, you will be in a nice pine forest. Later—higher—the forest becomes more interesting as you hike through stands of oak, aspen, fir and spruce. Lava cliffs and groups of boulders big as boxcars that have tumbled from the cliffs add visual interest.

The Oldham Trail ends at 3.3 miles *5.28 km*, where it meets the Elden Lookout Road, FR 557, at the cattle guard. Just before the road you will pass spectacular basalt cliffs loved by rock climbers.

A nice way to enjoy this hike is to use two cars. Take both to Buffalo Park. Then everybody gets into one of the cars and drives it to the parking area beyond the cattle guard, a point 2.7 miles *4.32 km* up the Elden Lookout Road. This way you hike mostly downhill.

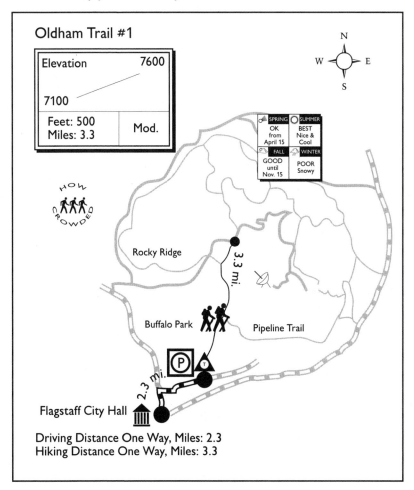

Mangum

Overland Road

General Information
Location Map F1
Davenport Hill & Williams South USGS Maps
Kaibab (Williams District) Forest Service Map

Driving Distance One Way: 41.3 miles *66.08 km* (Time 60 minutes)
Access Road: All cars, Last 0.9 miles *1.44 km* good gravel road
Hiking Distance One Way: 5.5 miles *8.8 km* (Time 3.0 hours)
How Strenuous: Moderate
Features: Historic road, Cabin ruins

NUTSHELL: This hike takes you over a portion of the 1863 Overland Road south of Williams.

DIRECTIONS:
From Flagstaff City Hall Go:
     West, then south on Route 66 under the railroad overpass. See Access Map, page 10. Follow Route 66 when it turns right at the second stoplight. In about five miles *8.0 km* you will merge onto I-40 West and stay on it to the 30.3 miles *48.5 km* point, the Williams Exit, #165. Take that exit and at the stop sign go left to Williams. Go into town on Railroad Avenue to the 32.9 mile point *52.6 km* where you will find Fourth Street. Turn left on Fourth Street. As it leaves town its name changes to the Perkinsville Road (County 73). Stay on this road to the 40.4 miles *64.6 km* point, where you turn left onto FR 139. Take FR 139 to the 41.3 mile *66.08 km* point, where you will see a parking area to your left. It is paved and fenced.

TRAILHEAD: You will see cairns marking the trail next to the road. Go east.

DESCRIPTION: Gold was discovered in Prescott in 1863 and with the ensuing gold rush there came a clamor for a north-south road into the gold fields. The sensible way to approach this was to use the 1859 Beale Road (which ran east-west) as far as possible and then branch off of it to the south. This was done and the resulting route was called the Overland Road. After the railroad arrived in 1882, few people used the Overland Road and it was abandoned.

     You will find that the path of the Overland on the route of this hike is marked with posts, cairns and blazes. Every quarter of a mile there is a brass cap. The old stage coaches could not handle steep grades, so the route is as level as the trailblazers could make it. Increases in elevation are gradual and most of the time the trail hugs the 7000 foot contour line.

At 2.5 miles *4.0 km* you will come to a clearing where you will find the ruins of a cabin. This was a stage coach station called Big Spring. The spring forms a scenic pool and flows through a lovely canyon behind the cabin. The trail swerves around the head of the canyon, crosses it and then comes back and begins a gradual descent.

At 4.25 miles *6.8 km* you come upon a big meadow with an old barn, a railroad-tie cabin and a pond. This is the historic Whiting Ranch. There is a modern facility nearby. From the Whiting Ranch walk to the end of the meadow, where the trail intersects FR 109. We stop the trail here for a nice day hike. The entire Overland Road was eighty-five miles long, of which thirty miles have been traced through the Kaibab Forest, with parking spots at suitable entry points. The Kaibab Forest Service has done a nice job since 1995 in improving the access to this historic road. We recommend doing this as a two-car hike, parking one at the beginning and one at the end.

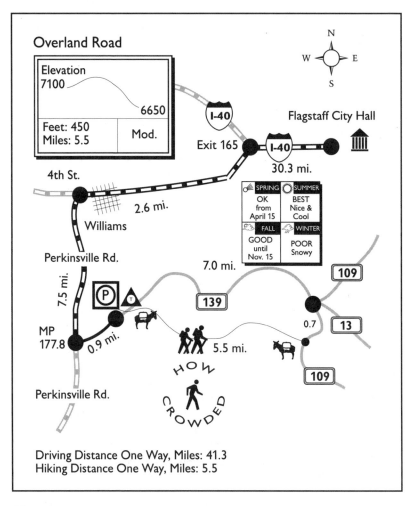

Mangum

Pipeline Trail #42

General Information
Location Map F3
Flagstaff East and Flagstaff West USGS Maps
Coconino Forest Service Map

Driving Distance One Way: 2.3 miles *3.7 km* (Time 10 minutes)
Access Road: All cars, All paved
Hiking Distance One Way: 4.0 miles *6.4 km* (Time 2 hours)
How Strenuous: Moderate
Features: Views

NUTSHELL: This trail is part of a trail system developed by the Forest Service around Mt. Elden. Located just north of Flagstaff, this moderate hike takes you around the base of Mt. Elden to connect with the Elden Lookout trailhead in East Flagstaff.

DIRECTIONS:
From Flagstaff City Hall Go:
   North on Humphreys Street to the stoplight at 0.60 miles *1.0 km.* See Access Map, page 10. Turn right here onto Columbus Avenue and go one block east to the next stop sign, which is at Beaver Street. Turn left onto Beaver Street and go up the hill. At the 1.0 mile *1.6 km* point you will reach Forest Avenue. Turn right on Forest and follow it over a hill. On top of the hill, at 1.9 miles *3.0 km*, you will find Gemini Drive. Turn left onto it and at 2.3 miles *3.7 km* you will come to Buffalo Park. Park in the parking lot.

TRAILHEAD: There are trail signs and a map at the gate in the parking lot fence.

DESCRIPTION: The Forest Service has developed a trail system around the Dry Lake Hills\Mt. Elden areas in Flagstaff and this trail connects with others in that system. You will find trail information at the trailhead.
   Buffalo Park is an open plain extending back about a half mile *0.8 km* from the gate. In the 1960s it was run as a sort of living zoo but failed due to lack of funds. You can see some vestiges of this operation near the entrance, where a welcoming arch and buffalo statue survive. Lately the City of Flagstaff has turned the area into a public park for joggers and walkers.
   Start by taking the main jogging path which goes straight back to the fence at the rear of the park. It is wide and graveled, until you reach the natural gas substation and the rear fence, at 0.50 miles *0.8 km*. Here the trail goes through the fence, narrows and becomes the **Oldham Trail No. 1**.
   Hike the Oldham Trail No. 1 to the 1.25 miles *2.0 km* point where you

will reach the junction of the Oldham Trail and the Pipeline Trail. The two trails are marked. Turn right here onto the Pipeline Trail.

Although the trail comes very close to some houses as you get into East Flagstaff, it feels quite remote in places. At about the 1.75 mile *2.8 km* point there is a side trail going to the left. Someone has painted "Satan's Cave" on a boulder there. It is a short jaunt over to the cave and worth taking a look.

The Pipeline Trail comes close to many interesting boulder formations, with intriguing caves and crannies. Mt. Elden is essentially a giant lava pile and the lava did some interesting things as it settled and cooled.

The trail terminates at a place where it links with the **Elden Lookout Trail** in East Flagstaff. A good way to do this hike is to use a two-car shuttle. Park one car at Buffalo Park and the other at the Elden Lookout trailhead parking lot in East Flagstaff.

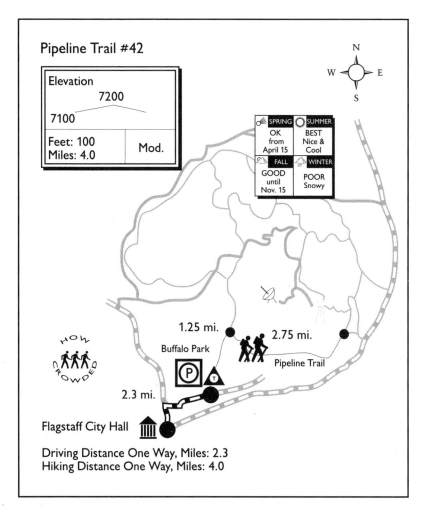

Pipeline Trail #42

Elevation
7200
7100
Feet: 100
Miles: 4.0
Mod.

SPRING	SUMMER
OK from April 15	BEST Nice & Cool
FALL	WINTER
GOOD until Nov. 15	POOR Snowy

1.25 mi.
Buffalo Park
2.75 mi.
Pipeline Trail
HOW CROWDED
2.3 mi.
Flagstaff City Hall

Driving Distance One Way, Miles: 2.3
Hiking Distance One Way, Miles: 4.0

Mangum

Pivot Rock Canyon & Wildcat Spring

General Information
Location Map G4
Pine, Calloway Butte USGS Maps
Coconino Forest Service Map

Driving Distance One Way: 65.7 miles *105.12 km* (Time 1.25 hours)
Access Road: All cars, Last 3.35 miles *5.36 km* good dirt road
Hiking Distance One Way: **Pivot Rock**: 1.5 mi. *2.4 km* (1 hour), **Wildcat**:
     1.4 mi. *2.24 km* (1 hour)
How Strenuous: Both hikes are Easy
Features: Beautiful pristine stream, Rain forest, Remote canyon

NUTSHELL: Starting from the same point, both hikes take you along hidden canyons located in the Mogollon Rim area, just south of Clint's Well. You follow little streams through lush canyons.

DIRECTIONS:
From Flagstaff City Hall Go:
     West, then south on Route 66, under the railroad overpass. At 0.5 miles *0.8 km*, go straight on Milton Road. See Access Map, page 10. At 1.7 miles *2.72 km* you will reach a stoplight at Forest Meadows Street. Turn right here onto Forest Meadows and go one block to Beulah. Turn left on Beulah and follow it south. Beulah merges onto Highway 89A. At 2.4 miles *3.84 km* (MP 401.6), turn left onto the Lake Mary Road. Follow the Lake Mary Road (also known as FH 3) to its end at the junction with State Route 87, 56.6 miles *90.6 km*. Turn right here on Highway 87, a paved road, and follow it to the 62.35 mile *99.76 km* point (MP 284.7), where you turn right on FR 616, which is posted. FR 616 is surfaced with gravel and is a good road. Follow it to the 65.7 mile *105.12 km* point, where you will see a little campground downhill to your right. Turn down into this and park.

TRAILHEAD: Pivot Rock: At the far end the campground, notice a blocked road. This is the entrance to the trail. **Wildcat**: Just before you drive down into the campground, there is a closed road to your left. This closed road is the Wildcat Spring trail .

DESCRIPTION: Pivot Rock: (This was the site of a big CCC camp in the 1930s). You hike along a closed road through a green and wonderful canyon. The road ends and a foot path goes down to creek level. There is water in the creek most of the time. At the end of a mile *1.6 km*, the plant life thins out. You will reach the end of the hike at 1.5 miles *2.4 km*, where you will find the ruins of a log cabin on a bench of land. The trail continues, but becomes less interesting. We followed it down to the 2.5 mile *4.0 km* point, before deciding that ending the hike at the cabin was perfect.

Wildcat Spring: As you enter this little canyon, you will be walking on a closed road. In 0.15 miles, *0.24 km*, you will reach a fork. Go downhill on the lower, dimmer road. You will soon see another road going uphill to your right. Stay down on the canyon bottom, where you will pick up a foot path at stream level.

For the next 0.5 miles *0.8 km*, you will walk through a beautiful little rain forest—yes, it's possible, even in dry Arizona. At the 0.7 mile *1.12 km* point, the foot path merges with the old road and you will walk the road to the end. You will reach Wildcat Spring at the 1.4 mile *2.24 km* point. There was a sign for the spring when we made the hike. It is to your left, uphill a bit, and is channeled into a concrete box.

The spring is the place to stop, though the road goes a bit farther.

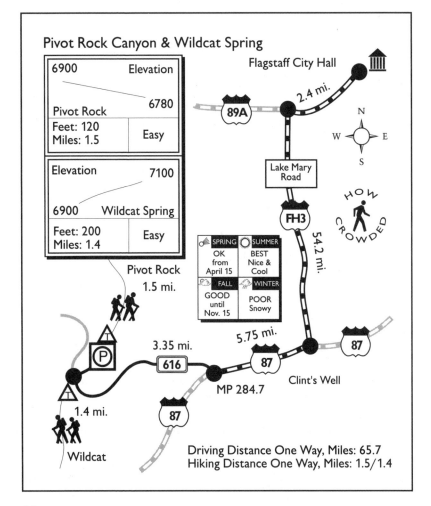

Point Trail

General Information
Location Map G4
Pine, Calloway Butte USGS Maps
Coconino Forest Service Map

Driving Distance One Way: 78.25 miles *125.2 km* (Time 1.5 hours)
Access Road: All cars, Last 6.75 miles *10.8 km* good dirt roads
Hiking Distance One Way: 0.5 miles *0.8 km* (Time 40 minutes)
How Strenuous: Hard, due to steepness, rocks
Features: Beautiful pristine stream, Remote canyon

NUTSHELL: This hike takes you into the scenic canyon through which West Clear Creek flows, an unspoiled Shangri-La.

DIRECTIONS:
From Flagstaff City Hall Go:
     West, then south on Route 66, under the railroad overpass. At 0.5 miles *0.8 km*, go straight on Milton Road. See Access Map, page 10. At 1.7 miles *2.72 km* you will reach a stoplight at Forest Meadows Street. Turn right here onto Forest Meadows and go one block to Beulah. Turn left on Beulah and follow it south, where it merges onto Highway 89A. At 2.4 miles *3.84 km* (MP 401.6), turn left onto the Lake Mary Road. Follow the Lake Mary Road (also known as FH 3) to its end at the junction with State Route 87, 56.6 miles *90.6 km* (MP 290.4). Turn right here onto paved Highway 87, and follow it to the 68.4 mile *109.44 km* point (MP 278.3), where you turn right on paved FR 260. Follow FR 260 to the 71.5 mile *114.4 km* point (MP 249), where you turn right on gravel road FR 144. Drive FR 144 to the 73.3 mile *117.28 km* point, its junction with gravel FR 149. Turn left on FR 149 and take it to the 74.55 mile *119.28 km* point, the junction with gravel FR 142. Turn right on FR 142 and follow it to the 75.55 mile *120.88 km* point, where you turn left on gravel FR 142E. Follow FR 142E to the 78.25 mile *125.2 km* point, the parking area at the tip of the Point. On this last leg you will see a couple of secondary roads branching to the left. Stay on the best road, which is graveled.

TRAILHEAD: At the NW corner of the parking area. There is no trail sign, but there is a trail register notebook in a little stand.

DESCRIPTION: The **Tramway**, **Maxwell** and **Willow Crossing** trails all go into West Clear Creek not too far away, but this trail is different. At the beginning it looks like an ordinary trail, but in a few yards it angles into a side canyon and then follows the canyon to the bottom—no zigzags, no moderation of the grade, just hiking down the bed of the canyon, a sharp drop. You must pick your way from boulder to boulder, watching every step carefully, grateful for trees that offer a handhold. So, although the mileage is short, the hike is as strenuous as one that is much longer.

Although it is difficult, the trail is very interesting. The canyon is moist and supports a cover of mixed flora—everything from flowers to ferns to fir trees. At the end you will emerge onto the rocky bank of the creek.

While all of the West Clear Creek hikes take you to beautiful sites, we think that this is the most scenic, a lush tranquil scene framed by high colorful walls. There is good exploring up or down the creek. Upstream you will come to a point in 1.5 miles *2.4 km* where you can see the Tramway and Maxwell trails on the other side. Downstream there is an area with a plant-hung undercut ledge fronted by a deep pool. If you want to explore, bring shoes that you can wade in, as you will have to cross the creek several times.

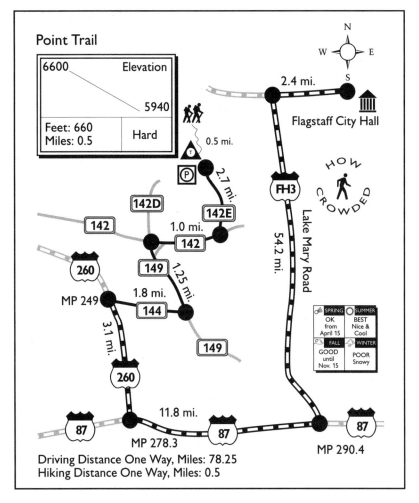

Mangum

Pumpkin Trail #39

General Information
Location Map E2
Kendrick Peak, Moritz Ridge and Wing Mt. USGS Maps
Kaibab Forest Service Map

Driving Distance One Way: 25.5 miles *40.8 km* (Time 1 hour)
Access Road: All cars, Last 11.1 miles *17.8 km* good gravel road
Hiking Distance One Way: 5.5 miles *8.8 km* (Time 4.0 hours)
How Strenuous: Hard
Features: Ten thousand foot peak, Views

NUTSHELL: This trail winds to the summit of Kendrick Peak for great views. Horrible fire damage in 2000 altered it, causing closure for the balance of the year. Call 800-863-0546 for current trail conditions.

DIRECTIONS:
From Flagstaff City Hall Go:
    North on Humphreys Street for 0.60 miles *1.0 km*. See Access Map, page 10. Turn left at the stoplight onto Columbus Avenue, which becomes Highway 180 and drive 180 to the 14.4 miles *23.04 km* point (MP 230.1), where you turn left on a a gravel road, FR 245, and follow it to the 17.4 mile *27.84 km* point where it intersects FR 171. Turn right on FR 171 and follow it to the 24.6 mile *39.36 km* point, where you will see a sign for the Pumpkin Trail. Turn right on the drive to the trailhead, which you will reach at 25.5 miles *40.8 km*. Park in the parking area.

TRAILHEAD: Well marked with a sign at the parking area.

DESCRIPTION: Unlike the nearby **Kendrick Mt. Trail**, which was made to provide access to a fire lookout tower by the Forest Service and was consequently engineered and built with an eye to making best use of the terrain, the Pumpkin Trail seems to have been built by and for sheepherders and just grew like topsy. It is rough and has some very sharp grades.
    From the parking lot you will climb along the side of a canyon for 1.0 miles *1.6 km* to a fence. Here you will turn right and begin going up a ridge. At 1.4 miles *2.24 km* you will meet the **Connector Trail** coming over from the **Bull Basin Trail.**
    Not far from this intersection you will climb into a more interesting forest, with many varieties of conifers and lots of aspens. The trail gets very rocky and rough in this stretch. At about 3.0 miles *4.8 km* you will find breaks in the forests punctuated by meadows. The meadows provide good viewpoints, though the footing can be hard due to the fact that the grass in

the meadows hides the rocks along the trail.

From the 4.0 mile *6.4 km* point the trail gets really steep and is hard going. You will reach the ruins of a log cabin at 5.0 miles *8.0 km* located at the edge of the biggest meadow. The slope of this meadow falls away so steeply that they must have issued spiked shoes to the sheep.

Beyond this meadow the trail becomes primitive and even harder, clawing its way to the top just below the base of the lookout tower at 5.5 miles *8.8 km*. Go on up to the tower for its superlative views.

This is a much harder trail than the Kendrick Mt. Trail or Bull Basin Trail. We think Bull Basin is the best of the three trails to the top, with the Kendrick Mountain Trail being next best.

A ranch near the trailhead is named Pumpkin Center, and there was a time when pumpkins were grown there.

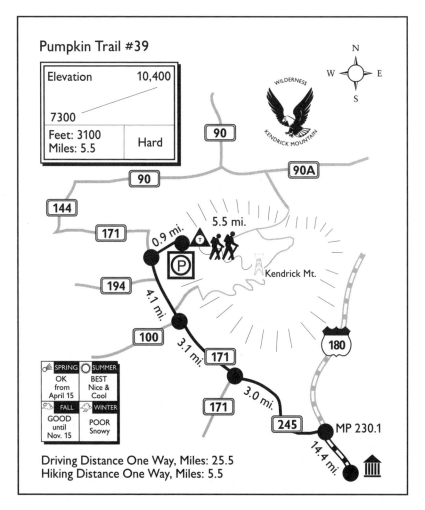

Mangum

Railroad Tunnel Trail

General Information
Location Map G4
Dane Canyon, Kehl Ridge USGS Maps
Coconino Forest Service Map

Driving Distance One Way: 78 miles *125 km* (Time 2 hours)
Access Road: All cars, Last 12.2 miles *19.5 km* good dirt road
Hiking Distance One Way: 0.6 miles *1.0 km* (40 minutes)
How Strenuous: Moderate
Features: Beautiful Mogollon Rim, Historic railroad tunnel

NUTSHELL: After enjoying a portion of the Rim Drive, you will take a refreshing hike to see a historic relic, an unfinished railroad tunnel boring into the side of the Mogollon Rim.

DIRECTIONS:
From Flagstaff City Hall Go:
    West, then south on Route 66, under the railroad overpass. At 0.5 miles *0.8 km*, go straight on Milton Road. See Access Map, page 10. At 1.7 miles *2.72 km* you will reach a stoplight at Forest Meadows Street. Turn right here onto Forest Meadows and go one block to Beulah. Turn left on Beulah and follow it south. Beulah merges onto Highway 89A. At 2.4 miles *3.84 km* (MP 401.6), turn left onto the Lake Mary Road. Follow the Lake Mary Road (also known as FH 3) to its end at the junction with State Route 87, 56.6 miles *90.6 km*. Turn right here on Highway 87, a paved road, and follow it to the 65.8 mile *105.3 km* point MP 280, where you turn left on FR 300, which is posted. FR 300 is surfaced with gravel and is a good road. Follow it to the 78 mile *125 km* point, where you will see a monument to the Battle of Big Dry Wash. Park near the monument.

TRAILHEAD: Across the road from the battle monument.

DESCRIPTION: You will see the trail running beneath the power line that goes down a canyon. On the way down the trail, be sure to leave the power line at the second pole and move to your left, where you will find an old service road that was built for the purpose of tunnel construction.
    The hike is steep, but the footing is not bad. It is short. The trail goes down about 0.33 miles *0.53 km*, and then makes a sharp turn to your left, going uphill. There were markers for the trail when we took the hike.
    After you make the turn, the trail doubles back uphill, going up 0.25 miles *0.4 km* to the tunnel, which sits on a scenic shelf of land. In front of the mouth are the remains of a hut built of sandstone slabs, and evidence of

the tunnel construction all around. The sight of the tunnel is quite a shock, as it sits in isolation, far from the world. The first reaction of any visitor is to ask, "How in the world did this get here?"

The tunnel was part of an 1885 plan to build a railroad from Flagstaff to Globe. Rim area residents were recruited to dig this tunnel in advance of the rails, taking their wages in stock rather than cash. After reaching Mormon Lake, the bankrupt railroad was abandoned, leaving this tunnel high and dry, miles away from anything, and sorrowful crews holding worthless paper.

The Rim Drive is a scenic must for northern Arizona—highly recommend. To take it continue east on FR 300 after the hike. The entire drive is 34.5 miles *55.2 km.* The drive ends at Highway 260, a good paved highway, where you turn right and go to Payson. From Payson you can return to Flagstaff via Camp Verde or on Highway 87. A detour to the Tonto Natural Bridge is well worthwhile. Take a long full day to do all this.

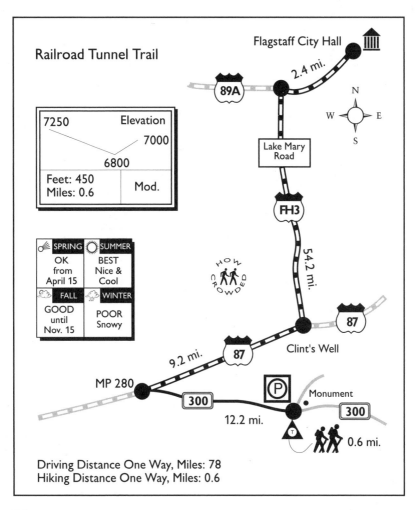

Mangum

Red Butte

General Information
Location Map C2
Red Butte USGS Map
Kaibab (Tusayan) Forest Service Map

Driving Distance One Way: 63.6 miles *102 km* (Time 90 minutes)
Access Road: All cars, Last 2.7 miles *4.3 km* good dirt road
Hiking Distance One Way: 1.2 miles *1.92 km* (Time 45 minutes)
How Strenuous: Moderate
Features: Unusual formation, Views of Grand Canyon country

NUTSHELL: This mountain stands alone near the Grand Canyon. A good trail makes a moderate climb worthwhile to enjoy the view.

DIRECTIONS:
From Flagstaff City Hall Go:
   North on Humphreys Street 0.60 miles *1.0 km* to a stoplight. See Access Map, page 10. Go left on Columbus Avenue and follow the curve north. Street signs will show the street first as Ft. Valley Road, then Highway 180. This is a major road to the Grand Canyon. At 50.4 miles *80.64 km* (MP 265.8), you will intersect Highway 64, coming out of Williams, at a place called Valle. Go right at this junction. At 60.9 miles *97.44 km* (MP 224), you will see a dirt road to the right. Turn right here. On our last trip there were no signs. At 62.3 miles *99.7 km*, you turn left. At 63.2 miles *101.1 km*, you go right. At 63.6 miles *102 km* you will be at the parking lot.

TRAILHEAD: This is a marked, maintained trail with signs.

DESCRIPTION: Although it is a small mountain for Northern Arizona, Red Butte dominates its area. Geologists speculate that because it had a thicker lava cap than the surrounding lands had, everything else eroded away, leaving Red Butte at the original ground level.
   On the south side of Red Butte you can see some red cliffs with white cliffs above them, capped by gray lava rock. These strata form interesting layers. The red stone is the Moenkopi formation, which abounds in Flagstaff. The county courthouse in Flagstaff was built of the stone in the 1890s, as were many other landmark Flagstaff buildings of that era. There was even a lively turn-of-the-century sandstone quarrying industry in Flagstaff to exploit the stone.
   The trail was built in 1976-77 and is well designed. Rather than trying to go straight up the mountain, it zigzags. The climb is fairly gradual at first, then gets steep going to the top. The trail takes you to the edge of the red

cliffs and then veers away from them.

The area at the top is small, about four acres, and bald, so that there are good views all around. Unfortunately, you can't see into the Grand Canyon—you can only see the cliffs of the North Rim and the line of the South Rim. The best views are to the SE, where you see the San Francisco Peaks and a long line of lesser mountains and hills. The land around Red Butte is a flat plain and the vegetation on it is sparse. You can see signs of cattle ranching activity. Decades ago when the sheep raising business was at its zenith, there would be many hundreds of sheep quartered on this plateau.

There is a fire lookout on top, and you can climb it and walk along its deck for the best views. Twenty minutes spent looking at the landscape from there is a better geology lesson than many hours in the classroom.

There is a helicopter landing pad at the top if you are a member of the jet set.

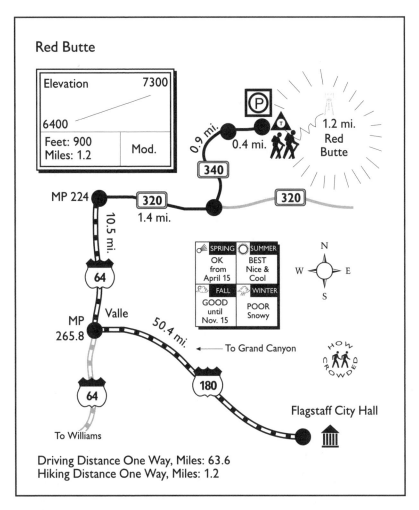

Mangum

Red Mountain

General Information
Location Map D2
Ebert Mountain USGS Map
Coconino Forest Service Map

Driving Distance One Way: 31.7 miles *50.72 km* (Time 40 minutes)
Access Road: All cars, Last 0.3 miles *0.48 km* good gravel road
Hiking Distance One Way: 1.25 miles *2.0 km* (Time 40 minutes)
How Strenuous: Moderate
Features: Unique experience—you go into the heart of a cutaway volcano

NUTSHELL: Located 31.7 miles *50.72 km* north of Flagstaff, this moderate hike takes you into the heart of Red Mountain to enjoy its otherworldly sculptures and formations. **A personal favorite.**

DIRECTIONS:
From Flagstaff City Hall Go:
   North on Humphreys Street for 0.60 miles *1.0 km*. See Access Map, page 10. Turn left at the stoplight onto Columbus Avenue and follow it around a big curve to the north. You will see the street signs call this road Columbus at first, then Ft. Valley Road and then Highway 180. Stay on Highway 180 to the 31.4 miles *50.24 km* point (MP 247), where an unpaved road, FR 9032V, takes off to the left. You will see a sign reading, "Red Mountain Geological Area." Turn left onto FR 9032V and follow it to the 31.7 mile *50.72 km* point, where there is a parking lot.

TRAILHEAD: The trailhead is the gate at the parking lot.

DESCRIPTION: The Forest Service has done some nice work on this trail. When we first did this hike in 1985 there was no trail and hikers had to thread their way through a maze of bad roads. The trail is now well maintained and easy to follow. Look for white plastic diamonds nailed to trees; these mark the path.
   Your objective will have been in sight for miles. Red Mountain looks just like hundreds of other cinder hills in the area north of Flagstaff except for one thing: its east face is sheared off cleanly, as if someone had done a cross-section of it to expose its red innards. Geologists tell us that all red cinder hills are like this in their interior.
   This is juniper country and the land is pretty flat. It is an easy walk though the trail rises constantly. At 0.75 miles *1.2 km* the trail leaves the old road it has been following and goes into the bed of a wash. This makes for fine walking as the bed is hard sand, and it makes a perfect entrance into Red

Mountain. As you come nearer, the streambed becomes the bottom of a V flanked by high black cinder shoulders. Then you see some strange black lava formations forming a sort of gate at the entrance to the insides of the mountain. The area has an Easter Island appearance of mystery.

At the 1.2 mile *1.92 km* point, you will see a rock dam full of silt. You can climb up the dam (our route) or go up the black cinders to your right. Once on top, you are in a basin surrounded by weird hoodoos. You don't see black lava on the inside. The prevailing color is red. You will also see an unexpected mustard colored rock in the lower formations. The place is like a mini-Bryce Canyon.

Once on the inside, the trail disappears. No worries. You can explore all around, enjoying the colors, shapes, play of light and other features that make this place so special. You feel cut off from the world. Everywhere you look there is something to delight your eye.

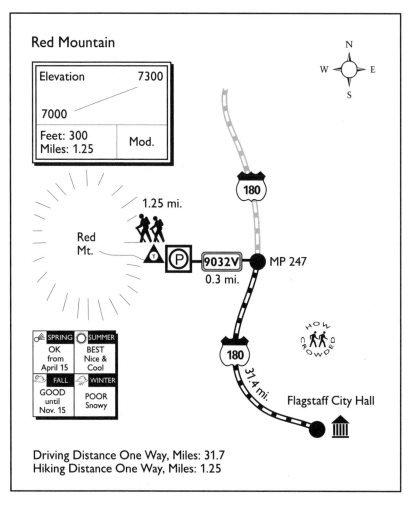

Mangum

Rio De Flag Trail

Driving Distance One Way: 1.2 miles *1.92 km* (Time 5 minutes)
Access Road: All cars, All paved
Hiking Distance One Way: 1.2 miles *1.92 km* (Time 30 minutes)
How Strenuous: Easy
Features: Urban trail

NUTSHELL: This urban trail in south Flagstaff is a pleasant 1.2 mile *1.92 km* walk.

DIRECTIONS:
From Flagstaff City Hall Go:
    East on Route 66 for one block. Turn right on Beaver Street and go south four blocks to Butler Avenue, where there is a stoplight. Turn left on Butler Avenue and follow it east for five blocks to Lone Tree Street (stoplight). Turn right on Lone Tree Street and follow it four blocks south to Brannen Circle. Turn left onto Brannen Circle and then immediately turn to your left on a graveled apron. Park on the apron.

TRAILHEAD: This is a marked and maintained trail. You will see it dipping down into the canyon from the parking area.

DESCRIPTION: Flagstaff is developing an ambitious system of urban trails. This trail shares a common trailhead with the **Sinclair Wash Trail**, which goes west from the parking lot, toward the Northern Arizona University campus, while the Rio de Flag Trail goes east toward a shallow canyon. The Rio de Flag trail was opened in the fall of 1989. The Sinclair Wash Trail was added to the trail system in the fall of 1990 and extended in 1991.
    The trail follows an old road. A row of boulders across the entrance now keeps vehicles from the road, as this path is for pedestrian use (and bicycles) only. The trail follows along the course of the whimsically named Rio de Flag as it curves and recurves along a canyon. The rio's streambed is usually dry, containing water only after the spring snowmelt in April or May or after a summer cloudburst of rain.
    The trail is built mostly above the bottom and the riverbed (riobed?) has been banked and channeled so that the trail should stay dry except in the time of a truly major flood.

The trail is the width of a single lane road and has been graded and surfaced so that the footing is very good.

After the first two hundred yards, you pass out of sight of habitation. Although you are surrounded by industry on the north and residences on the south, the canyon is deep enough so that you don't see any of this and it feels as if you are out in the country.

The walls of the canyon are mostly a buff colored limestone, some of which was crushed to make the surface for the trail. This sedimentary rock is a fairly soft stone that formed in layers. As these layers have eroded they have made ledges. Here and there you will find some interesting formations.

At the end of the hike you are jarred when you come out of the canyon under the roaring traffic of Interstate 40 on bridges overhead at the 1.2 mile *1.92 km* point. Just beyond the second bridge is a sewage treatment plant—an unwelcome return to "civilization" after a rustic respite.

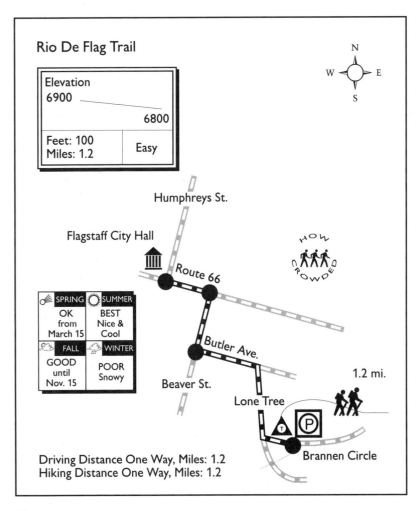

Mangum

Rocky Ridge Trail #153

General Information
Location Map E3
Flagstaff West, Humphreys Peak & Sunset Crater West USGS Maps
Coconino Forest Service Map

Driving Distance One Way: 3.9 miles *6.24 km* (Time 20 minutes)
Access Road: All cars, Last 0.25 miles *0.4 km* medium gravel road
Hiking Distance One Way: 3.0 miles *4.8 km* (Time 1.5 hours)
How Strenuous: Moderate
Features: Shady forest in the hills

NUTSHELL: This is a marked and maintained trail that hugs the base of the south face of the Dry Lake Hills about 4 miles *6.4 km* north of Flagstaff and goes from the Schultz Pass Road to the Elden Lookout Road.

DIRECTIONS:
From Flagstaff City Hall Go:
North on Humphreys Street for 0.60 miles *1.0 km*. See Access Map, page 10. Turn left at the stoplight onto Columbus Avenue and follow it around a big curve to the north. You will see the street signs call this road Columbus Avenue at first, then Ft. Valley Road and then Highway 180. Stay on Highway 180 to the 3.1 miles *5.0 km* point (MP 218.6), where the Schultz Pass Road, FR 420, goes to the right. Follow the Schultz Pass Road. As it starts around a curve to the left, at the 3.6 miles *5.76 km* point, you will see the Elden Lookout Road going straight. Ignore this and stay on the Schultz Pass Road. The paving will end soon and the road will become gravel. At the 3.9 miles *6.24 km* point, you will see a gate, which closes the road in winter. Just beyond the gate is FR 9128Y which goes downhill to your right. Take this. At the bottom turn left and follow the road a few yards to a fence, where you park.

TRAILHEAD: You will see a wooden sign for the Rocky Ridge Trail in the fence opening to your right.

DESCRIPTION: This trail starts at the same place that the **Schultz Creek Trail** ends. There are two distinct openings in the fence for the respective trails. They are both signed.
The trail climbs gradually until it reaches a point about three hundred feet higher than the beginning and then pretty well holds that contour. You will walk through a pine forest which is so thick that you are able to get only a few views through the trees. You will see Buffalo Park and the NAU campus clearly, but most of Flagstaff is below a mesa that cuts off your view of

the town.

The trail takes you around the west toe of the Dry Lake Hills and then follows along their south face. From the one mile *1.6 km* point onward you will be aware that the Elden Lookout Road is nearby on your right. Sometimes you can only hear sounds coming from it, while in other places you can see the road and will be a stone's throw from it. Mountain bikers love the road and many of them use the Rocky Ridge Trail as well.

The trail ends where it intersects the Elden Lookout Road at a point that is 3.0 miles *4.8 km* from its beginning.

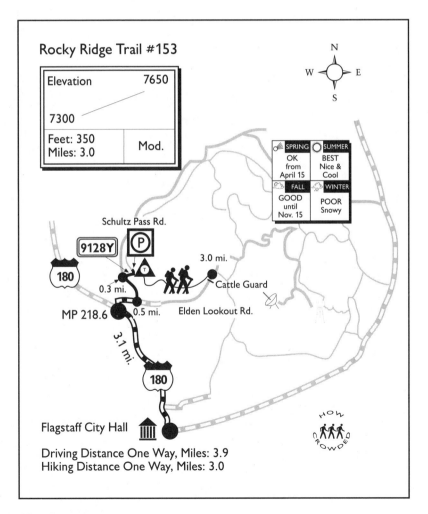

Mangum

Route 66

Driving Distance One Way: 18.9 miles *30.24 km* (Time 30 minutes)
Access Road: All cars, Last 0.5 miles *0.8 km* good gravel road
Hiking Distance One Way: 0.75 miles *1.2 km* (Time 30 minutes)
How Strenuous: Easy
Features: Walk along a 1931 portion (now closed) of fabled Route 66.

NUTSHELL: A closed strip of Route 66 near Parks has been turned into a hiking trail. You make an easy walk through a pleasant forest to enjoy a bit of history, then drive the old road.

DIRECTIONS:
From Flagstaff City Hall Go:
   West, then south on Route 66, beneath the railroad overpass. See Access Map, page 10. At 0.50 miles *0.8 km* go right Route 66. You will soon leave town. At the 5.0 mile *8.0 km* point you will merge onto Interstate-40 West. Drive I-40 West to the Parks Exit 178 at the 18.0 mile *28.8 km* point, and take it. Turn right and go up to the next stop sign, which intersects old Route 66. Turn right and drive to the 18.9 mile *30.24 km* point, where you will see a signed parking area to your left.

TRAILHEAD: At the parking place.

DESCRIPTION: Route 66 came through this area from its first days, but over the years engineers changed its right-of-way in the Williams area, constantly looking for a better, more manageable path. The bit of paved road that still goes by the Parks Store is the 1941 alignment and was used until I-40 was built in 1964. You will walk the 1931 alignment when you make this hike.
   This little walk starts at an interpretive sign for a Route 66 Auto Tour. Just east of here was the point where Highway 66 crested at the shoulder of 49 Hill, the absolute high point of Route 66 in its two thousand-plus miles, and the old cars really strained to pull this grade. Because of the steepness, engineers changed the alignment in the area to go around a flank of 49 Hill instead of over its top.
   You will walk along a disused stretch of old 66 that runs straight downhill. The old pavement survives most of the way, but it is crumbling. At about the 0.5 mile *0.8 km* point you will see a funky stone building to your

left. It was a spring house that provided water to a Forest Service campground. The hike ends near the present paved road, at a point where the 1941 route meets the 1931 route. There are a couple of concrete culverts showing how the roads merged here.

When you finish the hike, we suggest that you drive back to Flagstaff on the old highway rather than Interstate 40. You will pass through scenic Brannigan Park, once an active farming area. To do this, keep driving east beyond the trailhead parking spot. At 5.0 miles *8.0 km* from the parking area you will find an interpretive sign to your left at a pullout marked by a pole fence. At about 7.4 miles *12.0 km* you will come to Bellemont, where you re-enter Interstate 40.

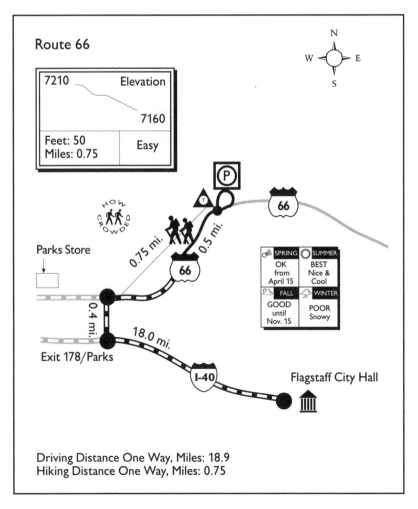

Mangum

SP Crater

General Information
Location Map D3
East of SP Mtn., SP Mtn. USGS Maps
Coconino Forest Service Map

Driving Distance One Way: 38.7 miles *61.9 km* (Time 1 hour)
Access Road: All cars, Last 6.5 miles *10.4 km* medium unpaved road
Hiking Distance One Way: 0.5 miles *0.8 km* (Time 1 hour)
How Strenuous: Moderate
Features: Volcano and lava field in midst of volcano belt

NUTSHELL: Located north of Flagstaff in flat country studded with volcanoes, this interesting crater is the most symmetrical of the group. It is relatively easy to climb, with great views from the top.

DIRECTIONS:
From Flagstaff City Hall Go:
    East and then north on Highway 89. See Access Map, pages 10-11. Stay on Highway 89 to the 32.2 mile *51.5 km* point (MP 445.9), where you will see an unpaved road to your left (west) just before you reach MP 446. Hank's Trading Post is in sight to the north. This area is in the middle of a huge ranch run by the Babbitt interests and there are many roads going to tanks and waterholes. The roads are not numbered on maps nor on the ground. Follow the main-traveled road. Be sure to turn left at the first Y. SP Crater will seem dead ahead of you. It stands out because of its shape: a flat top with sloping symmetrical sides. At the 37.0 mile *59.2 km* point, the road forks at the top of a little valley. Go right here, skirting around the valley. At the 38.2 mile *61.1 km* point, you will see a sideroad fork to the right and head straight for a saddle between the crater and SP Mountain, which is joined to the crater by the saddle. This jeep road goes all the way to the top of the saddle but washouts have made it dangerous. We recommend driving 0.50 miles *0.8 km* on it, to the point where it leaves the level land at the base and begins to climb. Park here, at the 38.7 mile *61.9 km* point.

TRAILHEAD: There is no foot trail. You hike the jeep road to the saddle. From the saddle to the top of SP Crater there is no path, but you will see what you have to do: climb straight up about 300 feet.

DESCRIPTION: The saddle offers good views. You will be surprised at the extensive lava field that runs from SP Crater to the north. The crater doesn't seem big enough to have poured out so much lava, but it did. We find that the easiest way to climb one of these cinder volcanic cones is to zigzag, as if you were doing switchbacks with a car. The cinders are loose and the footing is poor.

Your climb is well worth the effort. SP Crater itself (we are told that the initials stand for Shit Pot) is quite interesting, the model of what a volcano should be. It is a perfect cone with a depressed center. Many of the volcanoes blasted their sides away or took irregular shapes, but not this one.

Views to the north are splendid. The country is quite flat but dotted with small volcanic eruptions. You see the Painted Desert nicely. The large mesa farthest north is the Coconino Rim, behind which the Grand Canyon is located. To the south you see myriad volcanoes of all shapes and sizes. This place is like a living geology lesson. If you are not interested in the views from a scientific standpoint, then the aesthetics will suffice.

After you come back down to the saddle, you might want to climb to the top of the ridge on the other side of the saddle. This is SP Mountain.

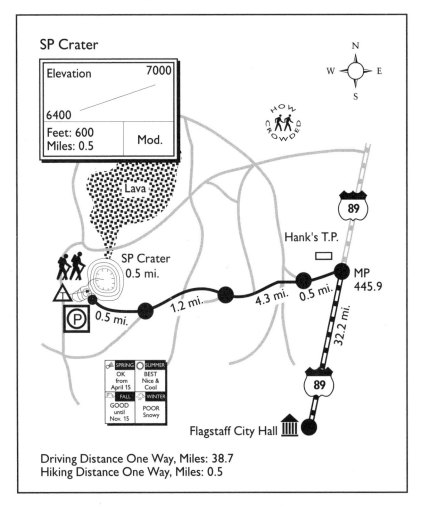

Mangum

Saddle Mountain

General Information
Location Map E3
Kendrick Peak & White Horse Hills USGS Maps
Coconino Forest Service Map

Driving Distance One Way: 25.3 miles *40.5 km* (Time 50 minutes)
Access Road: All cars, Last 4.5 miles *7.2 km* good dirt road
Hiking Distance One Way: 2.9 miles *4.64 km* (Time 90 minutes)
How Strenuous: Moderate
Features: Views, Volcanic field

NUTSHELL: Located 25.3 miles *40.5 km* north of Flagstaff, this hike takes you up an abandoned fire lookout road that corkscrews around a bare mountain, giving 360 degree views.

DIRECTIONS:
From Flagstaff City Hall Go:
    North on Humphreys Street for 0.60 miles *1.0 km*. See Access Map, page 10. Turn left at the stoplight onto Columbus Avenue and follow it around a big curve to the north. You will see the street signs call this road Columbus at first, then Ft. Valley Road and then Highway 180. Stay on Highway 180 to the 20.8 miles *33.3 km* point (MP 236.5), where the unpaved road FR 514 takes off to the right. Turn right onto FR 514 and drive it to the 23.4 mile *37.44 km* point where you will see FR 550 to the left. Turn left on FR 550 and take it to the 25.3 mile *40.5 km* point and park there.

TRAILHEAD: Hike the road up the mountain, FR 550A.

DESCRIPTION: Saddle Mountain is located in an ancient volcanic field. The excellent views from the top will show you the scope of the field. The mountains that you see in the region are all extinct volcanoes. Some of them, such as the San Francisco Peaks and Kendrick Mountain are high enough to catch clouds and get a lot of rain and snow. Because of this moisture they support abundant vegetation. In time soil forms on these favored mountains, covering the cinders and lava that formed the mountains with topsoil. On the lesser mountains, hills and cinder cones such as Saddle Mountain, there are only a few areas where soil has formed and most of the mountainsides are still bare cinders.
    A fire swept Saddle Mountain years ago and burned away most of its scant timber growth. The fire was a tragedy but it had its good side. As a result of it, you are able to get unobstructed views. The road circles around the mountain as it climbs, so you are able to see in every direction.

From the 1920s to the 1960s there was a fire lookout tower on the top of Saddle Mountain and the Forest Service built a decent road to the top of the mountain for access to the tower. The tower was replaced with a transmitter after the fire tower was removed. The road is still maintained so that the transmitter can be serviced. You could drive the road if you are a lazy bones, but this is a book of hikes.

At the top you can see all the way to the Grand Canyon when you look north. To the east you can see Sunset Crater and the Painted Desert. To the south you see the north face of the San Francisco Peaks. To the west you can see Kendrick Peak. This is an superb viewpoint.

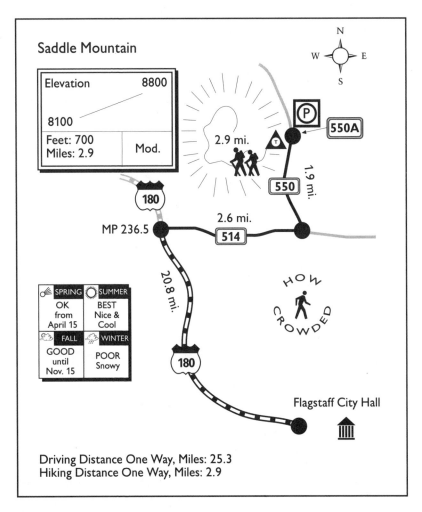

Sandy Seep Trail #129

General Information
Location Map E3
Flagstaff East & Sunset Crater West USGS Maps
Coconino Forest Service Map

Driving Distance One Way: 7.0 miles *11.2 km* (Time 20 minutes)
Access Road: All cars, Last 0.1 miles *0.16 km* good dirt road
Hiking Distance One Way: 2.0 miles *3.2 km* (Time 1 hour)
How Strenuous: Easy
Features: Strange white hills, Views

NUTSHELL: This hike in the Mt. Elden area northeast of Flagstaff, takes you to an unusual geological feature and provides a connection to other trails in the Mt. Elden system.

DIRECTIONS:
From Flagstaff City Hall Go:
East, then north on Highway 89. See Access Map, pages 10-11. At 6.5 miles *10.4 km* you will pass the last stoplight in town at the Townsend-Winona Road. Continue on Highway 89 to the 6.9 mile *11.04 km* point (MP 421.1), where you will see a dirt road, FR 9139, to the left. This is the first road beyond the Townsend-Winona Road intersection. Turn left onto this road and follow it to the parking place at 7.0 miles *11.2 km.*

TRAILHEAD: There is a trail sign at the parking lot at the gate.

DESCRIPTION: You will walk along in a northwesterly direction, toward Mt. Elden. The old road that used to take vehicles to Sandy Seep has been blocked off and made into a hiking trail. This means that the path is wide and that the grade is gradual.
As you walk, you can see that the side of Mt. Elden forms a big bowl and that you are heading toward the center of the bowl. Mt. Elden itself is obviously formed from lava and you can see rocks and cliffs on its face. You would think that the entire area would be covered with lava, and generally it is. However, there is one exception, and that is right in the heart of the bowl, where you will see a ring of low white hills. These are sandstone formations. In places the sandstone has eroded and made deposits of sand, which is what you will find at Sandy Seep.
Along the trail you will find many Cliff Roses. When these are in bloom, their fragrance fills the air. We have been here at times when it was almost overpowering. You will pass through an area that was burned by a small forest fire. Beyond, the road winds it way around the first hill, which you will

curve around. The trail is designed to end at 1.5 miles *2.4 km*, where it meets the **Heart Trail**, which comes down from the top of Mt. Elden.

We like to hike 0.5 miles *0.8 km* farther, to get to the actual Sandy Seep. This is a beautiful open area, where the ground really is sandy. Between the trail and the side of the tallest white hill, which is capped with a sharp peak, there is a depression. Water seeps into the bottom of the depression, as evidence of which you will see willows growing there.

Toward Mt. Elden you will see a long low hill formed from an unusual reddish soil. The red and white soils found in this basin are unusual for the Mt. Elden area. A geologist's delight.

Harrison Conrard, Flagstaff's renowned poet, had a little ranch here in the early part of this century. He did not actually run cattle, but used it for a retreat where he did his writing. What a beautiful hideaway it must have been.

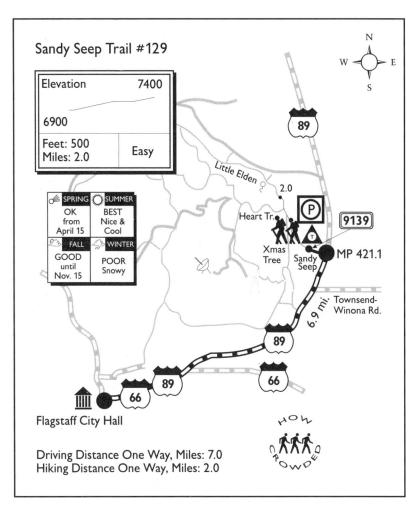

Mangum

Sandys Canyon Trail #137

General Information
Location Map F3
Flagstaff East USGS Map
Coconino Forest Service Map

Driving Distance One Way: 8.1 miles *13.0 km* (Time 20 minutes)
Access Road: All cars, Last 0.20 miles *0.32 km* good gravel road
Hiking Distance One Way: 3.6 miles *5.76 km* (Time 90 minutes)
How Strenuous: Moderate
Features: Beautiful canyon, Caves, Connection to The Arizona Trail

NUTSHELL: Located south of Flagstaff, only 8.1 miles *13.0 km* out on the
Lake Mary Road, this hike requires a brief climb into Walnut Canyon, then
an easy walk along the canyon bottom. It features impressive cliffs and a
cave that is fun to explore. We formerly called this hike *Fisher Point* but in
1992 the Forest Service created Sandys Canyon Trail, so we have changed
the description to match.

DIRECTIONS:
From Flagstaff City Hall Go:
    West and then south (left) on Route 66 under the railroad overpass. See
Access Map, page 10. At the 0.5 mile point *0.8 km*, go straight on Milton
Road. At 1.7 miles *2.72 km* you reach the stoplight at Forest Meadows,
where you turn right. At the next corner turn left on Beulah and follow it out
of town. Beulah will connect onto Highway 89A. At the 2.4 miles *3.84 km*
point (MP 401.6) you will see the turnoff to the Lake Mary Road to your
left, where the last stoplight in town is located. Take the turn and follow the
Lake Mary Road to the 7.9 mile *12.6 km* point where you will see a gravel
road to your left. This is just a few feet past the second cattle guard on the
Lake Mary Road. Turn left onto the gravel road and take it about 0.20 miles
0.32 km, through a camp site to get as close to the canyon as possible, at 8.1
miles *13.0 km*. Park there.

TRAILHEAD: Signed. Located near canyon rim.

DESCRIPTION: You will first walk along the rim of the canyon for 0.60
miles *1.0 km*, then descend a pretty side canyon to the floor of Walnut Creek,
which carves Walnut Canyon. The National Monument is several miles
downstream. There is 200 foot drop into the canyon bottom to reach the
streambed at 0.25 miles *0.4 km*. You cross it and hike an old road on the
other side. Go left on the road.
    The trail intersects the Arizona Trail at 0.75 miles *1.2 km*. From here

keep walking straight north to a bend, where you turn right (east), at 0.90 miles *1.44 km* from The Arizona Trail. At 1.65 miles *2.64 km*, to your left, is Fisher Point, with a half cave under a big rounded cliff. Walk on past the cliff to a place where the trail seems to end at a screen of willows.

This screen is at a bend in Walnut Canyon. The trail continues but changes character, from a jeep road to a foot trail. The canyon becomes very narrow and you wind your way back and forth across the streambed. At 1.9 miles *3.04 km* the trail goes past a large cave to your right. The cave is fun to explore, and even has an "escape hatch" out the back. At 2.1 miles *3.36 km* there is a smaller cave that is partly hidden, uphill to your right. Look for a short trail to it taking off from the streambed where the bed is wide and full of coarse sand.

We recommend stopping at the 3.6 miles *5.76 km* point, where you will find a large Ponderosa with a silver stripe painted around it.

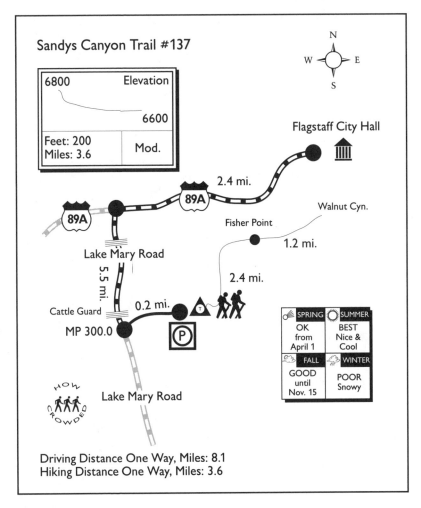

214

Schultz Creek Trail #152

General Information
Location Map E3
Humphreys Peak USGS Map
Coconino Forest Service Map

Driving Distance One Way: 8.5 miles *13.6 km* (Time 30 minutes)
Access Road: All cars, Last 4.9 miles *7.8 km* medium gravel road
Hiking Distance One Way: 4.25 miles *6.8 km* (Time 2.25 hours)
How Strenuous: Moderate
Features: Scenic creekside trail is easy to reach

NUTSHELL: This is a marked and maintained trail that starts high on the Schultz Pass Road north of Flagstaff and follows a creekside downward.

DIRECTIONS:
From Flagstaff City Hall Go:
    North on Humphreys Street for 0.60 miles *1.0 km*. See Access Map, page 10. Turn left at the stoplight onto Columbus Avenue and follow it around a big curve to the north. You will see the street signs call this road Columbus Avenue at first, then Ft. Valley Road and then Highway 180. Stay on Highway 180 to the 3.1 miles *5.0 km* point (MP 218.6), where the Schultz Pass Road, FR 420, goes to the right. Follow this road. At 3.6 miles *5.76 km* it curves to the left and you will see the Elden Lookout Road going straight. Ignore this and stay on the Schultz Pass Road. The paving will end soon and the road will become gravel. As you drive, look down into the canyon to your right and you will see a trail running along the canyon parallel to the road. This is the Schultz Creek Trail. Follow the road to the 8.3 mile *13.3 km* point, where you will see a sign for the Sunset Trail. Turn right on this access and park in the parking area, by the sign board, at 8.5 miles *13.6 km*.

TRAILHEAD: You will see a wooden sign for the Sunset Trail. The Schultz Creek Trail runs in the opposite direction and is marked with a lath showing it to be a trail closed to motor travel but giving no name.

DESCRIPTION: The Schultz Creek Trail follows the course of the old Schultz Pass Road. That road was so near the bottom of the creek that it often flooded, so in the 1930s the present road was built higher up the shoulder, requiring much blasting and earth removal.
    Down at creekside you will have a delightful ramble. The path is easy to walk, made of soft soil with few rocks. You will see many wildflowers growing in the upper reaches of the trail where the forest is an interesting mixture of pine, aspen, fir and spruce, with willows in the creek.

Flagstaff Hikes

This is not really a hiking trail, but a motorcycle trail maintained by a motorcycle club. The members wanted to have at least one trail in this region so an agreement was worked out for them to have this one if they would maintain it. Bicyclists also love the trail.

The trail is always just a stone's throw from the road, which is to your right, and you will see and hear cars pass. This and the presence of bikes mar the natural feeling of this otherwise fine trail.

Near the end of the trail, you will encounter several concrete slabs on the site of a 1930s CCC camp. The workers who lived there built the present road.

Forest Service maps measure this hike at 3.5 miles *5.6 km*, which seems too short. The best way to do this hike is as a two car shuttle, parking one at the Sunset trailhead and the other at the low end on FR 9128Y as shown on the map.

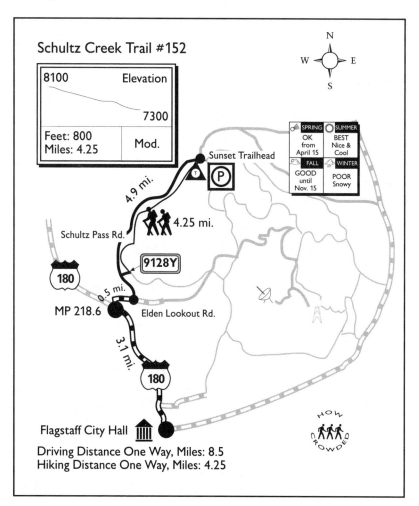

Schultz Creek Trail #152

8100	Elevation
	7300
Feet: 800 Miles: 4.25	Mod.

SPRING — OK from April 15
SUMMER — BEST Nice & Cool
FALL — GOOD until Nov. 15
WINTER — POOR Snowy

Sunset Trailhead

4.9 mi.

4.25 mi.

Schultz Pass Rd.

9128Y

180

0.5 mi.

MP 218.6   Elden Lookout Rd.

3.1 mi.

180

HOW CROWDED

Flagstaff City Hall

Driving Distance One Way, Miles: 8.5
Hiking Distance One Way, Miles: 4.25

Mangum

Secret Mountain Trail #109

General Information
Location Map F2
Loy Butte, Sycamore Point USGS Maps
Coconino Forest Service Map

Driving Distance One Way: 28.9 miles *46.2 km* (Time 1.5 hours)
Access Road: All cars, Last 25.3 miles *40.5 km* dirt road, rough spots
Hiking Distance One Way: 1.9 miles *3.0 km* (Time 1 hour)
How Strenuous: Moderate
Features: Historic cabin, Pristine first growth forest, Views

NUTSHELL: Located 28.9 miles *46.24 km* southwest of Flagstaff, this hike takes you from a scenic lookout on the Mogollon Rim across a ridge to Secret Mountain where you will find a historic cabin and another lookout. **A personal favorite.**

DIRECTIONS:
From Flagstaff City Hall Go:

West, then south on Route 66, beneath the railroad overpass. See Access Map, page 10. At 0.5 miles *0.8 km* go right on Route 66. You will soon leave town. At 2.6 mile *4.2 km* you will reach a road going to the left. This is the Woody Mountain Road, FR 231. Take it. It is paved about a mile *1.6 km* and then turns into a cinder road. At 16.6 miles *26.6 km* you will intersect FR 538. Turn right onto FR 538 and follow it to the 22.3 mile *35.7 km* point, where FR 538E branches off to the right. Take FR 538 to the left. At 27.7 miles *44.3 km* you will come to the intersection of 538K. Go left here, staying on 538. At 28.9 mile *46.2 km* you will come out onto a ridge. Park by the wilderness boundary sign at the end of the road.

TRAILHEAD: Marked and signed. Go east to the toe of the ridge.

DESCRIPTION: The trail is maintained and is easy to follow even though it is not posted. You will find trail-marking blazes on trees along the route as you go. See page 123 for a drawing of a blaze.

At 0.4 miles *0.64 km*, you drop off a knob onto a saddle where there is a gate. Here the trail splits. The fork to the right is the Loy Canyon Trail (see *Sedona Hikes*) and the fit hiker can follow it about five miles *8.0 km*, descending 2,000 feet. Instead, turn left and go uphill. You will reach the top of a knob at 0.6 miles *1.0 km,* then go downhill. In this area you will see damage from an August 1994 forest fire.

At 1.0 miles *1.6 km* you will enter a fold between three hills. On a small bench of land here you will find an old log corral and a dam. Beyond the corral you will at all times have a ravine to your right as you hike. Enjoy this forest. It has never been logged. Imagine what northern Arizona would look like if it were all like this. It is breathtaking.

At 1.8 miles *2.9 km* you will come to another shelf of land, with Secret Cabin and another corral. There is also a pond. The cabin is about 20 by 12 feet and only 5 feet high. This remote place was homesteaded unsuccessfully by a family in the 1870s. It was then used by Mormons hiding from polygamy prosecution. After that it was used by horse thieves, who stole horses around Sedona, led them to this hideout via the Loy Canyon Trail and eventually took them to Flagstaff and points north.

From the cabin go west into the ravine and across it. Walk up 0.1 mile *0.16 km* to a viewpoint on the rim for sensational views. The trail continues, another 2.8 miles *4.5 km,* to the top of Secret Mountain and over to its south face, but we like to stop at the viewpoint.

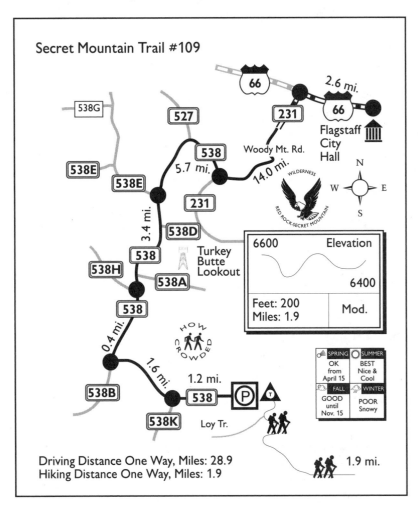

Secret Mountain Trail #109

Driving Distance One Way, Miles: 28.9
Hiking Distance One Way, Miles: 1.9

Mangum

Secret Pocket Trail #58

General Information
Location Map F1
May Tank Pocket USGS Map
Kaibab (Williams District) Forest Service Map

Driving Distance One Way: 53.4 miles *85.5 km* (Time 1.25 hours)
Access Road: High clearance needed for last 3.0 miles *4.8 km*
Hiking Distance One Way: 1.0 miles *1.6 km* (Time 30 minutes)
How Strenuous: Moderate
Features: Remote country, Hidden oasis

NUTSHELL: You will drive through miles of beautiful forest, then hike an old cattle trail from the top of the Mogollon Rim to a hidden pond in a "secret" pocket.

DIRECTIONS:
From Flagstaff City Hall Go:
West, then south on Route 66 under the railroad overpass. See Access Map, page 10. At 0.5 miles *0.8 km*, turn right on Route 66. In about 5.0 miles *8.0 km* you will merge onto I-40 West and stay on it to the 30.3 miles *48.5 km* point, the Williams Exit, #165. Take that exit and at the stop sign go left to Williams. Go into town on Railroad Avenue to the 32.9 mile point *52.6 km* where you will find Fourth Street. Turn left on Fourth Street. As it leaves town its name changes to the Perkinsville Road (Highway 73). Stay on this road to the 42.2 mile *67.5 km* point, where you will turn left on FR 354. Stay on FR 354 to the 49.4 mile *79.0 km* point, where FR 354 makes a 90 degree turn to the right. Stay on FR 354. In another mile the road will become quite rough, with lots of exposed rocks. At the 53.4 mile *85.5 km* point, you will see a lath-type marker for Trail 58 on your left, at an old road junction.

TRAILHEAD: Marked by a fiberglass lath.

DESCRIPTION: Once you leave the paved Perkinsville Road, you will drive on FR 354 to reach the trailhead. FR 354 used to be the Perkinsville Road and carried lots of traffic until the present paved road was built in the 1960s. You will see many culverts and other structures indicating the importance of the old road. The road now receives no maintenance and there are many rough spots on the last three miles. If you have a good high clearance vehicle, you might want to follow the road down to its junction with the present paved road after the hike. It's about 10.0 miles *16 km* to the bottom, from where you can turn left and go to Jerome (a great scenic drive) or turn right and go back up the present Perkinsville Road.

The trail is an old ranch road that is now closed to motor vehicles. You will hike over rocky but level ground through a cedar (juniper) forest. As you proceed, the country will open up and you will see that you are on a point near the edge of the Mogollon Rim. Government Canyon, which meets Sycamore Canyon, is prominent before you.

Near its end, the trail dips down and takes you into a fold where you will see green deciduous trees peeking up above the cedars. The hike ends at the pond, the waters of which support the growth of these water-loving trees. It is a delightful place, an open green oasis with a small pond.

We looked hard but could not find any trail going from here to the bottom of the Rim, even though some Forest Service maps indicate that there is such a trail.

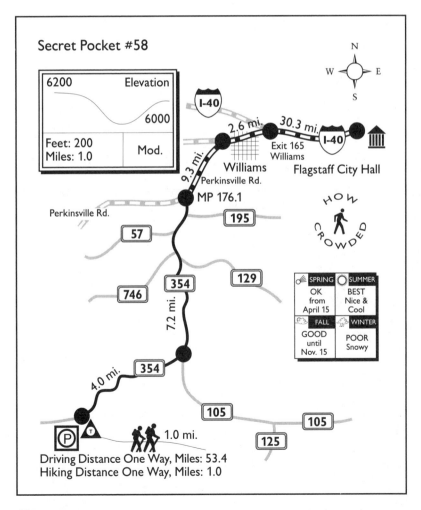

Sinclair Wash Trail

General Information
Location Map F3
Flagstaff West USGS Map
Coconino Forest Service Map

Driving Distance One Way: 2.2 miles *3.52 km* (Time 5 minutes)
Access Road: All cars, All paved
Hiking Distance One Way: 3.0 or 1.0 miles *4.8 or 1.6 km* (Time 1.5 or 0.5 hours)
How Strenuous: Easy
Features: Urban trail

NUTSHELL: This is an urban trail in the south part of town. Starting from the point we have selected, you can go east for an easy one mile hike through NAU's South Campus to Lone Tree Road, or southwest to Ft. Tuthill.

DIRECTIONS:
From Flagstaff City Hall Go:
    West, then south on Route 66. See Access Map, page 10. Follow Route 66 beneath the underpass. At 0.5 miles 0.8 km, go straight on Milton Road. Continue on Milton Road to the 1.7 mile *2.72 km* point, where you meet Forest Meadows Street. Turn right. In a block, turn left on Beulah. In another couple of blocks, you will see the Wal-Mart shopping center on your right. Turn right on Woodlands Village Boulevard, and immediately turn right into the Wal-Mart parking lot, parking near the street.

TRAILHEAD: This is a marked and maintained trail. You will see trail signs. Pole fences mark the Flagstaff urban trails.

DESCRIPTION: Flagstaff is developing an ambitious system of urban trails, with several excellent trails already on line, and more to come.
    Using Wal-Mart as a starting point, you can go east toward NAU or southwest toward Ft. Tuthill. The scenery is quite different depending on your choice.
    The east (NAU) leg is just under one mile. It skirts along the South Campus. Most of the time it stays in a band of trees, but you are always aware that you are in an inhabited area. The trail is kept in good condition and there are no major grades. It is a nice easy walk if you just want a little exercise.
    The other leg, going to Ft. Tuthill, is a three-miler. It goes south through more wooded areas. The first portion of this trail passes by the University Heights subdivision, and then through part of the Mt. Dell subdivision, so it

is definitely not what you would call a wilderness experience. There are a few stretches where you cannot see any homes or other man-made artifacts, and these are enjoyable. The trail is much more interesting than the NAU leg.

Just beyond the Mt. Dell subdivision, the trail joins the roadbed of an old logging railroad and goes through a forest. Eventually you will enter the Ft. Tuthill area. At first you will see nothing but an equestrian trail, but soon afterwards, you will come to the main portion of the property.

Ft. Tuthill is an old National Guard camp that is now owned by Coconino County. It is the home of the Coconino County Fair, and other events are sometimes held there.

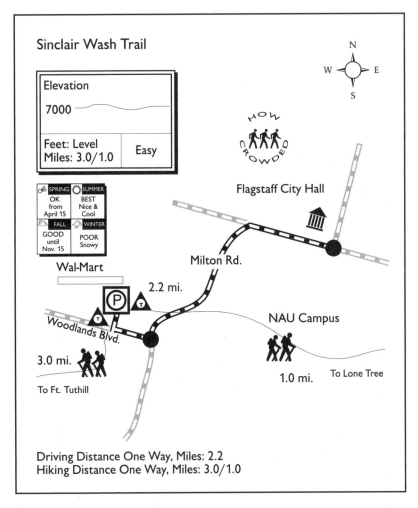

Mangum

Slate Mountain #128

General Information
Location Map E2
Kendrick Peak USGS Map
Coconino Forest Service Map

Driving Distance One Way: 29.1 miles *46.56 km* (Time 40 minutes)
Access Road: All cars, Last 2.2 miles *3.5 km* good gravel road
Hiking Distance One Way: 2.1 miles *3.36 km* (Time 80 minutes)
How Strenuous: Moderate
Features: Excellent views, Nature trail with explanatory signs

NUTSHELL: Located 29.1 miles *46.56 km* north of Flagstaff, this moderate hike follows an old road to the top of a mountain, with signs identifying local flora posted along the way.

DIRECTIONS:
From Flagstaff City Hall Go:
   North on Humphreys Street for 0.60 miles *1.0 km*. See Access Map, page 10. Turn left at the stoplight onto Columbus Avenue and follow it around a big curve to the north. You will see the street signs call this road Columbus at first, then Ft. Valley Road and then Highway 180. Stay on Highway 180 to the 26.9 miles *43.0 km* point (MP 242.4), where an unpaved road, FR 191, takes off to the left. Turn left onto FR 191 and follow it to the 28.8 mile *46.1 km* point. There you will see a road to your right that is marked as the trail access. Turn right onto this road and drive it to the 29.1 mile *46.56 km* point, where you will park.

TRAILHEAD: Hike the road going up the mountain.

DESCRIPTION: Like some other hikes in the book, this road was built to provide access to a fire lookout tower that was later dismantled. The road is now closed for vehicular traffic and makes a fine hiking trail.
   Slate Mountain is an extinct volcano called a rhyolite lava dome. When magma moved up through the Earth's crust to produce this volcano, it tilted up some of the rocks overhead. Along the first several hundred feet of your hike the path and the cut in the adjacent hillside are covered with the dark-rusty-red color of tilted up sandstone and siltstone of some of the same rock formations that are exposed in the walls of the Grand Canyon. Farther up the mountain slope, the rocks are the uniform pale gray of the rhyolite lava dome. Some pieces of the rhyolite exhibit large flat surfaces that mimic those typical of slate (blackboard) which gives the mountain its name.
   As you climb the mountain you wind around the two knobs that form a

saddle, so that you are able to see in all directions. You will have some great views as you go and will have even better views at the top.

One thing you can count on when you take one of these hikes to a spot where there was (or presently is) a fire lookout tower is that you will have great views, because the Forest Service located the towers in places where you can see forever. At the top of Slate Mountain there are just a few low-growing pines, so you can see freely to the north, south and west.

Immediately to the north you will see **Red Mountain**. Just a few years ago there was a bit of a stir in Flagstaff when a mining company indicated that it thought that there was gold in the red cinders of Red Mountain and it was going to set up a gold mining operation. Red cinders do contain minuscule quantities of gold, but you have literally to move mountains of it to recover any of the precious metal.

A big fire in 1996 scorched the bottom of Slate Mountain.

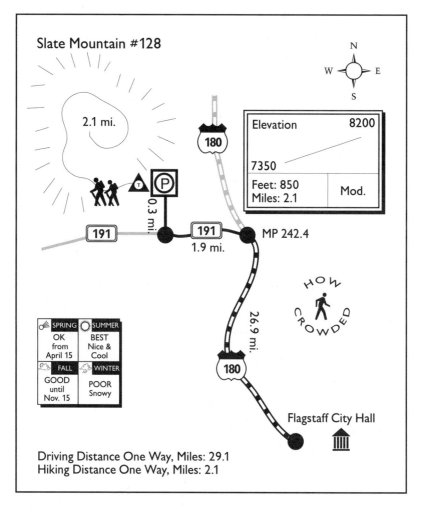

Soldiers Trail

General Information
Location Map F3
Flagstaff West USGS Map
Coconino Forest Service Map

Driving Distance One Way: 5.15 miles *8.24 km* (Time 15 minutes)
Access Road: All cars
Hiking Distance, Complete Loop: 6.0 miles *9.6 km* (Time 3 hours)
How Strenuous: Moderate
Features: Easy to reach, Design permits many variations

NUTSHELL: Opened in April 2000, this trail is part of Coconino County's recreation complex located at Ft. Tuthill south of town.

DIRECTIONS:
From Flagstaff City Hall Go:
    West and then south (left) on Route 66 under the railroad overpass. See Access Map, page 10. At the 0.5 mile point *0.8 km*, go straight on Milton Road. At 1.7 miles *2.72 km* turn right on Forest Meadows and then left on Beulah. You are now lined up to go south on Highway 89A. Stay on Highway 89A to the 4.8 miles *7.68 km* point MP 408.8, where you will see the turnoff to Ft. Tuthill, a county park. Turn right (W) onto the main entrance road and go to the 5.0 mile *8.0 km* point, where the paving turns to your left. Go straight ahead into the big gravel parking lot, turn right and then park at the second parking bay.

TRAILHEAD: There is a big sign marking the trailhead, with a map.

DESCRIPTION: Follow the Sinclair Wash Trail at first, turning left and walking north along a raised roadbed surfaced with gravel. The structures you see in the forest are obstacles for an equestrian course. At 0.5 miles *0.8 km* the Solders Trail cuts across the Sinclair Wash Trail making loops on either side of the it, like the wings of a lopsided butterfly. The Soldiers Trail is marked with green laths and accurate mileage markers. To hike the west wing, turn left. You will walk a gentle grade west along the park's northern fence, then turn south, where you climb a steeper grade.
    At 1.4 miles *2.24 km* you reach a trail junction where you can take a shortcut left to the campground. Turn right and go up the canyon. Just beyond mile 1.5 you will see a side-trail to the left. This goes 1.25 miles *2.0 km* south to join your trail again at the 3.6 miles *5.76 km* point. (We like this side trail for variety. It is 0.75 miles *1.2 km* shorter than the regular trail). The main trail rises to its high point at mile 2.0 then moves west a bit before

starting a long leg south. At 3.25 miles *5.2 km* you cross a gravel road, and soon cross another one. When you cross the second road you begin walking along the bed of a 1903-1925 logging railroad. Look for old rotting ties and one small piece of rail. You leave the bed for a while then return to it. At 3.8 miles *6.08 km* you reach a gravel road. If you turn left here and walk north past the Luke AFB area, it is 0.5 miles *0.8 km* back to your car.

You pick up the east wing on the other side of this road, dipping down into a canyon. You then hike north parallel to Highway 89A. At MP 4 you will be hiking along another logging railroad bed, this one used from 1925-1966. You leave the RR bed and walk north through picnic grounds. At MP 5 you will be at the top end of the racetrack. From here you continue north, then veer west. You will reach MP 5.5 where the Soldiers Trail meets the Sinclair Wash Trail, completing the loop. Turn left and walk south back to the parking space, for a total of 6.0 miles *9.6 km*.

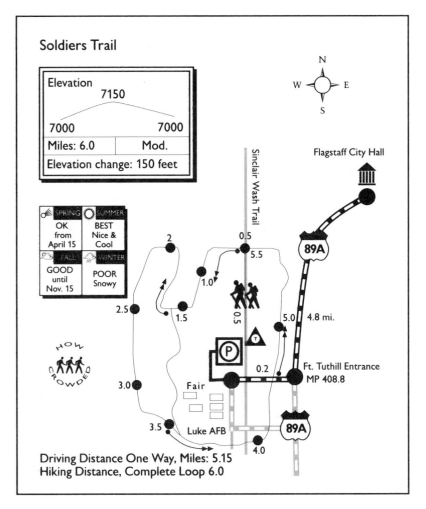

Mangum

South Kaibab Trail

General Information
Location Map B2
Phantom Ranch USGS Map
Kaibab (Tusayan) Forest Service Map

Driving Distance One Way: 81.4 miles *130.2 km* (Time 2 hours)
Access Road*:* All cars, All paved
Hiking Distance One Way*:* 1.5 miles *2.4 km* (Time 3 hours total)
How Strenuous*:* Hard
Features*:* Magnificent views of the Grand Canyon

NUTSHELL: This trail is maintained and heavily used. The first leg of the trail, down to Cedar Ridge, makes a perfect day hike.

DIRECTIONS:
From Flagstaff City Hall Go:
    North on Humphreys Street 0.60 miles *1.0 km* to a stoplight. See Access Map, page 10. Go left on Columbus Avenue and follow the curve north. Street signs will show the street first as Ft. Valley Road, then Highway 180, a major road to the Grand Canyon. At 50.4 miles *80.7 km* (MP 265.8), you will intersect Highway 64, coming out of Williams, at Valle. Go right at this junction and follow the highway to the south entrance to the Grand Canyon National Park, where you pay an entrance fee. Then drive on to the East Rim Drive, which you reach at 79.8 miles *128 km*. Turn right (east) on East Rim Drive, away from Grand Canyon Village. At the 80.9 mile *129.4 km* point, you will see the entrance to Yaki Point. During the high season you can't drive directly to the trailhead but must park in a designated area and take a shuttle to the trailhead.

TRAILHEAD: At the east side of the parking area. It is posted.

DESCRIPTION: This is the next most famous trail at the Grand Canyon, after the Bright Angel Trail. It is in constant use by hordes of people. Freight-bearing mules coming up from Phantom Ranch use this trail, so it is a busy place, with corrals for the mules at the top. The trail was built by the Park Service 1925-1928, to avoid the tolls charged on the privately-owned Bright Angel Trail. It goes to the river, a trip of 6.5 miles, *10.4 km* with a drop of 4,780 feet, then crosses the river on a bridge, and goes to the top of the North Rim on the other side of the river.
    Overnight backpacking trips in the Grand Canyon require permits (which are scarce and hard to get) and much preparation. Day hikes, such as the one we describe here, do not require permits. You do not need to notify

the Park Service that you are going to be on the trail. Just help yourself. Please take plenty of water. This is a *hot* trail in summer. We avoid it then.

The first part of this trail is an impressive set of switchbacks blasted out of a cliff face, with lots of rock work. Tremendous views open up to the hiker immediately, looking directly into the wide, colorful part of the main canyon.

The footing on the trail is generally good—sandy, with only a few loose rocks, and with many aprons at viewpoints.

The natural stopping point for a day hiker on this trail is at Cedar Ridge, a trip of 1.5 miles *2.4 km*. Here you are in red rock formations, with even better views into the canyon. There is a trail toilet here and a fossil exhibit, as well as hitching posts for the mules. Going out to the toe of the ridge, where you have superb views and a place to sit and soak them in, makes an unforgettable day hike.

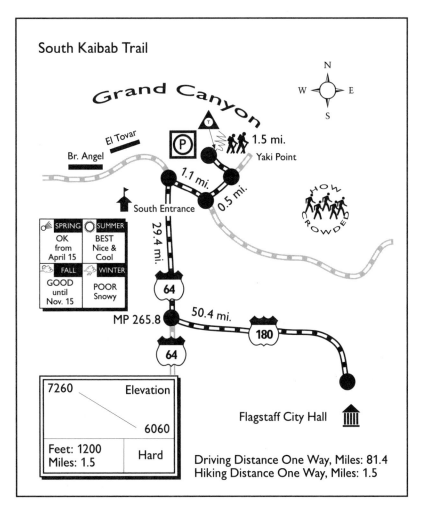

Mangum

Strawberry Crater

Driving Distance, One Way: 26.0 miles *41.6 km* (Time 40 minutes)
Access Road*: All cars, Last 5.6 miles *9.0 km* gravel, medium condition
Hiking Distance One Way*: 0.75 miles *1.2 km* (Time 45 minutes)
How Strenuous*: Hard
Features*: Volcano, Indian Ruins, Painted Desert Views

NUTSHELL: This hike takes you to an extinct volcano located 26.0 miles *41.6 km* north of Flagstaff. You hike up the south face of the crater to enjoy great views and Indian ruins.

DIRECTIONS:
From Flagstaff City Hall Go:
    East, then North on Highway 89. See Access Map, pages 10-11. Follow Highway 89 north out of town. At 20.4 miles *32.64 km* (MP 434.4), nearly at the bottom of a long downgrade, take FR 546 (unpaved) to the right. Follow FR 546 easterly to the 24.0 mile *38.4 km* point, where it meets FR 779. Here FR 546 veers to the right. Go straight on FR 779, which will take you to Strawberry Crater. You will soon see the crater ahead. At 26.0 miles *41.6 km*, you will reach a huge power line. Just beyond it, roads go left, right and straight ahead. Park at this intersection. High clearance cars can go ahead on a jeep trail about 0.1 miles *0.16 km* to park at the fence.

TRAILHEAD: At the fence. We have not seen any signs on our visits, except wilderness markers, but the path is clear and easy to follow.

DESCRIPTION: This trail has changed since we last hiked it. The trail formerly went north, along the side of the crater, and then curved to the east around the bottom of the crater wall, into the blown-out center. Now it climbs the steep—and only remaining—west wall. This is a harder hike, but we think it is an improvement. It is a return to the hiker-made path we used to follow before the official trail was built. Step over the fence and keep following the jeep trail. As you get near the crater, there is a road fork. Take the fork to the right. You will soon see cairns and as you come even closer to the crater, you will see that a path has been shoveled out, making a groove that moves counterclockwise around the crater.
    Next you will come to the point where the trail begins its climb to the top. Even though Strawberry is not terribly high, the trail is on a very steep

pitch and there are patches of loose cinders, causing us to rate the trail as hard. The trail winds up the wall of the crater, cresting out at the top, where there is a rim of crusty red lava. Low walls made of stacked red rock dot the rim of the crater. They are Indian ruins, but their nature is uncertain. They appear to be too low for habitations.

The walls of the bowl are decorated with layers of hard rock whose ribs roughly contour around the bowl. If you look closely at these rocks you will see that they contain clots of lava-fountain spatter that adhered, or welded, to each other when they fell back to Earth, simply because the clots were still hot and pasty. Had the clots totally solidified before falling back, they would have accumulated as a pile of loose cinders and volcanic bombs.

Once on top, you will be glad you made the climb, for the views from Strawberry Crater are great, with extensive volcano fields on all sides. To the north you can see the Painted Desert.

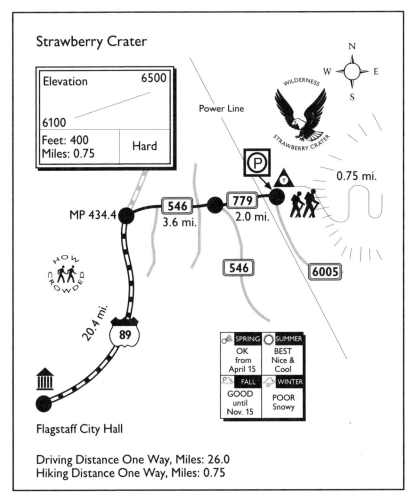

Mangum

Summit Mountain Trail

General Information
Location Map F1
Davenport Hill & Williams South USGS Maps
Kaibab (Williams District) Forest Service Map

Driving Distance One Way: 43.8 miles *70.08 km* (Time 60 minutes)
Access Road: All cars, Last 2.6 miles *4.16 km* good gravel roads
Hiking Distance One Way: 1.1 miles *1.76 km* (Time 45 minutes)
How Strenuous: Moderate
Features: Views

NUTSHELL: This hike takes you to the top of Summit Mountain south of Williams for some great views.

DIRECTIONS:
From Flagstaff City Hall Go:
    West, then south on Route 66 under the railroad overpass. See Access Map, page 10. Follow Route 66 when it turns right at the second stoplight. In about five miles *8.0 km* you will merge onto I-40 West and stay on it to the 30.3 miles *48.5 km* point, the Williams Exit, #165. Take that exit and at the stop sign go left to Williams. Go into town on Railroad Avenue to the 32.9 mile point *52.6 km* where you will find Fourth Street. Turn left on Fourth Street. As it leaves town its name changes to the Perkinsville Road (County 73). Stay on this road to the 41.2 miles *65.92 km* point (MP 177), where you turn left onto FR 110, the White Horse Lake Road. Take FR 110 to the 43.2 mile *69.12 km* point, where you turn right on FR 706. Follow FR 706 to the 43.8 mile *70.08 km* point, where you will see a parking area surrounded by a pole fence to your right, at the base of Summit Mountain. Park there.

TRAILHEAD: At the parking place. Marked and signed.

DESCRIPTION: This trail was opened in 1997, and is another effort by the Kaibab Forest people to create some shorter hiking trails for people who are looking for an interesting but moderate hiking experience. We think they have met their objectives superbly on this fine new trail, opened in August, 1997.
    Summit Mountain is not particularly tall as mountains in northern Arizona go, but it is well situated and its top in many places is clear due to steep lava cliffs on which no trees grow.
    Ranger John Eavis laid out this trail and told us of his astonishment when he saw that very old rock lines were evident if he looked hard enough. He

eventually found enough of these so that he could connect the dots and voilá, there was a nicely designed trail. He did some research and found that a ranger had laid out a horse trail to the top, where he had a lookout perch in a tree, in 1912. The trail had been abandoned and overgrown for many years when John rediscovered it.

In any event, the trail winds up the east face through a very nice forest. There are several places where you have good views to the east.

You will reach the top on the west wide of the mountain, from where you will have great views out over the landscape to the south and west. You can easily see the Black Hills and the location of Jerome. The craggy cliffs of Sycamore Canyon are also very evident. In this area you can walk back and forth around an unobstructed rim for some very fine viewing. There are a couple of big transmission towers on top of the mountain. We prefer to stay in the trees and enjoy the sights of nature.

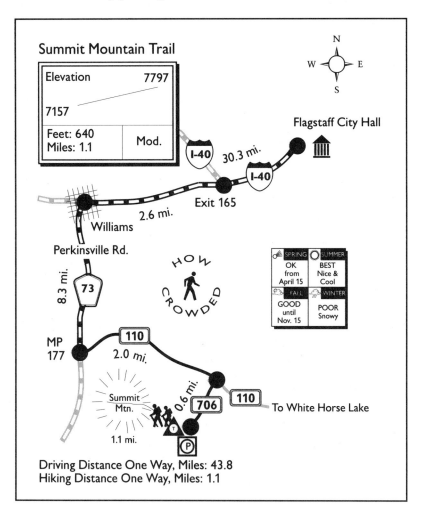

Sunset Trail #23

Driving Distance One Way: 8.5 miles *13.6 km* (Time 30 minutes)
Access Road: All cars, Last 4.9 miles *7.8 km* medium gravel road
Hiking Distance One Way: 3.6 miles *5.76 km* (Time 2 hours)
How Strenuous: Hard
Features: Views, Variety of scenery, Excellent forests

NUTSHELL: This is a marked and maintained trail that starts high on the Schultz Pass Road north of Flagstaff and winds to the top of Mt. Elden. **A personal favorite.**

DIRECTIONS:
From Flagstaff City Hall Go:
     North on Humphreys Street for 0.60 miles *1.0 km*. See Access Map, page 10. Turn left at the stoplight onto Columbus Avenue and follow it around a big curve to the north. You will see the street signs call this road Columbus Avenue at first, then Ft. Valley Road and then Highway 180. Stay on Highway 180 to the 3.1 miles *5.0 km* point (MP 218.6), where you turn right on the Schultz Pass Road. At 3.6 miles *5.8 km* where it curves to the left, you will see the Elden Lookout Road going straight. Ignore this and stay on the Schultz Pass Road. The paving will end soon and the road will become gravel. From here you have 4.9 miles *7.8 km* of gravel road to reach the 8.3 mile *13.3 km* point, where you will see a sign for the Sunset Trail. Turn right and go to the parking area at 8.5 miles *13.6 km*, parking by the sign board.

TRAILHEAD: Signed at the parking area.

DESCRIPTION: The beginning of this trail can be a bit confusing. Go east on the trail nearest the sign.
     At 0.3 miles *0.48 km* you will find a trail fork. The left trail goes to Schultz Tank, a pond to the north. Go right, away from the water, and then go up a side canyon. Since the canyon faces north and gets lots of water, it is lush and supports a nice forest.
     At the 1.2 mile *1.92 km* point you will cross a road and soon break into a clearing from where you have good views behind you of the San Francisco Peaks. Beyond this point you go over the crest of a hill and from that point onward will be unable to see the Peaks. You follow a shoulder of the Dry Lake Hills to the 1.85 mile *2.96 km* point, where there is a junction with the

Brookbank Trail. Take the fork to the left, downhill. It is signed.

The trail will take you down a fold between the Dry Lake Hills and Mt. Elden and then you will climb steeply to the top of a ridge on Mt. Elden. On the way up you will pass through a very attractive alpine mixed forest. Once you reach the ridge line you will drop over the other side slightly and walk along just below the ridge. At 3.1 miles *4.96 km* you will find the head of the **Heart Trail** to the left. Keep going to a trail junction at 3.6 miles *5.76 km*— just above the Elden Lookout Road. We have the trail stop here, though officially it goes on for another mile to the lookout tower.

This is a hard hike if you go back the way you came. We love it as a two-car shuttle, parking one car at the Sunset Trailhead and the other at a point 5.75 miles *9.2 km* up the Elden Lookout Road; then hiking down from the top.

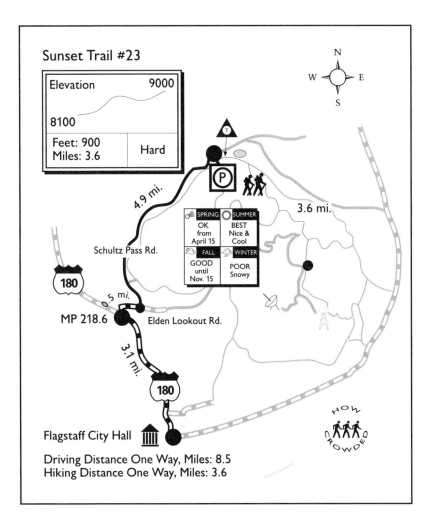

Sunset Trail #23

Elevation 9000

8100

Feet: 900
Miles: 3.6

Hard

N
W E
S

T

P

4.9 mi.

3.6 mi.

SPRING
OK from April 15

SUMMER
BEST Nice & Cool

FALL
GOOD until Nov. 15

WINTER
POOR Snowy

Schultz Pass Rd.

180

.5 mi.

MP 218.6

Elden Lookout Rd.

3.1 mi.

180

Flagstaff City Hall

HOW CROWDED

Driving Distance One Way, Miles: 8.5
Hiking Distance One Way, Miles: 3.6

Mangum

Sycamore Basin Trail #63

General Information
Location Map G2
Sycamore Basin USGS Map
Prescott Forest Service Map

Driving Distance One Way: 76.4 miles *122.3 km* (Time 2 hours)
Access Road: High clearance needed for last 13.4 miles *21.5 km*
Hiking Distance One Way: 3.0 miles *4.8 km* (Time 1.5 hours)
How Strenuous: Moderate
Features: Gorgeous remote scenic basin framed with redrocks

NUTSHELL: A long drive takes you to the magnificent basin of Sycamore Canyon.

DIRECTIONS:
From Flagstaff City Hall Go:
     West, then south on Route 66 under the railroad overpass. See Access Map, page 10. Follow Route 66 when it turns right at the second stoplight. In about five miles *8.0 km* you will merge onto I-40 West and stay on it to the 30.3 miles *48.5 km* point, the Williams Exit, #165. Take that exit and at the stop sign go left to Williams. Go into town on Railroad Avenue to the 32.9 mile point *52.6 km* where you will find Fourth Street. Turn left on Fourth Street. As it leaves town its name changes to the Perkinsville Road (County 73). Stay on this road to the bottom of the hill, where the paving ends, at 57.4 miles *92 km* and keep going east on FR 492. At 60.6 miles *97.0 km* you will reach an intersection where FR 354 comes down off the rim from your left. Turn right here and stay on the main road to the 63.0 mile *101 km* point, where you turn left at the sign for Henderson Flat on FR 181. Up to this point the roads have been fine for all cars. FR 181 has some rough spots and requires a high clearance vehicle. The road winds around until it reaches an old ranch house at Henderson Flat at the 70.8 mile *113.3 km* point. Keep going on FR 181 to its end at 76.4 miles *122.3 km*, where you will park at the Sycamore Canyon Wilderness boundary.

TRAILHEAD: At the parking spot. There are signs, one reading "Cow Flat 2, Taylor Cabin 8." Go through the fence.

DESCRIPTION: As you begin the hike, you will see how the Sedona area looked in its pristine condition. You drop down gradually into a vast basin rimmed with colorful cliffs, shaded red in the lower levels, tan and white on the higher levels. The trail is in good condition and makes for good walking.
     As you go, you may feel that you are in Sycamore Canyon, but you are

not. The basin is so vast that huge Sycamore Canyon occupies only a small part of it, to your right (east). At 1.6 miles *2.6 km*, you will come to Cross D Tank, where there is a corral made of juniper poles. This is about the halfway point of the hike.

At the 2.0 mile *3.2 km* point, we found a trail marker, "Yew Thicket Trail No. 52," with an arrow pointing NW. (According to maps, this trail climbs the rim and meets the **Lonesome Pocket Trail** at its trailhead in 5.3 miles *8.5 km*).

At the point where we end this hike, you climb up a long grade to top out on Lookout Ridge at 3.0 miles *4.8 km*. Here you will enjoy really splendid views. We especially enjoyed bushwhacking to the right, to a little redrock knob. Beyond the ridge, the trail makes a steep descent, and is much more difficult. We think that stopping at Lookout Ridge makes a good, moderate day hike, and suggest stopping there.

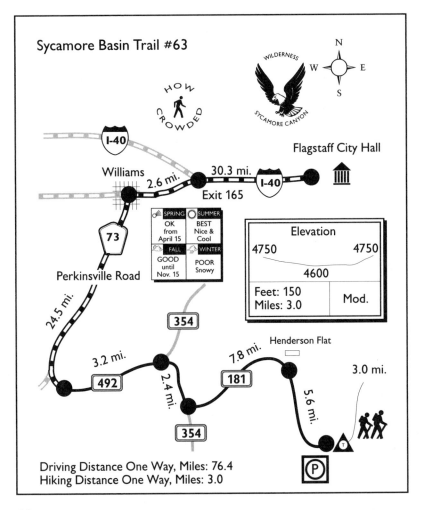

Sycamore Basin Trail #63

WILDERNESS
SYCAMORE CANYON

HOW CROWDED

N
W · E
S

I-40

Flagstaff City Hall

Williams   2.6 mi.   30.3 mi.   I-40
Exit 165

73

Perkinsville Road

SPRING	SUMMER
OK from April 15	BEST Nice & Cool
FALL	WINTER
GOOD until Nov. 15	POOR Snowy

Elevation
4750   4750
4600
Feet: 150
Miles: 3.0   Mod.

24.5 mi.

354

3.2 mi.

492

2.4 mi.

354

7.8 mi.

181

Henderson Flat

3.0 mi.

5.6 mi.

P   T

Driving Distance One Way, Miles: 76.4
Hiking Distance One Way, Miles: 3.0

Mangum

Sycamore Rim Trail

General Information
Location Map F2
Davenport Hill and Garland Prairie USGS Maps
Kaibab (Williams District) Forest Service Map

Driving Distance One Way: 28.2 miles *45.12 km* (Time 50 minutes)
Access Road: All cars, Last 10.2 miles *16.32 km* good gravel roads
Hiking Distance, Complete Loop: 12.0 miles *19.2 km* (Time 7.0 hours)
How Strenuous: Hard, due to length and rocky places
Features: Cabin and mill ruins, Lily ponds, Canyon springs, Views,
    Waterfall

NUTSHELL: This long hike displays the features of the Sycamore Canyon area southwest of Flagstaff, including spring-fed canyon pools, a waterfall, a huge canyon, a prairie and a hill climb.

DIRECTIONS:
From Flagstaff City Hall Go:
    West, then south on Route 66, beneath the railroad overpass. See Access Map, page 10. At 0.50 miles *0.8 km* turn right on Route 66. At the 5.0 mile *8.0 km* point you will merge onto Interstate-40 West. Drive I-40 West to Exit 178, "Parks" and take the exit—at the 18.0 mile *28.8 km* point. From the exit turn left and go south to Garland Prairie. When you cross the railroad tracks you will be on FR 141, the main road through Garland Prairie. Stay on it to the 27.6 miles *44 km* point, where it meets FR 131 and FR 13. Turn left (S) on FR 131 and drive to the 28.2 mile *45.12 km* point where you will see a paved drive and parking area to your right marked Dow Springs. Park there.

TRAILHEAD: Signed. Go through the opening in the fence.

DESCRIPTION: The Sycamore Rim Trail is a loop. You can start it at five places (see map), but we prefer the Dow Spring entry. Dow Spring comes out of a pipe projecting from the rim wall below the trail and flows into a small canyon, feeding into gigantic Sycamore Canyon. The trail crosses the canyon and moves along the opposite rim. Soon you will see water from LO Spring forming a chain of rock basin pools in which water lilies grow.
    Beyond these ponds, the canyon deepens dramatically as you continue along its rim. Sycamore Vista, coming up, provides a view into the immensity of Sycamore Canyon and some of its tributaries. From here you will leave the big canyon, climb a rocky hillside and go down into smaller Big Spring Canyon.
    The next point of interest is Sycamore Falls, a sharp chasm known to

climbers as Paradise Forks. When the falls run, they are spectacular. The most likely time for this is during the spring snow melt, though the trail may be very muddy for hiking then. From the falls, you walk north along the canyon until you come to Pomeroy Tanks, another series of scenic ponds.

Beyond Pomeroy Tanks, the land is more level. You will cross the **Overland Trail**, marked by cairns and burro symbols burnt into posts. Soon after this, you will go over FR 13 and make the 687 foot climb up KA Hill, from the top of which you will have great views over the countryside. Then it's down KA Hill heading back to the starting point. On the way you will pass the site of a 1910-1920 sawmill with interpretive sign. Beyond that— just as you reach the side trail back to the parking lot—you will see the remains of two old cabins.

By using two entry points and two cars, hikers can divide this long trail into smaller portions, as shown on the map.

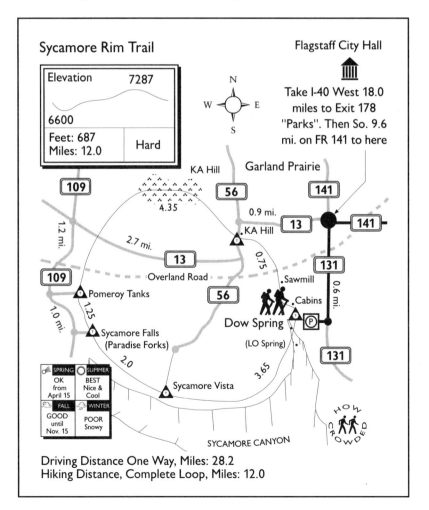

Taylor Cabin Trail #35

General Information
Location Map F2
Loy Butte, Sycamore Point USGS Maps
Coconino Forest Service Map

Driving Distance One Way: 29 miles *46.4 km* (Time 1.5 hours)
Access Road: High clearance, 25.4 miles *40.6 km* unpaved, rough spots
Hiking Distance One Way: 2.85 miles *4.6 km* (Time 2.5 hours)
How Strenuous: Hard, Very steep rocky trail
Features: Views, Tremendous wild canyons

NUTSHELL: Located 29.0 miles *46.4 km* southwest of Flagstaff, this hike plunges from the top of Buck Ridge to the bottom of Sycamore Canyon.

DIRECTIONS:
From Flagstaff City Hall Go:
    West, then south on Route 66, beneath the railroad overpass. See Access Map, page 10. At 0.50 miles *0.8 km* turn right on Route 66. At 2.6 miles *4.16 km* you will reach the Woody Mountain Road, FR 231, where you turn left. It is paved about a mile and then turns into a cinder road. At 16.6 miles *26.56 km* you will intersect FR 538. Turn right onto FR 538 and follow it to an intersection at 22.3 miles *35.7 km*. Turn left here, staying on FR 538. At 25.7 miles *41.1 km* you will pass the turn to Winter Cabin. Go straight ahead to the 26.1 mile *42 km* point, where FR 538B branches to the right. Take FR 538B. It follows the path of a huge power line. FR 538B is decent down to the 28.5 mile *45.6 km* point but from there it is one of the worst roads we have seen, virtually impassable, with lots of exposed chassis-ripping rock. Many hikers will want to walk this last half mile. The road ends at 29 miles *46.4 km* at a bare spot on the ridge, where you must park. **Caution**: do not drive down into the canyon, as the road is blocked by a big gate, trapping you in a place where you cannot turn around.

TRAILHEAD: Walk down the road 0.25 miles *0.4 km*.

DESCRIPTION: The trailhead is at a strategic point, located on a thin ridge where three trails come together: the Mooney Trail (see *Sedona Hikes*), the Taylor Cabin Trail and the **Casner Mountain North** trail. The views here are very fine. The ridge divides Sycamore Canyon from the Sedona back country, so you can see into both Sycamore and Sedona.
    There are some false trails at the beginning of the Taylor Cabin trail. From the rusty metal trailhead sign, walk behind it 15 paces to a tree to which a barbed wire fence and Wilderness sign are nailed. Turn right behind

the tree and then turn left at the next trail fork. You will go downhill on a zigzag course. Once established at the beginning, you can follow the trail.

The trail works its way down through a beautiful forest. It contains pockets of maple, beautiful in late October when their leaves are red. The trail is steep and littered with loose rocks, making for tricky footing.

When you have gone down about a mile *1.6 km*, it will seem that you have reached bottom. Not so. From here the trail follows the channel of a side canyon. In many places you walk right in the streambed. Look for cairns and blazes on this leg. Hiking here is slow, hard on the feet, and almost dangerous. As compensation, you pass through a beautiful red-walled canyon that is very colorful. This side canyon eventually merges into the awesome main canyon of Sycamore.

At the bottom you can visit Taylor Cabin, built of native stone and set against the canyon wall. It is a hard 1.5 miles *2.4 km* to your left (S).

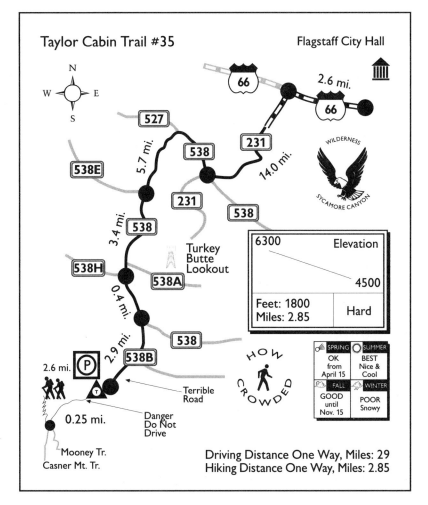

Mangum

Three Sisters

General Information
Location Map E1
Williams North USGS Map
Kaibab Forest Service Map

Driving Distance One Way: 38.85 miles *62.2 km* (Time 1.0 hour)
Access Road: All cars, Last 1.75 miles *2.8 km* good unpaved roads
Hiking Distance One Way: 0.50 miles *0.8 km* (Time 1.0 hour)
How Strenuous: Moderate
Features: Interesting volcanic formations, views

NUTSHELL: This group of three hills is a landmark near the City of Williams. You park at a saddle between two of the "sisters" and hike to the top of the tallest. On the way you will see huge boulders and volcanic outcroppings and at the top will enjoy tremendous views.

DIRECTIONS:
From Flagstaff City Hall Go:
   South on Route 66 under the railroad overpass. Be sure to turn right on Route 66 at the second stoplight. See Access Map on page 10. In about five miles *8.0 km* you will merge onto I-40 West and stay on it to the 34.5 miles *55.2 km* point, where you turn right on the Golf Course Exit, #161. You will come to a stop sign at 34.9 miles *55.9 km*. Turn right and go to the 35.4 mile point *56.6 km*, where there is another stop sign. Turn right and go under the railroad overpass. Stay on the main paved road. Go past the golf course. The paving ends at 37.1 miles *59.36 km* and you begin a good gravel road, FR 124, which winds around the last "sister" and begins to climb. At the 38.1 mile *61.0 km* point turn right on an unsurfaced unmarked road. The road is not maintained well but isn't bad when dry. Don't try it when it is wet. The road climbs to a saddle where at 38.85 miles *62.2 km* you will see a loop pullout to your right. Park there.

TRAILHEAD: There is no trail. You simply climb to the top of the "sister" to the north.

DESCRIPTION: Generally we like to hike on trails, but if we come across a good non-trail hike we think our readers can handle, we include it. This is such a hike.
   As you walk up the hill, you will find that the soil is composed of coarse red cinders. You will think that you see trails through the brush, but actually they are simply natural lanes between bushes. You will pick up game trails only to have them disappear. Don't worry. It is always easy to tell

where you are headed. Just keep moving uphill.

At the 0.25 mile *0.4 km* point you will reach the top of a cinder knob. Here you will have your first views, a taste of what is to come. You will see the higher crest before you, made of much different material. Instead of being a rounded cinder hill, it shows exposed volcanic rock, with huge tumbled boulders and a ridge of cliffs along the uplifted east face. It is easy to walk over to the base of this higher face of the hill and begin to climb it.

When you reach the base of the boulders you will have to pick your way more carefully, though we had no trouble finding a route. Once you are on top, you can navigate with ease. Because of bare boulders at places on the top you will have clear views in many spots. The views are splendid. You can see the City of Williams with Bill Williams Mountain behind it. The San Francisco Peaks, Sitgreaves Mountain and Kendrick Peak are all clearly in view. The top is about 0.50 miles *0.8 km* from where you parked.

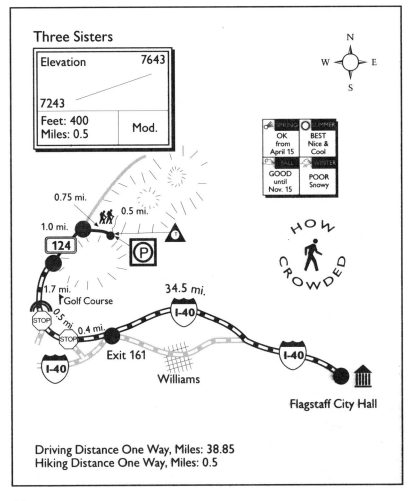

Three Sisters

Elevation	7643
7243	
Feet: 400 Miles: 0.5	Mod.

N
W — E
S

SPRING	SUMMER
OK from April 15	BEST Nice & Cool
FALL	WINTER
GOOD until Nov. 15	POOR Snowy

0.75 mi.
0.5 mi.
1.0 mi.
124
1.7 mi.
Golf Course
STOP
0.5 mi.
STOP
0.4 mi.
I-40
34.5 mi.
I-40
Exit 161
Williams
I-40
Flagstaff City Hall

HOW CROWDED

Driving Distance One Way, Miles: 38.85
Hiking Distance One Way, Miles: 0.5

Mangum

Tramway Trail #32

General Information
Location Map G4
Calloway Butte USGS Map
Coconino Forest Service Map

Driving Distance One Way: 57.5 miles *92 km* (Time 1.5 hours)
Access Road: High clearance vehicle mandatory, Last 1.7 miles *2.72 km*
     extremely rough
Hiking Distance One Way: 0.7 miles *1.12 km* (Time 45 minutes)
How Strenuous: Hard
Features: Views, Beautiful pristine stream, Remote canyon

NUTSHELL: This is one of the few trails into West Clear Creek, a remote canyon 57.5 miles *92 km* southeast of Flagstaff. The hike is short but steep and very beautiful.

DIRECTIONS:
From Flagstaff City Hall Go:

West, then south on Route 66 beneath the railroad overpass. See Access Map, page 10. At the 0.5 mile *0.8 km* point, go straight on Milton Road. At 1.7 miles *2.72 km* you will reach a stoplight at Forest Meadows Street. Turn right here onto Forest Meadows and go one block to Beulah. Turn left on Beulah and follow it south. Beulah merges onto Highway 89A. At 2.4 miles *3.84 km* (MP 401.6), turn left onto the Lake Mary Road at the stoplight. Follow the Lake Mary Road, going past Lower and Upper Lake Mary and Mormon Lake to the 48.9 mile *78.24 km* point (MP 297.7), where you turn right onto a dirt road, FR 81. The highway sign shows "V Bar V Ranch, Poor Farm and West Clear Creek." Follow FR 81 to the 52.0 mile *83.2 km* point, its junction with FR 81E, turning left on 81E and staying on it to the 55.8 mile *89.3 km* point, where you reach a fork. Take the right fork, on FR 693. You will see a sign for the Tramway Trail soon. FR 693 is a very rough road, requiring high clearance and tough tires. Keep driving FR 693 to the 57.5 mile *92 km* point, a parking area at the very rim of the canyon.

TRAILHEAD: There is a sign at the parking area.

DESCRIPTION: West Clear Creek is a tributary of the Verde River. Its headwaters are on the uplands of the Mogollon Rim, where this hike takes place. Located in a remote area, West Clear Creek canyon cuts a course running from east to west. At its low end it joins the Verde River near Camp Verde.

At the beginning of the hike, you will see a cable to your left. It goes down to the canyon bottom, and was part of the tram that gives this trail its name. You will see the cable again farther down the trail.

The canyon is open to view from the beginning. It is not very wide but is deep and colorful—buff sandstone with splashes of a light orangey rust.

The trail is very steep, with a bit of scrambling where you have to climb down ledges.

We were here in late May and there were all sorts of flowers; everything from cactuses to penstemons were blooming.

At the bottom, the vegetation is rich. You come out at a big pool at the base of an immense cliff. This is a favorite fishing hole for the speckled and rainbow trout that inhabit the water of Clear Creek. If you want to do any walking along the bottom, we recommend tennies or Tevas, as there are places where you will want to wade. The bottom is a peaceful, beautiful paradise.

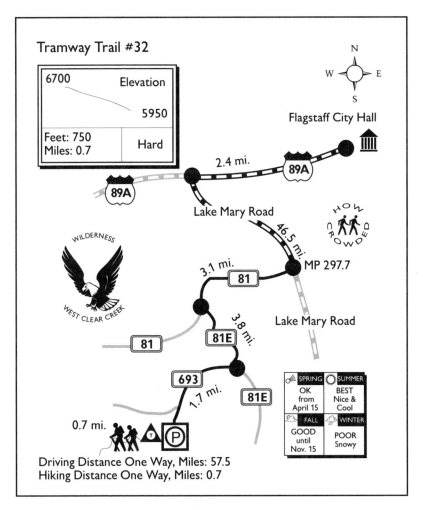

Mangum

Tunnel (Watershed) Road

General Information
Location Map E3
Humphreys Peak & Sunset Crater West USGS Maps
Coconino Forest Service Map

Driving Distance One Way: 9.4 miles *15.1 km* (Time 30 minutes)
Access Road: All cars, Last 5.8 miles *9.28 km* good gravel road
Hiking Distance One Way: 8.5 miles *13.6 km* (Time 4.5 hours)
How Strenuous: Hard if you go full distance
Features: High mountains, Interesting tunnel, Excellent views

NUTSHELL: Located about 10 miles *16 km* north of Flagstaff, this moderate but long hike takes you through beautiful forests and meadows on the San Francisco Peaks.

DIRECTIONS:
From Flagstaff City Hall Go:
North on Humphreys Street for 0.60 miles *1.0 km*. See Access Map, page 10. Turn left at the stoplight onto Columbus Avenue and follow it around a big curve to the north. You will see the street signs call this road Columbus at first, then Ft. Valley Road and then Highway 180. Stay on Highway 180 to the 3.1 miles *5.0 km* point (MP 218.6), where you turn right on the Schultz Pass Road. Turn right and follow this road. At 3.6 miles *5.76 km* it curves to the left and you will see the Elden Lookout Road going straight. Stay on the Schultz Pass Road. The paving will end soon and the road will become gravel surfaced. Follow it to the 8.8 mile *14.1 km* point, just beyond the **Weatherford Trail** sign, where FR 146 intersects the road from the left. Turn left onto FR 146 and take it to the 9.4 mile *15.1 km* point where you will reach a locked gate. Park off the road by the gate.

TRAILHEAD: Not a marked trail. You walk FR 146 beyond the gate.

DESCRIPTION: The City of Flagstaff and Forest Service use FR 146 for access to the city's watershed, particularly the works at Jack Smith Spring, so it is maintained. The only vehicle travel allowed is for city maintenance trucks. Mountain bikers love this road, so stay alert.
The grade of this road is gentle, running along the 8000 foot contour of the mountain for the first couple of miles, then beginning a climb that terminates at about 9400 feet at Jack Smith Spring. When you take the **Inner Basin Trail** hike, you will visit Jack Smith Spring.
You will reach the tunnel for which the hike is named at 2.0 miles *3.2 km*. At that point the road builders hit a lava dike and decided to bore

through it rather than blast it away. The tunnel is about 25 feet long, 10 feet wide and 12 feet high, and adds a pleasing note of interest. Hikers who want a mild but rewarding hike might want to turn back at the tunnel.

There are many fine views from the road, especially off to the hiker's right, into the Sunset Crater area. The volcanic nature of the terrain is plainly displayed and you will see a myriad of cinder cones, which are the remains of small volcanoes.

You can hike all the way to Jack Smith Spring, 8.5 miles *13.6 km*, if you are hardy and quick, but this requires a 17.0 mile *27.2 km* round-trip hike at high elevations, which may be too arduous for many readers. So, pick your spot anywhere and turn back at your own comfort point.

The road doesn't end at the spring. It continues climbing 5.5 miles *8.8 km* farther to the north face of the Peaks. The **Bear Jaw** and **Abineau Canyon** trails terminate on the far reaches of FR 146.

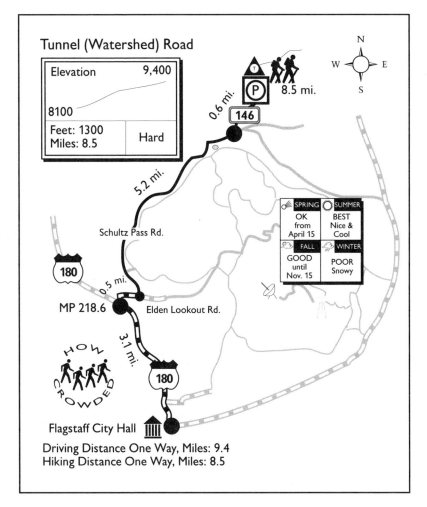

Turkey Hills

General Information
Location Map F3
Flagstaff East USGS Map
Coconino Forest Map

Driving Distance One Way: 8.65 miles *13.8 km* (Time 20 minutes)
Access Road: All cars, Last 1.1 miles *1.8 km* rough cinder road
Hiking Distance One Way: 1.0 miles *1.6 km* (Time 30 minutes)
How Strenuous: Moderate
Features: Easy access, Views

NUTSHELL: This cinder hill is located so as to give good views around the Flagstaff area. You hike an abandoned road that goes around the hill to the top.

DIRECTIONS:
From Flagstaff City Hall Go:
    East on Route 66. See Access Map, pages 10-11. At 3.8 miles *6.1 km* (MP 418.2/MP 200) you will come to a fork, where Route 66 goes to the right. Turn right onto Route 66 and follow it to the 7.55 mile *12.1 km* point, where there is a cinder road to the left. Turn left onto this road, FR 791, and follow it to the 8.3 mile *13.3 km* point, where the road splits. Both the left and right forks are marked FR 510B. Take the left fork. Up to this point the road has been good, but it now turns pretty bad, as there are ruts and exposed rocks. If you are not in a high clearance vehicle, you should park at the 510B fork. If you can make it, go up to the 8.65 miles *13.8 km* point, where there is an unmarked road going to the left. Park on the right shoulder here.

TRAILHEAD: There are no trail signs. You hike the road.

DESCRIPTION: At one time there was a cinder pit operation on this hill. The road you will hike was built to service the pit. You will see a number of side roads as you walk along. At every junction take the right fork, always staying on the outside of the hill and moving upward.
    You will soon come to the pit. There you will see that a road keeps going up the hill to the right of the pit. Stay on it and continue the ascent. From this point onwards it is easy to tell what the roads are doing and to follow the correct one.
    The road literally winds completely around the hill as it climbs. The vegetation is mostly low so that you can see clearly. The views are good. You are looking at some interesting landscapes: volcano fields, and beyond them, the Painted Desert. You can get a good look at Anderson Mesa. To the west

you can see parts of Flagstaff.

The top of Turkey Hill is a true top. There are no false tops or benches. You suddenly pop up onto a small flat summit from which you can see out on all sides.

On the maps, you will see references to Turkey Hills. The other hill is quite a bit smaller and is to the north of the one you can hike.

You will also see the Turkey Hills Pueblo on maps. This is located north of the hiking hill also. The best way to reach it is by going east on the Townsend-Winona Road for 3.0 miles *4.8 km* from the stoplight, then turning right on an unmarked gravel road and following it for 0.15 miles *0.24 km*. There you will see a burglar-proof chain-link fence surrounding about a half acre of ground to your right. Unfortunately there isn't much to see: just low lines of rubble marking pit houses and you can't get inside for a closer look.

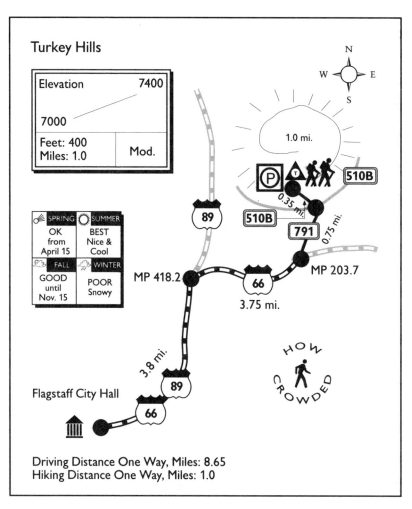

Upper Oldham Trail

General Information
Location Map E3
Humphreys Peak & Sunset Crater West USGS Maps
Coconino Forest Service Map

Driving Distance One Way: 7.1 miles *11.36 km* (Time 30 minutes)
Access Road: All cars, Last 2.5 miles *4.0 km* medium unpaved road
Hiking Distance One Way: 1.75 miles *2.8 km* (Time 1 hour)
How Strenuous: Hard
Features: Views, Forests

NUTSHELL: This is a marked and maintained trail that starts at a point on the Elden Lookout Road near the top of Mt. Elden north of Flagstaff and climbs to Sunset Park.

DIRECTIONS:
From Flagstaff City Hall Go:
    North on Humphreys Street for 0.60 miles *1.0 km*. See Access Map, page 10. Turn left at the stoplight onto Columbus Avenue and follow it around a big curve to the north. You will see the street signs call this road Columbus Avenue at first, then Ft. Valley Road and then Highway 180. Stay on Highway 180 to the 3.1 miles *5.0 km* point (MP 218.6), where the Schultz Pass Road, FR 420, goes to the right. Follow this road. At the 3.6 miles *5.76 km* point it curves left where you will see the Elden Lookout Road (FR 557) going straight. Take the right fork and follow FR 557 to the 7.1 mile *11.36 km* point, where you will park in an area off the left shoulder.

TRAILHEAD: Across the road from the parking place.

DESCRIPTION: This trail is part of the Dry Lake Hills/Mt. Elden trail system, so it is marked and maintained. You will follow an old road for the first 0.75 miles *1.2 km*. The climb on this stretch of the trail is gradual and doesn't really prepare you for the steep climb that is to follow. This part of the trail takes you through a dense spruce forest. Some of the trees have so much moss on their sides that you'd think you were in a rain forest.
    The old road ends where it bumps up against the flank of Mt. Elden. From there a footpath climbs the mountain. This second part of the trail is very steep, really a hard climb. It also passes through a heavy forest. The trees are so thick that you don't get many views even though you are climbing high enough to have excellent vantage points.
    Near the end of the trail you will come out into an open meadow called Oldham Park. You will cross it and reach the Elden Lookout Road at a place

that is 2.3 miles *3.68 km* up the road from where you parked. This is officially the end of the trail, but you will miss a splendid view if you stop here. Go across the road up to the skyline where you will see two trail signs. This place is Sunset Park. You can walk along the crest in either direction to enjoy the views.

The views from the top are excellent due to the Radio Fire that burned away many acres of timber in 1978. This was a terrible fire and we remember it well. Started by a teenager's campfire on a dry, windy June day, the fire roared up a canyon, burst over the top and raged out of control for days. At night Mt. Elden looked like a huge heap of glowing embers.

Our text depicts the trail as planned by the Forest Service. However, we think that this is a much better hike if you use two cars. Park one at the 7.1 mile *11.36 km* point and take the other one to the top and park it at the 9.4 miles *15.0 km* point. Then you start the hike from the top.

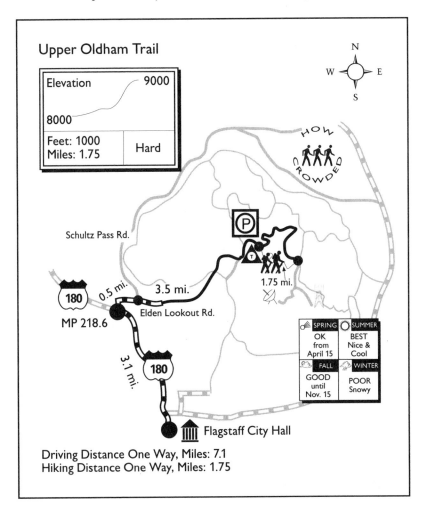

Veit Springs

General Information
Location Map E3
Humphreys Peak USGS Map
Coconino Forest Service Map

Driving Distance One Way: 11.8 miles *18.9 km* (Time 30 minutes)
Access Road: All cars, All paved
Hiking Distance One Way: 0.75 miles *1.2 km* (Time 30 minutes)
How Strenuous: Easy
Features: Alpine forests, Historical cabin, Rock art

NUTSHELL: The hike takes you to an old cabin site on the San Francisco Peaks about 11.8 miles *18.9 km* north of Flagstaff, a lush, peaceful Shangri-La. **A personal favorite.**

DIRECTIONS:
From Flagstaff City Hall Go:
    North on Humphreys Street for 0.60 miles *1.0 km*. See Access Map, page 10. Turn left at the stoplight onto Columbus Avenue and follow it around a big curve to the north. You will see the street signs call this road Columbus at first, then Ft. Valley Road and then Highway 180. Stay on Highway 180 to the 7.3 miles *11.68 km* point (MP 223), where the road to the Snow Bowl branches off to the right. It is well posted. Follow the Snow Bowl road to the 11.8 miles *18.9 km* point. There you will see a driveway to your right to the Lamar Haines Memorial Wildlife Area. Pull in and park there.

TRAILHEAD: Posted at the gate.

DESCRIPTION: At the parking area there is a gate. Go through it. There is a large sign beyond the gate telling about the area. The trail goes uphill to the right behind the sign, not straight ahead along the old jeep road.
    Although a lot of snow falls on the San Francisco Peaks, very little of the water produced by melting snow appears there in streams, ponds or springs. Due to their volcanic origin, the Peaks are quite porous and most of the water produced by snow melt sinks in and goes into underground rivers. Here and there you will find a spring. This hike takes you to the site of two springs, Veit and Canadian.
    The early settlers in the area looked carefully for springs and used most of them as sites for sheep or cattle operations. One such settler was Ludwig Veit, who homesteaded the area reached by this hike in 1892. If you look carefully you see his name chiseled into the face of a boulder to the right of the cabin.

As you walk the trail you will reach a fork at about 0.20 miles *0.32 km*. Go right here, downhill. You will follow an old road to the cabin from this point. At 0.70 miles *1.1 km* the road winds around to a set boulder on the face of which is a plaque honoring Lamar Haines, a Flagstaff outdoorsman.

Follow the road from the plaque up to the old log cabin. The cabin is very low, having been cut down so that adults can't stand up in it. Above the cabin is a pond formed by the water from the main spring. Between the pond and the cliff is a small stone shed. In the face of the cliff a frame has been built around the opening to Veit Spring. There is a basalt ridge running behind the cabin site, furnishing a wall or backdrop of lava cliffs.

If you walk the face of the cliff to your left (as you face the spring), you will go around a bend and find Canadian Spring. There are pictographs on the rock walls surrounding it.

This is a terrific place to enjoy changing aspen leaves in October.

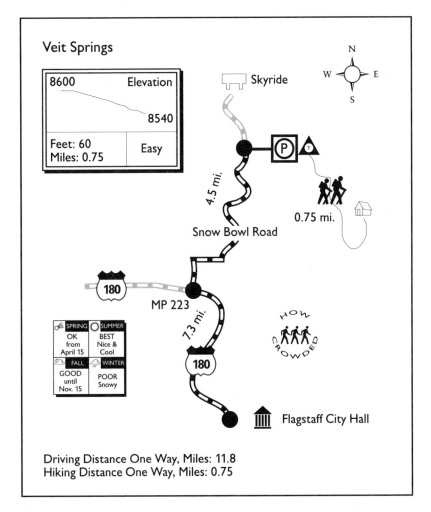

Vista Loop Trail

General Information
Location Map F3
Flagstaff East USGS Map
Coconino Forest Service Map

Driving Distance One Way: 8.1 miles *13.0 km* (Time 20 minutes)
Access Road: All cars, Last 0.2 miles *0.32 km* good gravel road
Hiking Distance One Way: 0.6 miles *0.96 km* (Time 20 minutes)
How Strenuous: Moderate
Features: Beautiful canyon, Rock climbing area, Easy to reach

NUTSHELL: Located south of Flagstaff, only 8.1 miles *13.0 km* out on the
Lake Mary Road, this hike requires a zigzagging descent into Walnut
Canyon on a well-made trail, then an easy walk across the canyon bottom to
the base of some impressive and beautiful sandstone cliffs, a favorite area
for local climbers. It's great fun to watch them at their work.

DIRECTIONS:
From Flagstaff City Hall Go:
    West and then south (left) on Route 66 under the railroad overpass. See
Access Map, page 10. At the 0.5 mile point *0.8 km*, go straight on Milton
Road. At 1.7 miles *2.72 km* you reach the stoplight at Forest Meadows,
where you turn right. At the next corner turn left on Beulah and follow it out
of town. Beulah will connect onto Highway 89A. At the 2.4 miles *3.84 km*
point (MP 401.6) you will see the turnoff to the Lake Mary Road to your
left, where the last stoplight in town is located. Take the turn and follow the
Lake Mary Road to the 7.9 mile *12.6 km* point where you will see a gravel
road to your left. This is just a few feet past the second cattle guard on the
Lake Mary Road. Turn left onto the gravel road and take it about 0.2 miles
0.32 km, through a camp site to get as close to the canyon as possible, at 8.1
miles *13.0 km*. Park there.

TRAILHEAD: Walk out toward the canyon rim, where you will see a sign
reading: "Vista Loop Trail/Sandys Canyon Trail".

DESCRIPTION: From the parking area you will see the canyon. Walk out
toward the rim on the obvious path. You will come to a trail junction at 0.1
miles *0.16 km* where there is a sign indicating that hikers turn left to use the
Sandys Canyon Trail and straight ahead for the Vista Loop Trail. Go
straight ahead. You will see a sign reading, "Climbing Area .4 mi."
    Stand at the rim and look across the canyon at the cliffs on the other side.
You will probably see rock climbers dangling from ropes, though sometimes

you can hear them before you can see them. Also notice the interesting lava flow to your left, spilling from the edge of the canyon down the side and into the canyon. A few aspens grow in the lava, making a picturesque contrast with their white trunks against the stark black of the lava.

The trail to the bottom is a good one, recently (1998) constructed and winding down a series of switchbacks. You will reach the bottom of the canyon at the 0.4 mile *0.64 km* point. The canyon itself is lovely, full of riparian growth—including a bit of poison ivy, so be careful.

You follow the trail across the creek channel to the other side, the base of the cliffs, where it turns to your left and goes on strongly for a bit, then dwindles down and disappears at the 0.6 mile *0.96 km* point. From this point you have another perspective of the climbing activity and can enjoy the cliffs up close and personal. They are tall, steep, and have a lovely pink tint atop a base color of creamy tan.

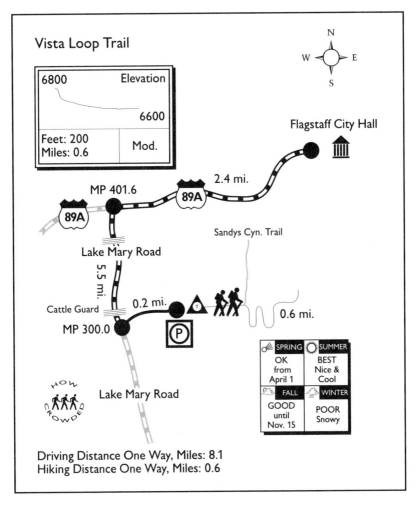

Mangum

Walker Lake

General Information
Location Map E3
Humphreys Peak, White Horse Hills & Wing Mt. USGS Maps
Coconino Forest Service Map

Driving Distance One Way: 21.6 miles *34.56 km* (Time 40 minutes)
Access Road: All cars, Last 2.2 miles *3.52 km* good dirt road
Hiking Distance One Way: 0.50 miles *0.8 km* (Time 1 hour)
How Strenuous: Easy
Features: Views, Scenic crater

NUTSHELL: This is a gentle hike to the crater of an ancient volcano located about 20 miles *32 km* north of Flagstaff.

DIRECTIONS:
From Flagstaff City Hall Go:
    North on Humphreys Street for 0.60 miles *1.0 km*. See Access Map, page 10. Turn left at the stoplight onto Columbus Avenue and follow it around a big curve to the north. You will see the street signs call this road Columbus at first, then Ft. Valley Road and then Highway 180. Stay on Highway 180 to the 19.4 miles *31.04 km* point (MP 235.2), where the unpaved upper Hart Prairie Road branches off to the right. Turn right onto this road, which is also identified as FR 151, and follow it to the 21.0 miles *33.6 km* point. There FR 418 branches to the left. Take FR 418 and follow it just 0.20 miles *0.32 km*, to the 21.2 mile *33.92 km* point. There you will reach an unmarked dirt road to the left. Turn left onto it and follow it to the 21.6 miles *34.56 km* point, where you will park.

TRAILHEAD: There are no trail signs. You will see a blocked road going up to the top of a cinder cone. You hike this road.

DESCRIPTION: The road is easy walking, being broad with a gradual grade. It is about 0.20 miles *0.32 km* to the top, where you will find yourself on the rim of a volcanic crater. This was a small volcano so the crater is fairly shallow. Walker Lake is in the center of the crater. The lake, never very big, often dries up completely in the summer. The best time of year to find water is in spring, after the snow melts, which is usually in April or May.
    The road forks at the top and you can walk either left or right on it. The left fork goes directly down to the lake, while the right fork sweeps around through a stand of aspen and firs and is more scenic. It is only about 0.10 miles *0.16 km* to the lake by the left fork, slightly longer than that by the right fork.

As you approach you will see that this area was burned. A monster forest fire raged through the area in the spring of 1996. At the top you can see the damage. About half of the trees were burned, but the fire was swirling so that it burned in irregular swathes. This is a good place to study erosion caused by removal of the tree cover.

The north rim of the crater is higher than the south rim. It is worth a climb up the north rim if you are willing to make the effort, for fine views from the top unimpeded by trees. There is no trail to the north rim but it is easy to bushwhack your way there. You can't get lost.

This is a pretty and little known spot. The San Francisco Peaks area is dotted with over one hundred volcanic craters. This is one of the most accessible and scenic of them, with the bonus of a lake. Most craters are pretty bare, but this one has lots of vegetation and a nice friendly feel.

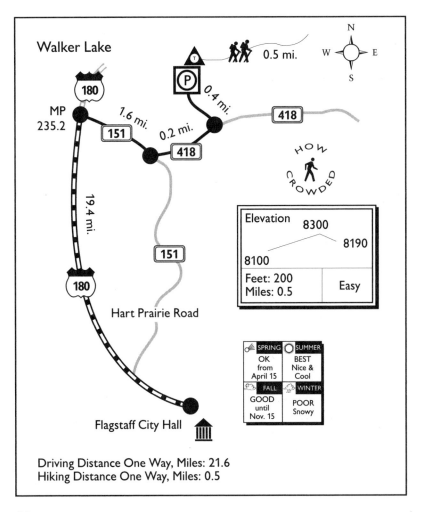

Mangum

Walnut Canyon Link (Arizona Trail)

General Information
Location Map F3
Flagstaff East USGS Map
Coconino Forest Service Map

Driving Distance One Way: 12.8 miles *20.48 km* (Time 25 minutes)
Access Road: All cars, Last 1.7 miles *2.72 km* good gravel road
Hiking Distance One Way: 5.75 miles *9.2 km*
How Strenuous: Moderate
Features: Scenic forest and canyons, easy to reach

NUTSHELL: This hike takes you over a segment of the Arizona Trail, which you join at a road near Walnut Canyon National Monument. You hike into a tributary canyon and then west along the Walnut Canyon rim to Fisher Point.

DIRECTIONS:
From Flagstaff City Hall Go:
East, then north on Highway 89. See Access Map, pages 10-11. At 4.2 miles *6.7 km* take the entrance to Interstate-40, turning left at 4.8 miles *7.68 km*, so that you are on I-40 headed east. At 8.3 miles *13.28 km* (MP 204), take the turn to Walnut Canyon, Exit 204. You will reach a stop sign at 8.6 miles *13.76 km*. Turn right and follow the Walnut Canyon access road. At the 11.1 mile *17.76 km* point, you will see a sign for the Arizona Trail at a gravel road, FR 303. Turn right on FR 303 and follow it to the 12.8 mile *20.48 km* point, where you will see a fenced parking area to your left. Pull in there and park.

TRAILHEAD: There is a link of the Arizona Trail to the north and to the south at the parking place. We consider the trail to the north to be a rather uninteresting connector. Take the trail to the south, toward Walnut Canyon. It is posted at the parking area.

DESCRIPTION:
The first leg of this hike is on an old road, the sides of which are lined with brush to delineate the trail. At 1.15 miles *1.84 km*, the junction with FR 3018, you will find a watering place that has been created for animals behind a fence to your right. A section of corrugated iron roofing on the ground catches rain and pours it into troughs. These devices are called trick tanks.

Just beyond this, the trail leaves the road and goes to the right (S) becoming a footpath. You will soon reach the rim of a tributary canyon, with Walnut Canyon to your left. The trail takes you about half way down the side canyon and then moves laterally to the west until it nears the head of the canyon. You cross the streambed at the bottom and then climb up the other side, heading south again. The trail is well engineered so that climbing down and up are gradual and easy. At the 2.0 mile *3.2 km* point you will come to a signed trail junction. There is a fork to the left to a Walnut Canyon viewpoint (not worth a visit).

Take the right fork, which takes you west along old roads. At the 4.0 mile *6.4 km* point, the trail leaves the road and moves south to the canyon rim, then west near the rim. At times the trail moves right on the rim of the canyon, allowing good views. At the 5.5 mile *8.8 km* point, the main trail branches off to the right at a signposted junction so that it can come down off the canyon rim. Stay on top, following the secondary trail to Fisher Point.

At Fisher Point you will enjoy fine views from a location high atop the bluff under which the first cave is located. (See **Sandys Canyon**).

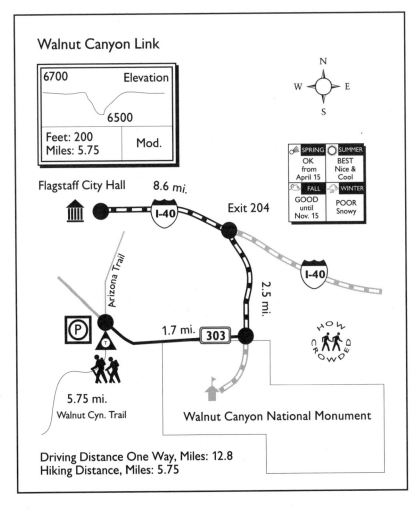

Walnut Canyon Trails (4)

General Information
Location Map F3
Flagstaff East USGS Map
Coconino Forest Service Map

Driving Distance One Way: 11.6 miles *18.56 km* (Time 25 minutes)
Access Road: All cars, All paved
Hiking Distances: See below
How Strenuous: Easy to Moderate
Features: Indian ruins, Scenic canyon

NUTSHELL: There are four hiking trails in the Walnut Canyon National Monument, located just a few miles east of Flagstaff. All allow the hiker to enjoy scenery and ruins.

DIRECTIONS:
From Flagstaff City Hall Go:
East, then north on Highway 89. See Access Map, pages 10-11. At 4.2 miles *6.7 km* take the entrance to Interstate-40, turning left at 4.8 miles *7.68 km*, so that you are on I-40 headed east. At 8.3 miles *13.28 km* (MP 204), take the turn to Walnut Canyon, Exit 204. You will come to a stop sign at 8.6 miles *13.76 km*. Turn right on this and follow the paved road to Walnut Canyon. You will reach the parking lot at the Visitor Center at 11.6 miles *18.56 km*.

TRAILHEAD: The Visitor Center.

DESCRIPTION:
Island Trail. Length, 0.8 miles *1.28 km* complete loop, moderate hike. Paved. Elevation change 300 feet. This is the main trail, and is really enjoyable. To take it, you must go into the Visitor Center and pay a fee. Then you go out the back door of the center, where you will find an endless flight of steps (there are 240). The steps take you down to a ledge that was undercut by erosion, creating a series of shallow caves. The trail winds around the toe of a ridge and loops back up to the Visitor Center. Along the way you are able to inspect the extensive ruins of ancient cliff dwellings.
Rim Trail. Length, 0.4 miles *0.64 km*, one way. Level. Paved. Interpretive signs along the trail. This trail moves east along the rim of the canyon. It is a very easy short walk. The scenery is beautiful. You will not walk right by ruins as you do on the other trails, but you can see many ruins across the canyon. On the way back, detour to the Pit House.
Ranger Cabin Trail. Reservation required. Summer only. Length 1.6

miles *2.56 km* complete loop, moderate hike. Elevation change of 300 feet. Unpaved except for last portion. This hike is guided by a ranger. Starting from the Visitor Center, you walk west along the rim to the old Ranger Cabin, a historic site that is fun to visit. Then you enter Walnut Canyon the old way, going down through a side canyon. From there you hike along a ruin-studded ledge to join the Island Trail at the foot of the steps and return to the Visitor Center. This is our favorite trail.

Ledge Trail. Reservation required. Summer only. Length 0.5 miles *0.8 km* complete loop, moderate hike. Elevation change of 300 feet. Half of trail is paved. This hike is guided by a ranger. Starting from the Visitor Center, you go down the steps on the Island Trail, then branch off to the west, where you visit a number of cliff dwellings, returning the way you came. This same ledge is included on the Ranger Trail.

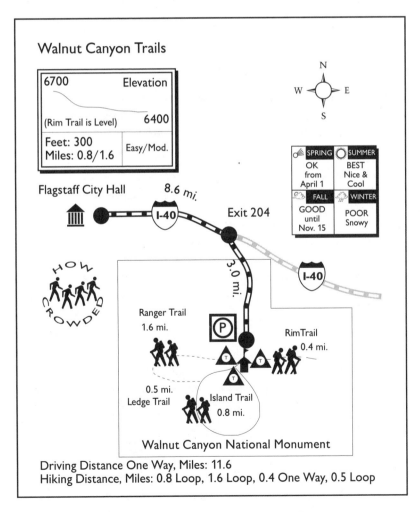

Weatherford Canyon

General Information
Location Map E3
Humphreys Peak USGS Map
Coconino Forest Service Map

Driving Distance One Way: 8.7 miles *13.9 km* (Time 30 minutes)
Access Road: All cars, Last 5.1 miles *8.2 km* medium gravel road
Hiking Distance One Way: 2.0 miles *3.2 km* (Time 1 hour)
How Strenuous: Moderate
Features: High mountains, Aspen groves

NUTSHELL: This trail climbs through a scenic canyon on the southeast face of the San Francisco Peaks 8.7 miles *13.9 km* north of Flagstaff.

DIRECTIONS:
From Flagstaff City Hall Go:
   North on Humphreys Street for 0.60 miles *1.0 km*. See Access Map, page 10. Turn left at the stoplight onto Columbus Avenue and follow it around a big curve to the north. You will see the street signs call this road Columbus Avenue at first, then Ft. Valley Road and then Highway 180. Stay on Highway 180 to the 3.1 miles *5.0 km* point (MP 218.6), where a paved road goes to the right. This is the Schultz Pass Road, FR 420. Turn right and follow this road. At 3.6 miles *5.8 km* you reach a curve to the left where you will see an paved road going straight. Stay on the Schultz Pass Road. The paving will end soon and the road will become gravel surfaced. Follow the Schultz Pass Road to the 8.7 mile *13.9 km* point, where you will see a sign for the **Weatherford Trail**. Park anywhere near the Weatherford trailhead.

TRAILHEAD: Begin this hike by taking the Weatherford Trail.

DESCRIPTION: The trailhead for this hike is also the "official" trailhead for the Weatherford Trail, the one indicated by the Forest Service on its maps and guides.
   You will hike the closed road for about 0.75 miles *1.2 km*, just beyond the place where a logging road takes off to the left.
   You will see a blocked road to your right going down into a shallow canyon at this point. Follow it. The canyon is Weatherford Canyon. Soon after you begin this new trail you will see a road forking to the right. Do not take it. Go straight up the canyon, walking along the canyon floor. The trail seems to have been an old wagon road, as it is broader than a footpath. Higher up it does turn into a footpath.
   You will pass through incredible aspen groves on this hike. In the lower

reaches of the canyon there is a stand of aspen saplings thick as hair that all seem to be the same height and age. This would indicate that they are the product of some bumper year, and from their age we would speculate that they are the result of the huge snowfall that hit the Flagstaff area in December, 1967. This dumped over twenty feet of snow on the San Francisco Peaks and caused a correspondingly wet spring in 1968.

Just before the trail ends you come to Aspen Spring, where a pond has been created. In a wet year this pond holds water year around and is a great place to spot animals.

The trail ends where it comes out into an open park and intersects the Weatherford Trail. The Weatherford Canyon Trail can be used as an interesting approach to or return from the Weatherford Trail. The trail through Weatherford Canyon is not a regular trail of the Forest Service system and is not maintained.

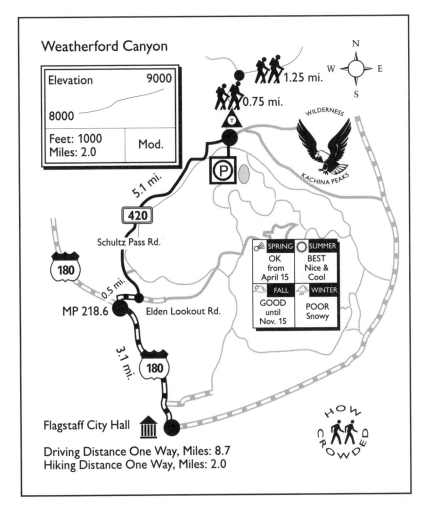

Weatherford Trail #102

General Information
Location Map E3
Humphreys Peak USGS Map
Coconino Forest Service Map

Driving Distance One Way: 13.7 miles *21.92 km* (Time 40 minutes)
Access Road: All cars, Last 4.0 miles *6.4 km* rough cinder road
Hiking Distance One Way: 6.0 miles *9.6 km* (Time 3.5 hours)
How Strenuous: Hard
Features: Highest mountains, Alpine forests, Excellent views

NUTSHELL: This is the easiest trail to the top of the San Francisco Peaks, 13.7 miles *21.92 km* north of Flagstaff.

DIRECTIONS:
From Flagstaff City Hall Go:
    North on Humphreys Street for 0.60 miles *1.0 km*. See Access Map, page 10. Turn left at the stoplight onto Columbus Avenue and follow it around a big curve to the north. The street signs call this road Columbus at first, then Ft. Valley Road and then Highway 180. Stay on Highway 180 to the 7.3 miles *11.7 km* point (MP 223), where the road to the Snow Bowl branches to the right. It is well posted. Follow the Snow Bowl road to 9.7 mile *15.52 km* point, where you will see an unpaved road, FR 522, branching to the right. Turn right onto FR 522, which is also known as the Freidlein Prairie Road. At 9.8 miles *15.7 km* this road will fork. Take the left fork and drive FR 522 to the 13.7 mile *21.92 km* point. There you will find a parking lot and road's end. Park in the lot.

TRAILHEAD: You will see a blocked road just beyond the parking lot. Hike the blocked road. There is a trail sign.

DESCRIPTION: These directions are for our easy way to the Weatherford Trail. For the "official" Forest Service way, which is longer and harder, see the entry for **Weatherford Canyon**.
    When you have hiked 0.33 miles *0.5 km* up the Weatherford Trail, take note of a trail coming onto the road from your left. This is the end of the **Kachina Trail**, a favorite hike. Beyond this is a big meadow. There are several roads branching off the main road. Follow the road that takes you across the meadow and moves uphill.
    At the end of the meadow the road will enter a shaded area framed by aspens and marked by a sign. When you see these you will know you are on the Weatherford Trail. Up the trail from here about 0.20 miles *0.32 km* you

will find a trail logbook in an ammunition can chained to a log. Please make an entry for yourself in this book. It is fun to read it and see who has been here, and it helps the Forest Service monitor trail use.

The Weatherford Trail was built as a private toll road, construction lasting from 1920 to 1928. The Great Depression wiped out any chances of success the road might have had. It fell into disuse and was incorporated into the Kachina Wilderness Area in 1984. The trail tops out at 6.0 miles *9.6 km* at Doyle Saddle (formerly called Fremont Saddle) where you get great views out over the countryside and down into the Inner Basin of the Peaks. No camping is allowed beyond Doyle Saddle.

The trail goes another 3.0 miles *4.8 km* to meet the **Humphreys Peak Trail,** from where you can go another half mile *0.8 km* to the highest point in Arizona, at 12,643 feet.

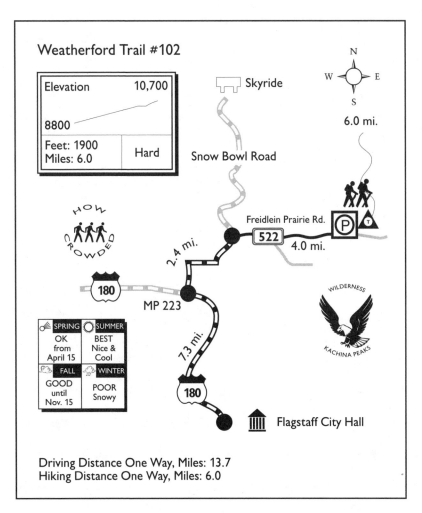

Mangum

West Fork Head

General Information
Location Map F2
Bellemont, Dutton Hill, Flagstaff West, Wilson Mt. USGS Maps
Coconino Forest Service Map

Driving Distance One Way: 21.1 miles *33.8 km* (Time 40 minutes)
Access Road: All cars, Last 17.5 miles *28.0 km* good gravel road
Hiking Distance One Way: 1.0 miles *1.6 km* (Time 40 minutes)
How Strenuous: Moderate
Features: Extremely attractive canyon, Lush vegetation

NUTSHELL: The West Fork of Oak Creek is a beautiful canyon. The hike at its end, where it meets Highway 89A is famous. See *Sedona Hikes*. This hike is at the beginning of the canyon, 21.1 miles *33.8 km* south of Flagstaff and has its own considerable attractions.

DIRECTIONS:
From Flagstaff City Hall Go:
    West, then south on Route 66, beneath the railroad overpass. See Access Map, page 10. At 0.50 miles *0.8 km,* go right on Route 66. You will soon leave town. At 2.6 miles *4.16 km* you will reach a road going to the left. This is the Woody Mountain Road, FR 231. Take it. It is paved about a mile and then turns into a cinder road. Stay on FR 231 to the 21.1 mile *33.8 km* point, where the road crosses a bridge. Go just past the bridge and park on the right shoulder.

TRAILHEAD: Not marked. Go down into the canyon.

DESCRIPTION: As you travel FR 231 you will encounter many side roads. The best way to describe the route is to tell you to stay on FR 231 at all times. It winds around in a bewildering way, but generally is the main traveled road everywhere. It is well posted.
    When you get to the bridge over West Fork you will see a canyon to your left which is fairly shallow right at the bridge. This is the head or beginning of West Fork. Those who are familiar with West Fork at its mouth where it meets Oak Creek will be surprised by West Fork's humble beginnings, as it seems to be just another ravine in country full of ravines. Go down into the canyon and start walking along the right hand bank of the streambed. You will pick up the trail there.
    At 0.2 miles *0.32 km* you will come to a large sign that reads, *"WEST FORK OF OAK CREEK. You are entering a very remote canyon. There is no developed hiking trail. Only experienced hiking parties should attempt*

this hike. DO NOT go alone." Don't worry. The first mile of the canyon does have a trail and is plenty safe. We feel that the warning on the sign is appropriate only if you go beyond the first mile. After the first mile the trail disappears and you have to hop the rocks in the streambed as the canyon narrows and the shoulders and shelves disappear.

It is possible for fit hikers to hike the whole length of the canyon in a day, about 12 miles *19.2 km*, meeting a car that they have previously parked at the West Fork trailhead in Oak Creek Canyon, but we do not recommend this for the average hiker.

This canyon is incredibly lush. You will think you are in a Pacific Northwest rain forest. Many of the trees are festooned with Spanish moss. The variety of plant life is mind boggling (including poison ivy). This is a special place and a magic hike.

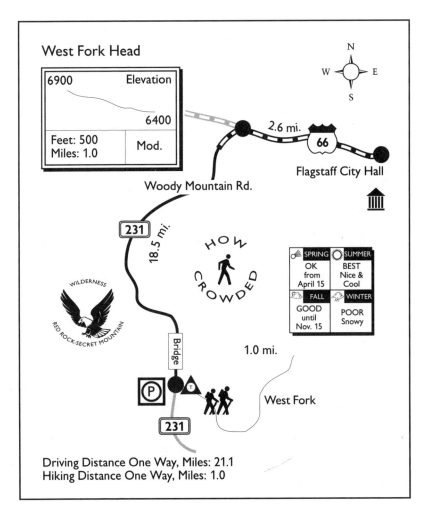

White Horse Hills

General Information
Location Map E3
White Horse Hills USGS Map
Coconino Forest Service Map

Driving Distance One Way: 23.15 miles *37.04 km* (Time 45 minutes)
Access Road: All cars, Last 3.75 miles *6.0 km* good gravel road
Hiking Distance One Way: 1.0 miles *1.6 km* (Time 45 minutes)
How Strenuous: Moderate
Features: Views

NUTSHELL: This moderately strenuous hike to the top of a mountain located just north of the San Francisco Peaks gives great views.

DIRECTIONS:
From Flagstaff City Hall Go:
North on Humphreys Street for 0.60 miles *1.0 km*. See Access Map, page 10. Turn left at the stoplight onto Columbus Avenue and follow it around a big curve to the north. You will see the street signs call this road Columbus at first, then Ft. Valley Road and then Highway 180. Stay on Highway 180 to the 19.4 miles *31.04 km* point (MP 235.2), where you will turn right onto the unpaved upper Hart Prairie Road, FR 151. Follow FR 151 to the 21.0 miles *33.6 km* point, where you turn left onto FR 418. Follow FR 418 to the 23.15 mile *37.04 km* point, where you will see a big sign on your left. Turn left, uphill, onto an old road there and park.

TRAILHEAD: Where you see a large sign depicting authorized uses.

DESCRIPTION: This trail climbs gradually at first on an old road. The whole area was badly burned in a May 1996 forest fire, marring its formerly beautiful appearance. You will soon reach a place where the road is badly eroded and steep, but beyond this the road climbs gradually and the footing is good. Watch for a place where the trail forks in a little saddle. The road you want goes to your left uphill and stays on the south side of the hill. You will reach a road junction higher up in a bare saddle. Go left here, to the top of the knob that is clearly seen before you. It is about 0.10 miles *0.16 km* to the top (8,700 feet high). One redeeming feature of the fire was that the tree cover was burned off so that you have great views. On the way back—at the road junction—you can take the trail to the other knob, which is 9,000 feet high. It is 0.20 miles *0.32 km* from the junction to the top of the second knob. The views are enough different to make the second climb worthwhile if you have the time and energy.

This trail provides magnificent views of the north face of the San Francisco Peaks. Mt. Humphreys, the tallest peak, really shows its stuff from here and is very imposing. This is a good hike to take when you want to enjoy seeing the changing aspen leaves in October.

From the top you can enjoy views of Kendrick Park, the Hochderffer Hills, **Saddle Mountain**, the Grand Canyon Plateau, the Vermilion Cliffs and countless cinder cones. To the east you can see sweeping views of Deadman Flat and **O'Leary Peak**.

While the soil looks typical for the area when you start climbing on this trail, you become aware about half way up that you have entered a zone where the earth beneath your feet has turned red. It looks rather like the soil in southern Utah or Sedona.

Near the top of the White Horse Hills is a white limestone layer. Some believe that it was this white stone that gave the hills their name.

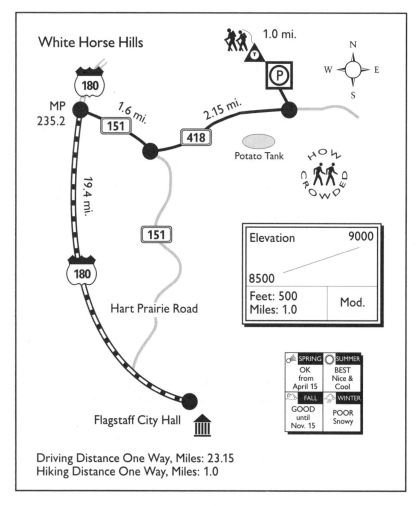

Mangum

Wild Bill Hill

General Information
Location Map E2
Wing Mountain USGS Map
Coconino Forest Service Map

Driving Distance One Way: 21.65 miles *34.64 km* (Time 40 minutes)
Access Road: High clearance only, Last 2.0 miles *3.2 km* rough dirt road
Hiking Distance One Way: 1.5 miles *2.4 km* (Time 1 hour)
How Strenuous: Moderate
Features: Hoodoos in volcano's center, Views

NUTSHELL: This mountain 21.65 miles *34.64 km* west of Flagstaff is located at the east edge of Government Prairie and is an extinct volcano. It is easily climbed to enjoy a look into the heart of the volcano and views over the prairie. **A personal favorite**.

DIRECTIONS:
From Flagstaff City Hall Go:
     North on Humphreys Street for 0.60 miles *1.0 km*. See Access Map, page 10. Turn left at the stoplight onto Columbus Avenue and follow it around a big curve to the north. You will see the street signs call this road Columbus at first, then Ft. Valley Road and then Highway 180. Stay on Highway 180 to the 14.4 miles *23.04 km* point (MP 230.1), where a gravel road takes off to the left. Turn left onto this road, FR 245, and follow it to the 17.4 mile *27.84 km* point where it intersects FR 171. Turn left onto FR 171 and follow it to the 19.5 mile *31.2 km* point, where FR 156 goes off to the right. Turn right on FR 156 and take it to the 21.15 mile *33.84 km* point. Turn left on a primitive unmarked road and follow it to the 21.65 miles point *34.64 km*, where you park. You will be 0.25 miles *0.4 km* away from the hill.

TRAILHEAD: You will see Wild Bill Hill to your left. There is no trail. Just walk across country to the hill and climb it to the saddle.

DESCRIPTION: This hill is shaped like a three-leaf clover. When you reach the top of the saddle, at an aspen grove, about 0.75 miles *1.2 km* from where you parked, you will see a bare knob to your right, a wooded knob (the highest) to your left, and the smallest knob to the north. We suggest that you climb the bare knob first. The views from there are great. You have good lines of sight in all directions except to the north, where the lowest knob blocks your view. Out over Government Prairie you can see for miles. If you know where to look, you can see the Beale Road coming across from Government Mountain. In fact, you can see it here better than you can as you walk the old road. See **Beale Road on Government Prairie**.

Then come back to the saddle. You will see a game trail there headed to the west. Follow it about 0.15 miles *0.24 km* and you will come to a place where you look down into the core of the volcano. Here is a wonderful moonlike landscape of hoodoos. You can walk to the north knob on a game trail from there, though the views are not so good because of the timber.

If you want to climb the highest knob, don't do it from the hoodoos even though you see a game trail going west, because it is very steep there. Come back to the first saddle and ascend it from there.

These three knobs are fascinating. The soil of which each is composed is quite different. The highest knob, loose red cinders; the lowest knob, brown cinders; the bare knob, red cinders.

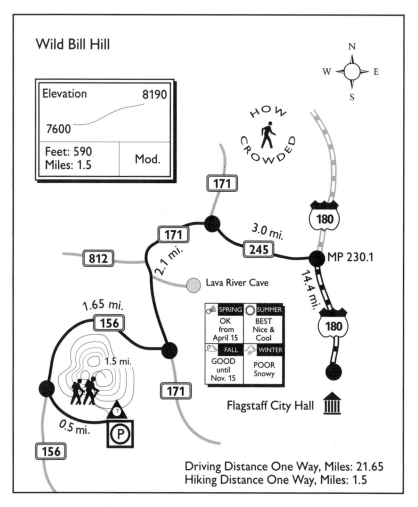

Mangum

Wildcat Hill

General Information
Location Map F3
Flagstaff East USGS Map
Coconino Forest Map

Driving Distance One Way: 7.0 miles *11.2 km* (Time 20 minutes)
Access Road: All cars, Last 0.20 miles *0.32 km* rough cinder road
Hiking Distance One Way: 0.1 miles *0.16 km* (Time 30 minutes)
How Strenuous: Moderate
Features: Cave, Pit house ruins, Rock Art, Scenic canyon

NUTSHELL: Located on the fringe of town, this canyon suddenly appears as a deep slash. On its steep lava walls are several panels of rock art and a cave. On top are the remains of several pit houses.

DIRECTIONS:
From Flagstaff City Hall Go:
     East, then north on Route 66. See Access Map, pages 10-11. At 3.8 miles *6.1 km* (MP 418.2/200) you will come to a fork, where Route 66 goes to the right. Turn right onto Route 66 and follow it to the 5.8 mile *9.3 km* point (MP 202) where you will see a street sign to your left marked *El Paso Flagstaff* and beyond that a sign for the *Wildcat Hill Waste Water Treatment Plant.* Turn left onto this good gravel road. At 5.95 miles *9.52 km* you will see a road going left. Ignore it. At 6.4 miles *10.24 km* you will see the turnoff to the El Paso Station. Ignore it. The road will curve around the back of the El Paso property and you will reach another fork at 6.8 miles *10.9 km*. You can see the canyon from here. Take the right fork, which runs along the rim of the canyon and follow it to the 7.0 mile *11.2 km* point where you will see an old barbed wire fence. Park here.

TRAILHEAD: There are no trail signs.

DESCRIPTION: You have parked on a high point just off the rim of the canyon. Walk over to the canyon and take a look at it. It is a strange gash in the earth. On each end of the canyon is gentle wide country; then suddenly the earth's crust split and made this steep narrow rock-lined canyon. You will see a stream flowing in the bottom of the canyon. Beware! The water you see there is treated sewage coming out of the wastewater treatment plant.
     You do not actually walk down to the bottom of the canyon on this hike, but stay up on a bench about a third of the way down.
     Begin by walking downhill, looking to your left. You will see the

remains of pithouses on the rim of the canyon to the left of where you parked, at a place where the canyon walls are not so steep and sheer. From there come back toward the parking spot, working your way down to a lower ledge at the base of the cliffs and boulders. You will see a fairly deep cave here, its roof blackened by the smoke of countless fires. Beyond, look on every smooth boulder face for rock art. The art seems scattered without a pattern.

There are several panels. We counted at least six. The art is rather basic, not as elaborate as that encountered at other sites.

When you reach the end of the area of the sheer cliffs, walk back up to the top and return to your car. There is a bit of rock art across the canyon, but it is hardly worth the effort. The most interesting sights are on your side.

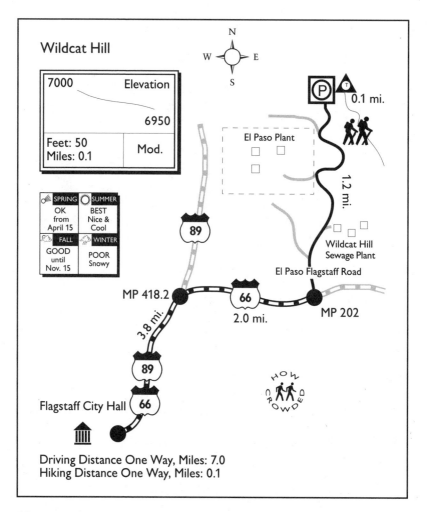

Mangum

Wildlife Trail

Driving Distance One Way: 20.0 miles *32.0 km* (Time 30 minutes)
Access Road: All cars, All paved
Hiking Distance, 2 Complete Loops: 0.25 miles *0.4 km* (Time 20 minutes),
      1.5 miles *2.4 km* (1 hour)
How Strenuous: Easy
Features: Views of Kendrick Park, Easy to reach, Parking Area, Toilet, and
      Universal Access

NUTSHELL: A perfect way to stretch your legs and make a rest stop while driving to the Grand Canyon. There are two loops here, one being 0.25 miles *0.4 km* long, and the other being 1.5 miles *2.4 km* long. The short trail has a hard surface and provides universal access for wheelchairs.

DIRECTIONS:
From Flagstaff City Hall Go:
    North on Humphreys Street for 0.6 miles *1.0 km*. See Access Map, page 10. Turn left at the stoplight onto Columbus Avenue and follow it around a big curve to the north. You will see the street signs call this road Columbus at first, then Ft. Valley Road and then Highway 180. Stay on Highway 180 to the 20.0 mile *32.0 km* point MP 235.6 where you turn left into an easy-to-see paved parking lot and park.

TRAILHEAD: There is a big sheltered sign with a map. Note, at the time of this writing, the sign on the trailhead says that this is the Walker Lake Trailhead. This is unfortunate because the trail does not go to Walker Lake and is not intended to go there ever. You can see the north side of the crater in which Walker Lake is contained from the trailhead, but otherwise there is no connection.

DESCRIPTION: The short hike has a hard surface and makes a gentle loop to the south of the parking lot, following level ground. It is very easy. At the top of the loop, the north end, you will be looking out onto Kendrick Park, a vast open plain ringed with hills and mountains, a very scenic spot. The Forest Service hopes to be able to place interpretive signs at strategic points along the trail.
    The longer loop starts at the same place as the short loop but veers away

to the west, hugging the south edge of Kendrick Park. It goes along a fence and at its westernmost point there is a gate through which hikers may pass for a side-trip of 0.25 miles *0.4 km* one-way to see a Ponderosa Pine Management Area. The trail then swings south, through an aspen grove and then curves around to the east before moving north again to link up with the short trail.

Both of these trails are located in a scenic area. We love the views to the north across Kendrick Park in the evening when the low light turns the prairie grasses a shimmering golden hue. The trail takes its name from the fact that this is a prime site for wildlife. Deer and elk love to graze the meadow and can dart into the safety of the cover of the woods in case of danger. Birds are also plentiful here.

In the 1930s, 1940s and 1950s there was some farming on Kendrick Park but it has long since been abandoned. You will see a few homesteads there now, but the rough winters make it a difficult place to live.

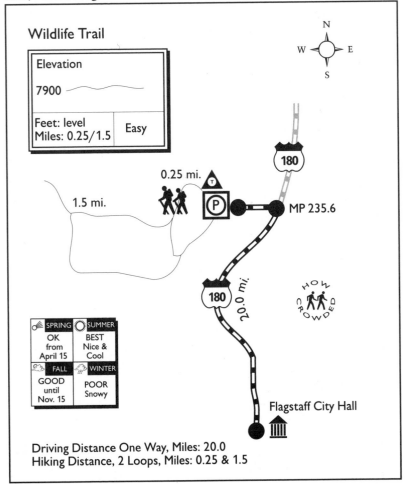

Wildlife Trail

Elevation

7900

Feet: level
Miles: 0.25/1.5   Easy

0.25 mi.

1.5 mi.

180

MP 235.6

180

20.0 mi.

HOW CROWDED

SPRING	SUMMER
OK from April 15	BEST Nice & Cool
FALL	WINTER
GOOD until Nov. 15	POOR Snowy

Flagstaff City Hall

Driving Distance One Way, Miles: 20.0
Hiking Distance, 2 Loops, Miles: 0.25 & 1.5

Mangum

Willow Crossing Trail #38

General Information
Location Map G4
Calloway Butte USGS Map
Coconino Forest Service Map

Driving Distance One Way: 53.65 miles *85.84 km* (Time 1.5 hours)
Access Road: High clearance best, Last 4.75 miles *7.6 km* unpaved road
Hiking Distance One Way: 1.0 miles *1.6 km* (Time 45 minutes)
How Strenuous: Moderate
Features: Beautiful pristine canyon, Back country

NUTSHELL: This little-used trail takes you into and across Willow Valley Canyon, a tributary to West Clear Creek. The canyon is beautiful, though fire-scarred, and the trail in and out is on a moderate grade.

DIRECTIONS:
From Flagstaff City Hall Go:
    West, then south on Route 66, beneath the railroad overpass. See Access Map, page 10. At 0.5 miles *0.8 km*, go straight on Milton Road. At 1.7 miles *2.72 km* you will reach a stoplight at Forest Meadows Street. Turn right here onto Forest Meadows and go one block to Beulah. Turn left on Beulah and follow it south. Beulah merges onto Highway 89A. At 2.4 miles *3.84 km* (MP 401.6), turn left onto the Lake Mary Road at the stoplight. Follow the Lake Mary Road, going past Lower and Upper Lake Mary and Mormon Lake to the 48.9 mile *78.24 km* point (MP 297.7), where you turn right onto a dirt road, FR 81. The highway sign shows "V Bar V Ranch, Poor Farm and West Clear Creek." Follow FR 81 to the 52.0 mile point *83.2 km*, its junction with FR 81E. Turn left on 81E and stay on it to the 53.15 mile *85 km* point, where you reach a fork. Take the left fork. This is FR 9366M, though we saw no markers. Go to the 53.65 mile *85.84 km* point, where you will see a barbed wire fence, with a cattle guard. Just beyond the cattle guard, to your left (east), is the trailhead. Park here.

TRAILHEAD: There is a sign and wire-bound cairn where you park.

DESCRIPTION: The first leg of this trail is the approach to the rim of Willow Valley Canyon. The approach is eastward along level ground. The trail is not very distinct here, but it is easy to find your way: all you have to do is walk along the fence. This part of the trail is rather drab.
    When you reach the 0.4 mile *0.64 km* point, you will enter into an area where a sheep wire fence creates an enclosure. You can see that you are very

near the canyon here. A big blaze on a pine tree marks the trail here, which dips down into the canyon, moving away from the barbed wire fence. From this point, the trail is clear and easy to follow.

You descend along the bank of a side canyon. The hike is not steep, and the area becomes more and more beautiful as you go. Finally, you drop down into the streambed, where you can enjoy some impressive views. The canyon walls here are very sheer, though not terribly deep. We saw a huge variety of plants, including many flowers.

Go straight across the canyon, where you will see the trail going up the other side. From this point, you climb to the opposite rim. Again, the grade is not very steep, and it is a pleasant hike.

The hike terminates in a park in a pretty valley, where you will find a trail marker sign. A reader reports an arch in a side canyon to the right.

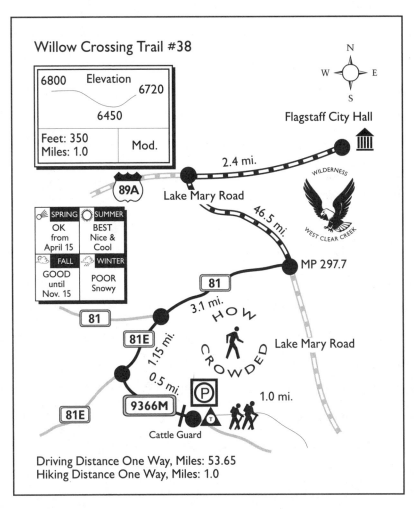

Mangum

Wilson Meadow

General Information
Location Map E3
Humphreys Peak and Wing Mountain USGS Maps
Coconino Forest Service Map

Driving Distance One Way: 14.9 miles *23.84 km* (Time 35 minutes)
Access Road: All cars, Last 4.7 miles *7.5 km* good gravel
Hiking Distance One Way: 1.0 miles *1.6 km* (Time 30 minutes)
How Strenuous: Easy
Features: Aspen groves, Meadow Views

NUTSHELL: Located on the San Francisco Peaks, 14.9 miles *23.84 km* north of Flagstaff, this easy walk displays the area's alpine beauty.

DIRECTIONS:
From Flagstaff City Hall Go:
   North on Humphreys Street for 0.60 miles *1.0 km*, to the stoplight. See Access Map, page 10. Then take a left onto a street marked Columbus Avenue, which changes to Ft. Valley Road as it makes a curve to the north. Outside the city limits, the road becomes Highway 180, a major route to the Grand Canyon. At 10.2 miles *16.3 km* (MP 225.1), turn right onto FR 151, the lower Hart Prairie Road, and follow it to the 14.7 miles *23.5 km* point, where an unmarked gravel road takes off to the right. This access is rough because of exposed rocks, but it is only 0.2 miles *0.32 km* long. Turn right and drive to the 14.9 miles *23.84 km* point, where you will find a fenced parking place. Park there.

TRAILHEAD: You will see a "Road Closed" sign at a gate in the parking area fence. Walk up this road.

DESCRIPTION: The sign at the parking lot identifies this merely as a "Wildlife Habitat Area" and it is not named on any map that we could find. You will see a reference to the Wilson Foundation on the sign. As we made this beautiful hike, enjoying the flowers, the meadow and the views, it occurred to us that it would be fitting to call it the Wilson Meadow hike in honor of The Wilson Foundation, for it spearheaded a fight two decades ago to prevent the commercial development of Hart Prairie, under the slogan, "Save the Peaks." Had it not been for it bearing the brunt of years of costly litigation, this pristine area would now be covered with condos. Thanks, folks! This is a wonderful place and we are grateful that you saved it for nature lovers.
   The hike consists of following a closed road up the meadow. This is a

wet area with underground water marked by lines of water loving shrubs. After one half mile *0.8 km* the tracks peter out near a large metal water tank lying on its side. No problem. Just keep hiking toward the top of the meadow, to the tree line.

From the half mile point *0.8 km* you begin to get wonderful views. Turn around every so often and enjoy them. Three major mountains and an infinity of hills cover the landscape. Beginning on your right hand, the tallest mountains are Kendrick, Sitgreaves and Bill Williams. The hike ends at a fence at the top of the meadow.

We made the hike in mid-August and the meadow was full of flowers and high grass. Instead of going to the fence, we veered to the right near the top, into a grove of spruce and aspen, so cool on a hot day. The rippling of the wind in the aspen leaves sounded like water running. Almost every aspen in the grove shows signs of having been rubbed by antlers.

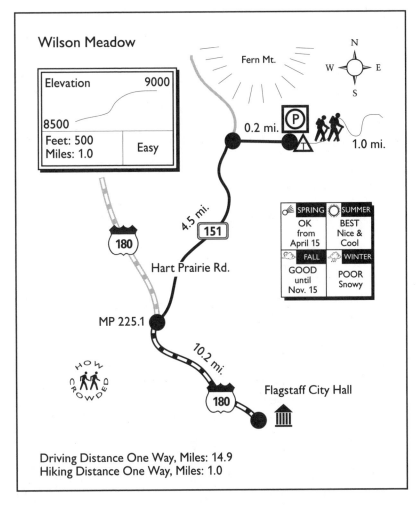

Wing Mountain

General Information
Location Map E2
Wing Mountain USGS Map
Coconino Forest Service Map

Driving Distance One Way: 12.4 miles *20 km* (Time 30 minutes)
Access Road: All cars, Last 3.7 miles *6 km* good gravel road
Hiking Distance One Way: 0.75 miles *1.2 km* (Time 40 minutes)
How Strenuous: Hard
Features: Landmark crater north of Flagstaff provides wonderful views

NUTSHELL: A hard climb straight uphill brings the hiker to the rim of a crater, the bowl of which is a grassy meadow with a lake (sometimes) in the bottom.

DIRECTIONS:
From Flagstaff City Hall Go:
   North on Humphreys Street for 0.60 miles *1.0 km*. See Access Map, page 10. Turn left at the stoplight onto Columbus Avenue and follow it around a big curve to the north. You will see the street signs call this road Columbus at first, then Ft. Valley Road and then Highway 180. Stay on Highway 180 to the 8.7 miles *14 km* point (MP 224.3), where an unpaved road takes off to the left. Turn left onto this road, FR 222, and follow it to the 10.4 mile *16.7 km* point where it intersects FR 519. Turn left on FR 519 and follow it to the 12.2 mile *19.5 km* point, where you turn right, on a primitive unmarked road. This is pretty rough, but you can probably follow it to the 12.4 mile *20 km* point, which is a good place to park.

TRAILHEAD: Unmarked. No official trailhead.

DESCRIPTION: From the point where you parked, the primitive road continues up the side of the mountain. You will see signs of tree cutting. It is hard to tell whether this was a logging operation or just tree thinning. Where the road ends, you will be part way up the mountain. From there, it is just a question of scrambling to the top, up the south face of Wing. The pitch is very steep, and you might want to zigzag rather than go in a straight line.
   Once at the top, turn around and enjoy the views behind you, to the south. You will find a large cairn of stones here, bound together with sticks and wire. This is a good marker. Use it to locate the place to go back down the mountain when you are finished. At this point, you will have hiked 0.75 miles *1.2 km*.
   From here, you can walk around the rim. We suggest going counter-

clockwise, to the northeast. You will find a clear place just in front of a fence, where you have good views of the San Francisco Peaks.

The barbed wire fence you will find here is unexpected. The Forest Service map does not show that it is private property.

Wing Mountain and **A-1 Mountain** are near neighbors. In Flagstaff's early years, the Arizona Cattle Company had a huge ranch in the Ft. Valley area. Its brand was the A-1, which is how A-1 Mountain got its name. Wing was one of the owners of the Arizona Cattle Company. There is a legend about this outfit's cook. Range cattle are not the tenderest of beef, so the chuckwagon cook invented a steak sauce to help the boys chow down on their staple protein. The sauce was so good that it was developed commercially. You can still go into a grocery store and buy A-1 Steak Sauce. When you do, think of the cowhands of Flagstaff long ago.

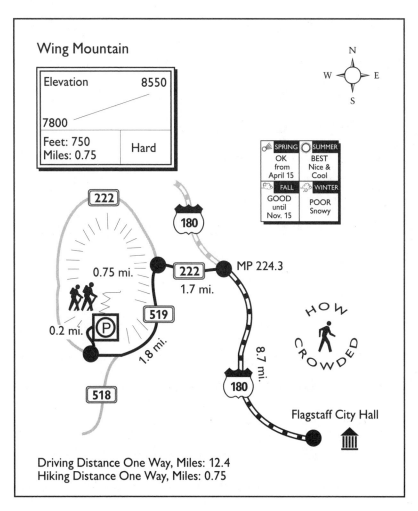

Mangum

Winter Cabin Trail

General Information
Location Map F2
Sycamore Point USGS Map
Coconino Forest Service Map

Driving Distance One Way: 26.3 miles *42.1 km* (Time 1 hour)
Access Road: All cars, Last 22.7 miles *36.3 km* dirt road, rough spots
Hiking Distance One Way: 1.1 miles *1.76 km* (Time 1 hour)
How Strenuous: Moderate
Features: Views, Sycamore Canyon access, Historic cowboy cabin

NUTSHELL: Located 26.3 miles *42.1 km* southwest of Flagstaff, this is a scenic trail in its own right as well as being an access trail into Sycamore Canyon. There is an interesting cabin in an idyllic glade at the end of this hike.

DIRECTIONS:
From Flagstaff City Hall Go:
    West, then south on Route 66 beneath the railroad overpass. See Access Map, page 10. At 0.50 miles *0.8 km* turn right on Route 66. At 2.6 miles *4.16 km* you will reach the Woody Mountain Road, FR 231, going to the left. Take it. It is paved about a mile and then turns into a cinder road. At 16.6 miles *26.56 km* you will intersect FR 538. Turn right onto FR 538 and follow it to the 22.3 mile *35.7 km* point, a T junction. Turn left, still on FR 538, and drive to the 25.7 mile *41.1 km* point, where it intersects FR 538H. Turn right on FR 538H and go to its end at 26.3 miles *42.1 km*. FR 538H is rather rough. Park at the end of the road.

TRAILHEAD: You will see a sign at the parking area.

DESCRIPTION: The trail is maintained and passes through an attractive mixed forest with oaks, maples and other trees adding variety to the prevailing Ponderosa pines. This is a colorful trail in mid-October. The trail is mostly soft, covered with soil, though there are a few rocky patches.
    Forest Service signs give the mileage to Winter Cabin as 1.5 miles *2.4 km*. We measured it as 1.1 miles *1.76 km*. The cabin is located in a peaceful glade on a little shelf of land, a remote peaceful paradise far from the cares of the world. You may not want to come back out.
    The cabin is an old log relic with a corrugated metal roof, and is still in good condition. It is hard to tell how the place got its name, Winter Cabin, because one can't imagine cowboys surviving the winter here. Heavy snows fall in this area and once the snow season begins in the autumn, this place

would be totally cut off from the outside world.

The cabin is a trail intersection. The trail to the southwest goes on down 1.5 miles *2.4 km* to Ott Lake, and from there goes another 2.0 miles *3.2 km* into the bottom of Sycamore Canyon. (Don't try hiking into Sycamore Canyon unless you are really prepared for it. Unprepared people have died there). The trail to the west goes to Dorsey Spring and then on to Kelsey Spring on the 5.5 mile *8.8 km* long **Kelsey-Winter Trail**.

Stopping at Winter Cabin makes a dandy day hike that can be handled by almost anyone who is reasonably fit.

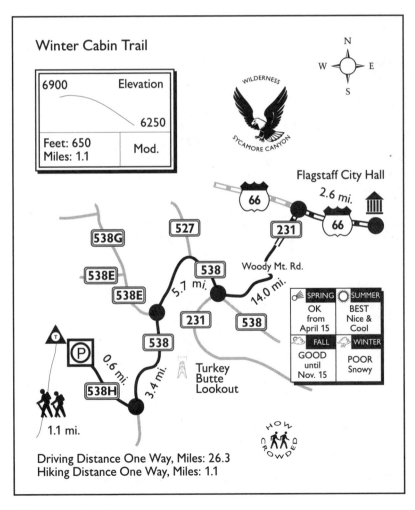

Wood Trail

General Information
Location Map F3
Ashurst Lake, Lower Lake Mary USGS Maps
Coconino Forest Service Map

Driving Distance One Way: 15.1 miles *24.16 km* (Time 25 minutes)
Access Road: All cars, All paved
Hiking Distance One Way: 0.5 miles *0.8 km* (Time 20 minutes)
How Strenuous: Easy for hikers, Moderate for wheelchair users
Features: Easy to reach, Lake Mary, Fishing, Wheelchair Accessible

NUTSHELL: Opened on October 16, 1998, this trail was specifically created for wheelchair access. It is paved, but the rather steep grade makes it an interesting challenge in a wheelchair.

DIRECTIONS:
From Flagstaff City Hall Go:
    West, then south on Route 66 under the railroad overpass. See Access Map, page 10. At 0.5 miles *0.8 km* you will reach a stoplight at a Y intersection. Leave Route 66 here and go straight on Milton Road. At 1.70 miles *2.72 km* you reach the stoplight at Forest Meadows, where you turn right. At the next corner turn left on Beulah and follow it out of town. Beulah will connect onto Highway 89A. At the 2.4 miles *3.84 km* point (MP 401.6) you will see the turnoff to the Lake Mary Road to your left at a stoplight. Turn left and follow the Lake Mary Road to the 12.6 miles *20.2 km* point (MP 331.6) where you will see the paved road to the right going down to the Lake Mary Narrows parking lot. Turn right and drive down to the farthest end of the parking lot at the 15.1 mile *24.16 km* point, where you park.

TRAILHEAD: At the parking place. You will see a trail sign.

DESCRIPTION: This all-paved trail starts out parallel to the lake. After following the shore for about 0.1 mile *0.16 km,* you come to a fork. The right hand fork goes about twenty yards to a viewpoint. The left fork is the main trail. On the main trail you will soon come to a boulder on the right side of the path. A plaque on the boulder reads as follows: "This trail built with support from the Wood Family in Memory of William C. Wood. 'Access for all.'" Mr. Wood, who worked for the Forest Service, was a staunch advocate of allowing everyone to enjoy the forest resources. Wood, unfortunately, was killed in an auto accident in 1992.
    Soon after you pass the boulder, you will reach another fork. Again the right hand fork goes a short distance to a pad, which is intended either to be

a viewpoint or a resting point. The main trail, to the left, turns away from the lake here and begins climbing up toward the Lake Mary Road.

Soon you will come to a big concrete culvert, which serves as an underpass for hikers. You walk right under the road. The passage is shaded and water flows through it, so watch your footing here, especially if it is cold enough for ice to form. On the other side of the culvert, the path winds uphill until it comes to a gravel road at the edge of the Lake Mary Narrows Campground. If a person were staying in the campground, this trail would make an ideal way to walk to the fishing ramp at the lake in safety.

We salute this trail as a welcome addition to the list of hiking trails around Flagstaff. We agree with William Wood that we should work to make the forest accessible to all.

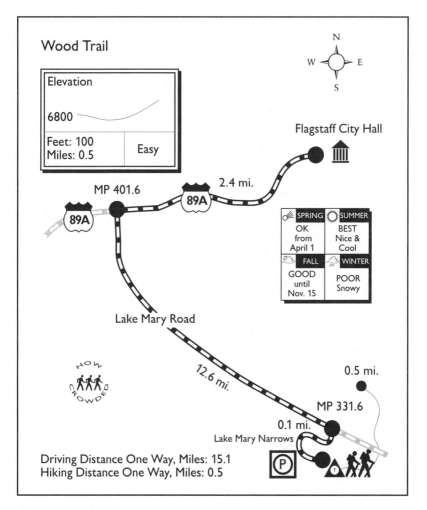

Mangum

Wupatki Ruin Trail

General Information
Location Map D4
Wupatki SW USGS Map
Coconino Forest Service Map

Driving Distance One Way: 37.8 miles *60.48 km* (Time 60 minutes)
Access Road: All cars, All paved
Hiking Distance, Complete Loop: 0.40 miles *0.64 km* (Time 45 minutes)
How Strenuous: Easy
Features: Views, Best pueblo Indian ruins in the Flagstaff area

NUTSHELL: This is a fascinating easy trail starting at the Visitor Center in Wupatki National Monument 37.8 miles *60.48 km* north of Flagstaff. It features pueblo ruins, a ball court, an amphitheater and a unique blow hole.

DIRECTIONS:
From Flagstaff City Hall Go:
East, curving to north on Highway 89. See Access Map, pages 10-11. Follow Highway 89 north out into the country. At 16.4 miles *26.24 km* (MP 430.3) you will reach the entrance to Sunset Crater National Monument. Turn right on the road into Sunset Crater. This road is also known as FR 545. At 18.4 miles *29.44 km* you will reach a ticket booth where you will have to pay admission. Just beyond that is the Visitor Center, which is worth a look. At 26.0 miles *41.6 km* you reach the Painted Desert Vista. This is a lookout point where we recommend stopping to enjoy the view. Under the right lighting conditions it is superb. At 37.8 miles *60.48 km* you enter the Wupatki National Monument, which adjoins Sunset Crater, and you will see the road to the Wupatki Visitor Center to your left. Take the road to the Visitor Center and park in the parking lot.

TRAILHEAD: The trail starts at the right hand side of the Visitor Center.

DESCRIPTION: Even though this is a "tame" hike, being the furthest thing from a wilderness adventure, it is very interesting and well worth taking. This is a favorite excursion for visiting relatives. It will keep even the small fry happy.
　　The setting is lovely. The ruins are situated on the side of a small valley, where exposed layers of red sandstone provided plentiful building materials. The Sinagua Indians, who built the pueblo, fitted their construction around some of the existing boulders in fascinating ways so that they could use the boulders as much as possible to serve as walls and buttresses. Across the valley you can see a couple of small pueblos, but you are not permitted to visit

them. Beyond the far end of the valley you can see the Painted Desert, a vast multicolored area.

From the pueblo at the top of the valley you walk downhill to an amphitheater, then to the valley floor to a ball court and a blow hole. The blow hole is wonderful. During the cool hours of the day, in the morning and evening, the blow hole draws in air. When the day is hot, during the afternoon, the blow hole expels air. It is like some giant breathing. The breaths can be quite forceful, causing a loud rushing noise.

Along the trail are posted several markers which are keyed into a trail guide. You pick up the guide at the beginning of the trail. If you want to keep it, you put fifty cents into the box at the end of the trail. If you do not want to keep it, you return it to the box.

We recommend visiting other Wupatki sites: Wukoki, Lomaki and the Citadel.

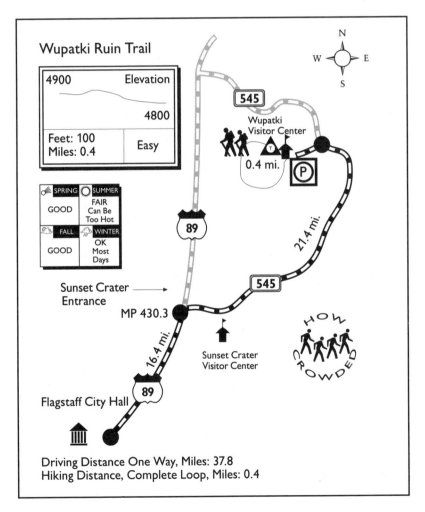

Mangum

Index

288